INVESTMENT MADE EASY

HOW TO MAKE MORE
OF YOUR MONEY

WARNING

Stock market investments (including gilts and loan stocks), unit trusts, investment trusts, insurance products, property and alternative investments, can go down as well as up. The income from most securities can also go down as well as up. When you seek advice, also ask about marketability. The shares, gilts, loan stocks, investment trusts and unit trusts referred to in the text of this book are for illustrative purposes only and are not an invitation to deal in them. This book was originally written in November 1993 and revised in August 1995. But market conditions change. Neither the publisher nor the author accept any legal responsibility for the contents of the work, which is not a substitute for detailed professional advice. Readers should conduct their own investment activity through an appropriately authorised person.

INVESTMENT MADE EASY

HOW TO MAKE MORE OF YOUR MONEY

JIM SLATER

CARTOONS BY

ORION

To Helen, who continues to be my best investment.

First published in Great Britain in 1994 by
Orion
An imprint of Orion Books Ltd
Orion House, 5 Upper St Martin's Lane, London WC2H 9EA

New Edition published in 1995

A CIP catalogue record for this book is available
from the British Library

ISBN 0 75280 056 6

Production: PLS
Cover Design: Orion

Printed in Great Britain by
Butler & Tanner Ltd., Frome, Somerset

CONTENTS

ACKNOWLEDGEMENTS

When I agreed to write this book, I did not realise the magnitude of the task I had undertaken. I soon found that I needed much more help than I had at first imagined.

I would like to thank, in particular, Tom Stevenson of the *Independent*, for editing my work on both the hardback and paperback version. He has also made many suggestions for improving the text and the structure of most of the chapters. His help has been invaluable.

Thanks are also due to Anthony Bailey who was, until recently, Personal Finance Editor of the *Investors Chronicle*. He has concentrated on the first part of the book, checked all the facts for me, edited the text and helped to update this paperback. He has also had many good ideas for lifting the final product.

I am indebted to my son, Mark, and my friends, Ralph Baber, George Finlay, Bryan Quinton and Peter Greaves for reading and checking the proofs of the second part of the book and for their many suggestions.

Roger Marshman of Roffe Swayne helped me to flesh out and substantially improve the taxation chapter and my son, Christopher, Colin Bray and Richard Collins made many constructive suggestions for the chapter on property. Thanks are also due to James McMullen for editing and improving the chapters that deal with mortgages, insurance, pensions and financial advisers and to Christopher Dennistoun for his help and suggestions for the chapter on alternative investment.

I would also like to thank Victoria Nye of The Association of Unit Trusts and Investment Funds Information Unit for checking through the unit trust chapter and Eleanor Burton of The Association of Investment Trust Companies for doing the same on investment trusts.

I must congratulate Edward McLachlan, who has drawn such superb cartoons. It amazed me how quickly he grasped the essence of each of the chapters and found a way of bringing them to life in his highly entertaining and inimitable way.

I would be in great personal danger if I failed to thank Pam Hall, my long-suffering secretary, who has typed most of the chapters even more times than those of *The Zulu Principle*. She has been a tower of strength.

SAFETY-FIRST INVESTMENT

PREFACE

You are reading this book because you want to manage your money better. My aim is to help you to achieve that objective.

Most people spend very little time thinking about their personal finances; they are bewildered by the increasing range of financial packages advertised every day and they have no idea how to protect their capital against the ravages of inflation.

Not many of us remember that shortly after the Second World War, in 1946, you could buy a family car for about £600; the comparable cost today is nearer £8,000. A loaf of bread cost 4p and a pint of milk 2p, against about 60p and 35p today. Anyone who has simply preserved the same amount of capital between 1946 and 1995 has no cause to celebrate – they are very much poorer.

No one will read the future for you. No one knows your present position and future aims better than you. If you want your money to work better, *you* must do something to make it happen. The skill you apply in making your decisions will be clearly reflected in the return you enjoy on your investments. This book will help to develop that skill.

If you have some surplus money to invest, you must first of all decide whether you wish to put safety first or to become a more active investor.

A safety-first investor will be content to leave most of the decision-making to professional managers. He or she needs to have little or no knowledge of the stock market and will be quite likely to invest in unit trusts or investment trusts, drawing great comfort from professional management and the wide spread of their investments.

However, safety-first investors still have to make a number of very important decisions. To name just a few: they need to decide whether to deposit their money with a building society or in a TESSA scheme; they have to weigh up the relative merits of unit and investment trusts, and once they have made that choice, they must select the right unit or investment trust and decide when they should add to their investment or take some profits. This book will help safety-first investors to manage their money better by giving them a clear idea of the fundamentals, helping them understand the jargon of finance and showing them how to navigate the maze of available options.

My hope is that after reading this book, you will have a better understanding of the bewildering array of investment propositions that fill the City pages of your newspapers and keep dropping through your letter box. You should also have a better idea of the financial packages that are most likely to meet your personal requirements. You will still need to consult an independent financial adviser, but at least you will not be starting from scratch. You should be better able to help your adviser to help you and be better able to judge the quality of the advice you receive.

I have not tried to cover every little detail and every option available. That would have been an almost impossible task and, even if I had succeeded, would have made this book impossibly boring. Also, it would not be long before it became out of date. The November 1995 and subsequent budgets may change the tax position, new financial products may reach the market, but the basic principles and the fundamental approach to managing your money are likely to remain the same.

I have tried to concentrate on the branches of the investment tree and I may, as a result, have missed out a few twigs. For example, you should know that the majority of unit trusts underperform the stock market in which they invest. It is crucial to understand why, and to grasp the importance of tracker funds which aim to match the market. This is a branch. In contrast, the precise make-up and performance of UK Balanced Unit Trusts is relatively unimportant. This is a twig.

The second part of this book is for active investors who like to manage their own funds. It is aimed at those people who have already made preparations for their basic financial health and now want to make the rest of their money work extra hard by accepting the risks and seeking the rewards of investing directly in shares. They spend a few hours a week considering their investments and, with or without professional advice, prefer to make the decisions. I hope to help them to acquire a much improved understanding of the financial news and to learn how to minimise downside-risk and maximise upside-potential. They will also learn how to read accounts, judge markets, manage their portfolios and, as a result, how to make their money work much better.

1

DEPOSIT ACCOUNTS AND NATIONAL SAVINGS

The absolute safety of your savings is of paramount importance. You can earn higher interest by shopping around, but should never take risks with your basic savings. Instead, try to increase your return by minimising your tax.

Before you buy your own home, or invest in unit trusts, investment trusts or shares, make sure that you have set aside an emergency fund for a rainy day. The amount will vary with individual circumstances. For many people, a few hundred pounds will suffice – kept on *instant access* in case of unexpected expenditure like major car repairs. You also need a strategic reserve for known future expenditure, or while you wait for the right long-term investment opportunity. The money must be reasonably accessible but, as you will not need it back quickly, you can afford to give longer notice of withdrawal. You will then receive higher interest and your money will be 'parked' more advantageously.

In addition, you should have adequate life insurance and money earmarked for illness, old age and, in some cases, school fees. These precious reserves should be invested with absolute safety for a certain return. Any surplus cash left over will be genuinely *patient* money, which might still be kept on deposit but, most of the time, would be better put into some form of bond or equity investment. The essential characteristic of patient money is that you should not need to withdraw it suddenly. Being forced to sell equity investments at the wrong moment can be a very painful experience.

BANKS AND BUILDING SOCIETIES

For instant access, your money could be kept in a strongbox or hidden under a mattress, but a safer and better place is in a bank or building society deposit account. Even when interest rates are very low, you will at least earn a small return.

When you come to choose a deposit account, you will find that there is a considerable difference between the interest rate offered on the worst instant access account and the best ninety-day account. It is worth shopping around. All the banks and building societies pay higher rates for large amounts, for example £5,000 and above, and more again for money which is locked up for several months at a time or longer. Keep the bare minimum in instant access, as banks and building societies pay derisory interest on small sums that can be immediately withdrawn.

A number of building societies operate postal accounts, which are not available through branches but only by post direct to head office. These usually pay more than an equivalent branch account as they are cheaper for the building society to administer.

I will not go into great detail on specific rates of interest because they are constantly changing. However, to show the range of deposit rates on offer, here is a table of just a few of the accounts available from some of the largest banks and building societies in April 1995:

	£1,000 Instant Access (%)	£1,000 90 Day Notice (%)
Banks		
Abbey National	3.8	4.6
Barclays	2.8	5.2 (min £2,000)
Lloyds	3.5	5.25 (min £10,000)
Midland	3.72	4.75 (min £5,000)
NatWest	3.75	4.0 (min £2,000)
Royal Bank of Scotland	3.8	4.75 (min £2,000)
TSB	4.1	4.5 (60 days)
Yorkshire	2.5	3.75
Building Societies		
Alliance & Leicester	4.4	4.65 (min £2,500)
Birmingham Midshires	3.6	4.35 (60 days)
Bradford & Bingley	2.15	6.4 (30 days)
Britannia	4.0	5.9
Bristol & West	0.5	4.25
National & Provincial	4.25	4.6
Nationwide	3.8	4.4
Woolwich	3.85	4.5 (min £5,000)

Source: *Moneyfacts*, April 1995

The above details are a small, representative sample that should be sufficient to give a general idea of the range of interest rates available at any time. Each of the banks and building societies offers a large number of options. For example, Barclays has four different types of account with interest rates that vary at several levels of deposit.

It is clear that in spring 1995 Bristol & West, for example, did not appear to be falling over themselves to attract small sums of money, especially on instant access. For 90-Day deposits of £25,000, however, Bristol & West paid 6.05%, a rate which gave the society a slight edge over some of their high street rivals.

TAX

Just as taxpayers can pay as much as 40% of an increase in salary to the Government, so a sizeable slice of deposit account interest is eaten up by tax. As well as hunting around for the best available rates of interest, make sure that you use all the legal means available to avoid paying tax.

Taxpayers should choose tax-free investments – TESSAs and National Savings Certificates. Non-taxpayers should make sure they claim their interest gross, without any tax deducted, to avoid having to wait until the end of the tax year to claim it back.

Married couples with one spouse paying no tax should ensure that they split their investments between them, so that the non-taxpayer makes use of the tax-free personal allowance, worth around £3,500 a year, and more for older people. The same applies to couples where one partner pays a higher rate of tax than the other. A non-taxpayer can have £70,000 on deposit and, at a rate of 5%, pay no tax on the interest of £3,500; a 40% taxpayer would face a bill of £1,400. Tax can be a dull topic, but anyone who is serious about investment needs to understand the basics. For this reason, Chapter 9 is devoted to the subject.

TESSAS

Taxpayers, and particularly higher-rate taxpayers with money to spare for the next five years, should look at *TESSAs* (Tax Exempt Special Savings Accounts). Introduced by John Major in his only budget as Chancellor, these are bank or building society accounts which are tax-free, albeit with some restrictions.

Anyone over eighteen can open a TESSA, but you can hold only one at a time. The most you can invest is £9,000, which must be spread over five years, either £1,800 a year, or £3,000 in year one followed by £1,800 a year for three years, ending with £600 in the fifth year. You can invest less in any year and catch up, if you wish, in a subsequent year, provided you never exceed £1,800 a year in years two to five.

One problem with TESSAs is that your money is tied up for five years. Investors in TESSAs can usually take all their money out before the five years are up, but only at the cost of losing the tax benefit. Partial withdrawals of capital are not allowed. Interest can be left to accumulate or be paid out annually, in which event it will be paid net of the basic rate of tax. The tax benefit plus interest thereon will follow as a lump sum at the end of the five-year period. You should also watch out for penalties of as much as three months' interest, imposed by some banks and building societies in cases of early withdrawal.

When a TESSA matures after five years, you can reinvest all the capital (but not any interest) in a new TESSA. You have six months from the date your old TESSA matures in which to take advantage of this concession. The annual investment limit remains the same for a replacement TESSA, and there is still an overall limit of £9,000 over five years. The main advantage is that you can invest the capital sum all at once instead of in driblets.

There are a few TESSAs available which pay a fixed rate of interest. These are most appealing when interest rates are high and likely to fall. At times when base rates are likely to go higher, their attractions are less obvious.

Fixed or floating, the rates on offer for TESSA accounts are much of a muchness. For the amounts involved (up to the limit of £9,000) the rates were better than those offered by deposit accounts, even without the tax advantage. Of course, with a five-year obligation, you would expect a good rate. Even compared with National Savings Certificates (which have a similar restriction), TESSAs offer some of the best available rates of interest. For those prepared to tie their money up for five years, they are a good thing.

Although TESSAs are meant to be simple deposit accounts, the financial institutions have managed to make them very complicated. They are fiendishly difficult to compare, without a cold towel around your head and a computer programme. Some pay loyalty bonuses at the end of five years; others offer slightly higher interest if you hand over the full £9,000 in one sum and drip feed it over the years into the TESSA from a 'feeder' account, which will be taxed in the normal way.

Newspapers and magazines occasionally publish guides to best-buy TESSAs but, for a full breakdown of what is available, check with a specialist publication such as *Moneyfacts*. This statistical magazine is packed full of information on interest rates on deposit accounts, TESSAs and mortgages. It is available monthly from Moneyfacts Publications, Laundry Loke, North Walsham, Norfolk, NR28 OBD, Telephone: 01692 500677. The annual subscription is £38.50, but first ask for a sample copy.

NATIONAL SAVINGS

The other main tax-free investments for cash are offered by National Savings, although not all National Savings products are tax-free. Those that are include Savings Certificates (both fixed-interest and index-linked), Children's Bonus Bonds, Premium Bonds and the first £70 of annual interest from an Ordinary Account (£140 for a joint account).

Quite substantial amounts can be invested in these tax-free accounts: up to £10,000 in both fixed-rate and index-linked certificates, plus a further £20,000 in each certificate, if you are reinvesting certificates that have matured.

Investment limits can vary as new certificates are issued and old ones withdrawn. With each new certificate, you can invest up to the maximum allowed, regardless of how much you hold in earlier issues. In April 1995, up to £1,000 can be put into Children's Bonds. Everyone can hold up to £20,000 in Premium Bonds and have £10,000 in a National Savings Ordinary Account.

The National Savings scheme, along with gilts and taxation, is used by the Government to raise the money it needs to run the country. So when Government borrowings are high, National Savings usually pays generous rates to attract extra funds.

Each National Savings certificate pays a guaranteed rate of interest. When the Government wants to alter rates of interest for National Savings, it makes a new issue but continues to pay interest at old rates on all previous issues until their five-year life is up. You will know when a new issue is on offer by reading the personal finance pages of the newspapers.

Interest rates will be very much in line with banks and building societies, but the tax-free aspect enhances the return to taxpayers. A tax-free interest rate of 5.85% is worth 7.8% to savers who pay 25% tax and 9.75% to those paying 40% tax.

Only the Government can dictate which National Savings investments are tax-free; it usually ties up money for five years and also places tight limits on how much investors can save that way.

In April 1995, the 42nd issue fixed-interest savings certificates pay 5.85% a year over five years. The return falls if you cash in early, although there is still no tax to pay. The 8th issue index-linked savings certificates pay a bonus of 3% above inflation if the certificates are held for five years; when inflation is 4%, the return would therefore be 7% tax-free. The minimum investment for both certificates is £100 and the maximum £10,000.

Index-linked savings certificates guarantee to increase the value of your investment in line with inflation. Each year the rate of interest increases from a low of 1.25% in year one to 6.07% in year five, so it is important that your money is left for the full five years.

The table shows how these attractive investments work, assuming an initial outlay of £1,000 and steady inflation of 4% per annum:

Year	Value of investment	Annual index-linking	Annual Interest
Year 1	£1000	£40	£12.50
Year 2	£1052.50	£42.10	£18.42
Year 3	£1113.02	£44.52	£27.83
Year 4	£1185.37	£47.41	£41.49
Year 5	£1274.27	£50.97	£77.35

Value after
five years: £1402.59

On the anniversary of purchase everything you earned in the previous year is added to your capital. In the next year, you earn index-linking and extra interest on the new amount of capital. Not only do you pay no tax on the income from index-linked certificates, but the capital gain is also completely tax-free.

As with fixed-rate TESSAs, fixed-interest certificates are a good buy when interest rates are about to come down; savers with the 35th issue are still earning 9.5% tax-free.

When inflation is high, or about to start rising, index-linked certificates are preferable. The best-paying issue was the 5th series, which paid 4.5% over inflation. I believe index-linked certificates are a good buy almost at any time because, even when inflation is low, other interest rates are also low, and there is the tax-free bonus on top. Also, inflation has a habit of returning and, with a floating pound, this is more likely.

Once National Savings certificates have completed their five-year stint, they move on to the General Extension Rate, which is a minimal rate of interest (3.5% in April 1995). Index-linked certificates continue to earn monthly index-linking, but with only an extra 0.5% a year. *Always remember the anniversary date* and either cash in or transfer your certificates to the latest issue available. *In April 1995, up to £20,000-worth of old certificates can be reinvested on top of the current £10,000 maximum investment.* However, limits change and may vary with each issue.

PREMIUM BONDS

Premium Bonds are another medium of tax-free investment, although they are essentially for gamblers. Like deposit accounts, they have a fixed yield (in April 1995, it was 5.2% per annum) but, instead of being allocated pro-rata, all of the interest is put in a pool and allocated in prizes to the winners every month on a computer draw. In other words, a few lucky winners get a return of well in excess of 5.2%, while most people receive nothing at all.

After a one-month eligibility period, every £1 Premium Bond has one chance of winning a prize in every draw; a £100 bond has a hundred chances. The minimum holding is £100 and the maximum £20,000. Monthly prizes range from £50 to £1 million. Around 315,000 prizes worth £20m are sent out each month. Great fun if you win.

The important point to bear in mind is that, if you were to hold Premium Bonds for a period of, say, five years, you would sacrifice a certain tax-free yield of 5.85% per annum which you could have enjoyed by investing in National Savings certificates. In April 1995, only 5.2% is distributed to Premium Bond winners, which means that you would be losing 0.65% per annum. This is 11% of 5.85%. At a casino, the house would have an advantage of less than 3% if you played roulette with your interest. That compares with the Government's 'take' of 11% for Premium Bonds. The tax benefit is the same in each case, because winnings from gambling are also tax-free.

I would like to make it absolutely clear that I am not suggesting that investors should foresake Premium Bonds and take up gambling, which can be addictive. However, I *am* pointing out that if you buy Premium Bonds, you must be aware that you are gambling with your interest at worse odds than you would obtain by playing roulette once a year in a gaming house. The important advantage of buying Premium Bonds is that you can gamble in the comfort of your own home and you cannot lose more than your interest. If you choose to cash in your bonds, you are guaranteed your capital back in full. You will not end up losing more than you can afford but, make no mistake, Premium Bonds are nothing more than a gamble at poor odds.

SAFETY

This brings me to an important point of principle that is worth dwelling upon. Taking a deliberate gamble, whether in a casino or with Premium Bonds, is a matter of personal choice. However, I have always been puzzled by the way so many people gamble, unintentionally, with their life savings by putting them on deposit with banks like BCCI.

If you are depositing money with a savings institution, the last thing you want to do is to risk any of your precious capital for a miserable 1% a year extra return. Here is an important financial health warning to help you avoid the next failure of a small bank:

✳ Never deal with a company unless the name is familiar and you know that it is well established. If you have not heard of the name before, avoid it; there are plenty of safe institutions, so why take any risk?

✳ Be very wary of any institution which is paying a much higher rate of interest than any of its competitors. The offer is far more likely to be a sign of distress than altruism.

COMPENSATION SCHEMES

Banks and building societies are protected by statutory compensation schemes, so if you have made a deposit with one of them and it fails, you will get back some of your money. 'Some' is the key word – you will not get *all* of your money back, because there are limits on how much the compensation schemes pay out.

All banks and building societies are covered by deposit protection schemes, unless they are trading illegally. Their offshore subsidiaries are also protected.

The building societies' scheme guarantees to return 90% of the money you have on deposit with any one building society, but only up to a ceiling of £20,000. So, the maximum you can be certain of getting back is £18,000. If your account was for £10,000, you would only receive £9,000. The limits are doubled for joint accounts. The protection includes any interest earned to the last accrual date before the society failed and, probably, interest between then and the date of collapse. However, your money will not earn any interest while you wait for it to be paid out.

A great comfort is that no building society has ever lost depositors' money. They are very tightly regulated by the Building Societies Commission and whenever one society has begun to look shaky another larger society has quickly stepped in to rescue it. However, you cannot rely upon this happening next time, so choose well-known, long-established societies and do not deposit more than £20,000 with any of them.

If one of the larger societies were to get into trouble, then the Government would be forced to intervene. The assets of the Halifax Building Society, the largest in the country, are over £72 billion and two households in every five have an account with them.

Unlike building societies, some banks have failed and depositors have lost some of their money as a result. The banks' deposit protection scheme was recently brought into line with the building societies' scheme and now also pays 90% of the first £20,000 deposited with any one bank, including interest earned to the date of collapse. You may receive more if the collapsed bank has sufficient funds to pay something to its depositors.

If you are ever tempted to run the risk of earning a rate of interest which is out of line with the rest of the market, just remember:

1. You can lose everything over £20,000.

2. You can lose 10% of your deposit up to £20,000.

3. You will experience a great deal of unnecessary aggravation and worry, with your capital locked up for a year or more while the failure is being investigated.

4. You will not earn any interest on your money while the mess is being sorted out.

All UK-based banks and deposit-takers, and foreign banks operating in this country, must by law be licensed by the Bank of England, although this does not in any way preclude failure, as depositors in BCCI know only too well.

Small banks often have important-sounding names and seduce depositors with an extra 1% a year. But if I offered you 1%, or even 2%, to put your life savings at risk, you would, rightly, tell me to get lost. When normal rates are 6% a year and someone offers you 7%, remember that you are only being offered an extra 1%. You can obtain the normal rate of 6% with relative safety, so why put any of your precious capital in jeopardy for a measly 1%?

The safety of your capital should be your first, second and third criteria when making a deposit. Shop around for the best rates by all means, but only choose solid institutions that are such an important part of the fabric of society that they would not be allowed to fail. Your capital will then be safe and so will your interest. Safe, that is, against all but the corrosive effect of inflation, which is a problem addressed in later chapters.

CHASING WINDFALLS FROM BUILDING SOCIETIES

The days of the traditional building society owned by its saving and borrowing members could be numbered, as more and more societies are converted to banks owned by shareholders. When this happens, the existing member-owners stand to make small windfalls as they are bought out with cash or free shares.

When Cheltenham & Gloucester was taken over by Lloyds Bank, members received quite large cash hand-outs, determined by the level of their savings. Members of Halifax and Leeds stand to gain free shares when their newly merged society converts to a bank, and it seems that many more societies are now candidates for takeover or conversion. The precise rules for qualifying for a windfall depend on the nature of each takeover or conversion. But there is usually a general minimum requirement that a saver has to have had not less than £100 in a qualifying account for at least two years. Not all accounts confer membership and qualify the holder for a payout.

There is an argument for spreading savings around a number of societies in a kind of speculative way, although a minimum £100 deposit may not qualify for the maximum payout. *Always check whether a particular account confers membership*. There is little to lose in depositing money amongst a number of societies in the hope of windfall gain, except that lower balances do not always obtain the highest interest rates. However, this may be a small price to pay in view of the prospect of disproportionate windfalls.

HOW TO INVEST IN A DEPOSIT ACCOUNT AND NATIONAL SAVINGS

These are the easiest investments to make because banks, building societies and the Post Office have numerous branches throughout the country.

When picking a bank or building society, you may be tempted to stick with one you have used in the past. However, it is advisable to put a little more research into your decision because there is no reason to stay loyal these days *just for the sake of it*.

If you decide to buy a TESSA, the bank or building society will provide the application form and deal with the Inland Revenue. You will have to provide your National Insurance number and proof of identity, such as a passport. Some will remind you to invest another tranche when the anniversary comes round each year; others do not seem to bother.

The personal finance pages of newspapers and consumer money magazines frequently carry articles about deposit accounts, although not necessarily in every issue. For more comprehensive details of all the accounts available, check with a statistical magazine such as *Moneyfacts*.

National Savings leaflets and application forms are available from every post office in the country. You can also respond to advertisements on television, in newspapers and magazines. For up-to-the-minute information on interest rates and products, telephone the National Savings Sales Information Unit free on 0645 645000.

SUMMARY

1. Before buying your own home, or investing in unit trusts, investment trusts or shares, make sure that you have some money on deposit for a rainy day.

2. Set aside money for life insurance, illness, old age and school fees.

3. Your overriding priority should be to keep your capital safe.

4. Funds being kept in reserve, for known future expenditure a few

years hence, can earn better interest rates by being invested for one to two years.

5. Married couples with only one spouse paying tax should split their deposits between them to use up the personal allowance of the non-taxpayer. They should also take advantage of one spouse paying a lower tax rate than the other.

6. Shop around for the best interest rates, but only consider well-established institutions with household names. Beware of institutions offering substantially more than their competitors.

7. There is an argument for spreading savings around a number of building societies in the hope of a windfall gain from a takeover or conversion to a bank. *Always check that a particular account confers membership.*

8. Building societies have a further advantage – no building society has failed so far.

9. Do not keep more than £20,000 on deposit in one name (£40,000 for a married couple's joint account) with any one building society or bank, unless its credit rating is unquestionable.

10. Consider an investment of up to £9,000 in a tax-free TESSA, particularly if you are a higher-rate taxpayer and can leave the money untouched for five years.

11. Consider National Savings certificates, especially if you pay tax at the top rate and can tie up your money for five years. Index-linked certificates are particularly attractive at times when inflation is likely to return.

12. Make a careful note of anniversary dates for National Savings. In April 1995, up to £20,000 can be reinvested in addition to the normal limit of £10,000 for both fixed-interest and index-linked savings certificates.

13. Bear in mind that with Premium Bonds you are gambling (at not particularly attractive odds) with the interest that you could otherwise receive tax-free.

14. Once you have made five-year investments in National Savings and TESSAs, there is little you can do except wait for maturity. However, money on short and medium-term deposit needs

monitoring and managing. Keep an eye on interest rates each week by checking the personal finance pages of the newspapers or subscribing to a statistical service such as *Moneyfacts*.

2

—

GILTS

Because of inflation, gilts have not always been the safe haven that might be expected from a Government security. They are free of capital gains tax, but most investors should only buy conventional gilts when interest rates are about to fall sharply. Index-linked gilts are more attractive when inflation is likely to rise.

We have already seen how the Government can raise money by issuing National Savings certificates. Apart from taxes, the other way it can generate funds to finance the difference between its annual income and expenditure is through the gilt-edged market. The Bank of England acts as the Government's agent in the gilt-edged market and sells, purchases and pays the interest on the gilt-edged stocks that are created by the Treasury.

A gilt is an IOU from the Government promising to pay you, the lender, interest at a fixed rate for a prescribed period at the end of which, if the gilt is dated, you will also receive back your capital. Most gilts are *dated* (redeemable at a fixed future date), but a few are *undated* (irredeemable). An undated gilt simply promises to pay interest at a fixed rate *ad infinitum* – your capital can only be recovered if the Government decides to redeem the stock or if you sell in the market at a profit or loss.

So far, gilts sound a little like National Savings certificates. A deposit is made with the Government for a fixed time and receives a fixed return. But there is a crucial difference – gilts are traded on a market and so their value can go up and down. They fluctuate for several reasons, but the most important influence on conventional gilt prices is the general level of interest rates. If interest rates rise, gilts fall in value and if interest rates fall, gilts appreciate. When you come to sell, the total return from a gilt will depend on two things: the interest you have received and any profit or loss on your original capital.

A good example of this is the infamous 3½% War Loan, which was issued undated. In 1916, you would have paid £100 for every £100 worth of stock and received, before tax, £3.50 per annum thereafter. In April 1995, an investor who could get a 6% return from a building society account would not be interested in 3½% from War Loan. The market price reflects this and, as a result, it has more than halved in value and in April 1995 stood at only £42¼. At that price, the £3.50 dividend represented a yield of 8.3%. This admittedly extreme example of how undated gilts work also illustrates a major drawback of conventional gilts. They offer no protection against the ravages of inflation.

Bearing in mind that the purchasing power of £100 in 1916 was thirty-five times greater than £100 in 1995 (and eighty times greater than £42¼) it is easy to understand why some of the original investors in 3½% War Loan might describe the stock with a stronger word than 'infamous'. What is true of 3½% War Loan is true, to a lesser extent, of all fixed-interest investments *including dated ones*, which goes part way to explaining the poor long-term performance of gilts compared with other forms of investment. As you will see from the chart below, on an income-reinvested basis, the stock market has vastly outperformed gilts and inflation as measured by the Retail Prices Index (RPI).

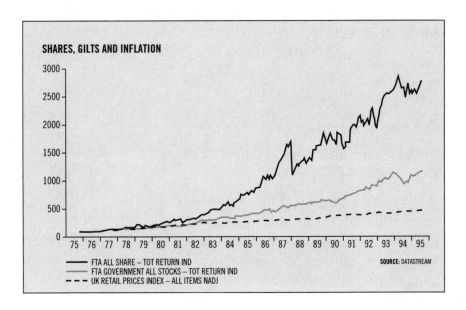

SHARES, GILTS AND INFLATION

— FTA ALL SHARE – TOT RETURN IND
— FTA GOVERNMENT ALL STOCKS – TOT RETURN IND
--- UK RETAIL PRICES INDEX – ALL ITEMS NADJ

SOURCE: DATASTREAM

THE LANGUAGE OF GILTS

Before we concentrate upon their attractions or failings as an investment, you need to understand the jargon of gilts:

1. **Treasury, Exchequer and Funding** – Gilts are usually named 'Treasury', 'Exchequer' or 'Funding'; for example 'Treasury 8¾% 2017' or 'Exchequer 12% 1998'. The names are interchangeable and mean the same thing – the Government guarantees repayment of the debt. The two examples also tell you that the years 2017 and 1998 are the dates that the stocks will be redeemed (repaid) and that 8¾% and 12% are the rates of annual interest investors will be paid six-monthly in the meantime.

2. **Classification** – Dated gilts are classified according to the number of years they have left to run before they become due for redemption (repayment). The *Financial Times* shows stocks with lives of up to five years as 'shorts', those with five to fifteen years remaining are sometimes called 'medium dated' and 'longs' have over fifteen years to run. This is how they appeared in mid-April 1995:

UK GILTS PRICES

Notes	Yield Int	Yield Red	Price £	+or –	1995 High	1995 Low
Shorts" (Lives up to Five Years)						
Exch 10¼pc 1995	10.14	6.31	101 3/32	.....	101 7/8	101 3/32
Treas 12¾pc 1995‡‡	12.31	6.50	103 9/16xd	.....	104 7/8	103 9/16
14pc 1996	13.30	6.84	105 1/4	–1/8	106 7/8	105 1/4
15¼pc 1996‡‡	14.09	6.98	108 7/32xd	–1/32	109 5/8	108 7/32
Exch 13¼pc 1996‡‡	12.46	7.01	106 3/8xd	–1/32	107 1/7	106 9/32
Conversion 10pc 1996	9.64	7.37	103 25/32xd	.....	103 27/32	103 3/32
Treas 13¼pc 1997‡‡	12.14	7.58	109 3/16	–1/32	109 9/16	108 11/16
Exch 10½pc 1997	10.01	7.56	104 15/16	.....	105 19/32	104 1/32
Treas cnv 7pc 1997‡‡	7.10	7.63	98 5/8	+3/32	98 5/8	97 1/8
Treas 8¾pc 1997‡‡	8.58	7.76	102	+1/16	102	100 1/32
Exch 15pc 1997	12.93	7.87	115 31/32xd	.....	116 3/16	114 15/16
9¾pc 1998	9.35	7.96	104 1/4	.....	105 13/16	102 3/4
Treas 7¼pc 1998‡‡	7.39	7.96	98 1/16	+1/16	98 1/16	96 3/16
Treas 6¾pc 1995-98‡‡	6.98	7.97	96 21/32xd	+1/32	96 21/32	94 13/16
14pc 1998-1	12.10	8.15	115 21/32	.....	115 21/32	114 9/32
Treas 15½pc '98‡‡	12.71	8.04	121 15/16	+1/32	122 3/32	120 3/8
Exch 12pc 1998	10.75	8.15	111 21/32xd	.....	111 21/32	109 21/32
Treas 9½pc 1999‡‡	9.11	8.13	104 1/4	.....	104 1/4	100 7/8
Treas Fltg Rate 1999	–	–	100 1/8	.....	100 1/8	99 13/32
Exch 12¼pc 1999	10.81	8.20	113 5/16	.....	113 5/16	111 7/16
Treas 10½pc 1999	9.74	8.20	107 13/16xd	.....	107 13/16	105 13/32
Treas 6pc 1999‡‡	6.50	8.12	92 11/32	+1/16	92 11/32	89 15/16
Conversion 10¼pc 1999	9.55	8.26	107 3/8	.....	107 3/8	105 1/8
Five to Fifteen Years						
Conv 9pc 2000‡‡	8.74	8.20	103 1/32	+3/32	103 1/32	100 23/32
Treas 13pc 2000	10.90	8.34	119 5/16	+1/32	119 3/8	117
8pc 2000‡‡	8.08	8.18	99 1/32	+1/16	99 1/32	96 9/16
10pc 2001	9.30	8.31	107 9/16	+3/32	107 9/16	104 25/32
7pc 2001‡‡	7.48	8.27	93 17/32xd	+1/8	93 17/32	90 21/32
9¾pc 2002	9.10	8.40	107 5/32	+7/32	107 3/4	103 31/32
8pc 2003‡‡	8.18	8.36	97 3/4	+9/32	98 11/32	94 5/8
10pc 2003	9.16	8.42	109 3/16	+5/16	109 3/4	105 7/8
Treas 11½pc 2001-4	10.12	8.49	113 5/8	+3/32	113 5/8	110 31/32
Funding 3½pc 1999-4	4.58	7.03	76 3/8	+1/2	76 1/2	73
Conversion 9½pc 2004	8.89	8.41	106 27/32	+11/32	107 7/16	103 5/16
Treas 6¾pc 2004‡‡	7.54	8.33	89 9/16	+5/16	90 5/32	86 7/16
Conv 9½pc 2005	8.86	8.40	107 3/16xd	+11/32	107 25/32	103 5/8
8½pc 2005‡‡	8.41	8.31	101 1/8	+11/32	101 3/4	97 5/8
Treas 12½pc 2003-5	10.14	8.59	123 1/4	+7/32	123 7/8	119 15/32
7¾pc 2006‡‡	8.11	8.33	95 19/32	+11/32	96 1/8	92 1/8
8pc 2002-6‡‡	8.22	8.36	97 9/32	+13/32	97 23/32	93 3/4
Treas 11¾pc 2003-7	10.02	8.61	117 5/16	+3/32	117 3/8	113 31/32
Treas 8½pc 2007‡‡	8.40	8.32	101 5/32	+3/8	101 5/32	97 17/32
13½pc 2004-8	10.38	8.59	130 1/32	+9/32	130 1/32	126 3/32
Treas 9pc 2008‡‡	8.55	8.32	105 7/32	+3/8	105 7/32	101 5/8
Treas 8pc 2009	8.23	8.32	97 5/32	+3/8	97 21/32	94
Over Fifteen Years						
Treas 6¼pc 2010	7.58	8.25	82 13/32	+9/32	82 13/32	79 9/32
Conv 9pc Ln 2011‡‡	8.51	8.32	105 3/4	+3/8	105 3/4	101 27/32
Treas 9pc 2012‡‡	8.49	8.31	106 1/32	+5/16	106 1/32	102 1/32
Treas 5½pc 2008-12‡‡	7.25	8.09	75 13/16	+5/16	75 13/16	72 3/4
Treas 8pc 2013‡‡	8.23	8.27	97 1/4	+5/16	97 1/4	93 15/32
7¾pc 2012-15‡‡	8.19	8.27	94 5/8	+3/8	94 5/8	91 21/32
8pc 2015	8.21	8.24	97 13/32	+5/16	97 13/32	93 21/32
Treas 8¾pc 2017‡‡	8.35	8.25	104 13/16	+11/32	104 13/16	100 21/32
Exch 12pc 2013-17	9.05	8.46	132 19/32	+3/8	132 19/32	127 9/16
Undated						
Consols 4pc	8.52	–	46 15/16	+7/32	47 3/32	45 1/8
War Loan 3½pc‡‡	8.28	–	42 1/4	+5/32	42 1/4	40 15/32
Conv 3½pc '61 Aft	5.96	–	58 11/16	+1/16	58 3/4	57 15/32
Treas 3pc '66 Aft	8.53	–	35 3/16	.....	35 21/32	34 1/4
Consols 2½pc	8.28	–	30 3/16	+1/16	30 3/16	28 23/32
Treas 2½pc	8.39	–	29 13/16	+1/4	29 13/16	28 3/8

The 'Treasury 8¾% 2017' are 'longs' of over fifteen years and the 'Exchequer 12% 1998' is a 'short'.

Some stocks, such as Treasury 6¾% 1995-8, have more than one possible redemption date. 1995, 1996, 1997 and 1998 are the years during which redemption might take place. The Government has the right to choose any time within those four years, and will do so according to the prevailing level of interest rates. For example, if market rates suddenly dropped to 4% per annum, the Government would redeem immediately to avoid having to pay the excess interest of 2.75% per annum.

3. **Cum and Ex-dividend** – Interest on gilt-edged securities is paid half-yearly. When you buy them cum dividend (with the dividend included) you will be entitled to the interest that has accrued (accumulated). If, for example, three months have passed since the last dividend payment, half of the next payment will have accrued. The quoted price will exclude the accrued income, and all yields will be calculated without taking it into account. You will pay extra for the accrued interest and be entitled to it. On some

occasions, when the stock is about to pay a dividend, it can be bought *ex-dividend* (xd; without the dividend). In that event, the dividend will be retained by the seller.

YIELDS

Because the prices of gilts move up and down, the interest return or yield is rarely the same as the percentage figure in their name. For example, to buy the return of 5.5% interest on £100 of Treasury 5½% 2008-12, you only had to pay £75¹³⁄₁₆ in April 1995. At that price the return is a more attractive 7.25%.

To complicate matters further, gilts have two different yields. Dated gilts have a *running yield* (sometimes called interest or flat yield) and a *redemption yield*. The running yield is easy to calculate – just take the interest rate of the stock, divide it by the market price and multiply by 100. That is how the 7.25% yield was calculated on the Treasury 5½% 2008-12.

Here is another example: in April 1995, Treasury 8¾% 2017 had a market price of £104¹³⁄₁₆ xd and a yield of 8.35%. The calculation works like this:

$$\frac{8¾ \text{ (the interest rate)}}{104^{13/16} \text{ (the market price)}} \times 100 = 8.35\%$$

Calculating the redemption yield is much more difficult. If you buy a gilt under par for, say, £80, you know that you will eventually be repaid at par of £100 and the difference of £20 will be an extra gain over and above your annual interest. That extra gain can be spread over the life of the stock and added to the running yield in a complicated calculation involving compound interest. For example, in April 1995 Funding 3½% 1999-2004 stock was priced at £76³⁄₈ and had a redemption yield of 7.03% compared with the running yield of 4.58%.

Conversely, if you buy a stock at more than par, the redemption yield will be lower than the running yield. The excess that you pay over par has to be deducted from the running yield to compensate for the fact that you have paid out more than you will receive on redemption. In the case of Exchequer 12% 1998, for example, the running yield in April 1995 was 10.75% and the redemption yield was lower, at 8.15%. The good news is that you do not have to worry about calculating either running or redemption yields. They are both shown clearly in the *Financial Times* and several other newspapers.

It is important to remember that redemption yields are only meaningful if stocks are held until they are repaid. Meanwhile, the market price will fluctuate, driven by the fears and hopes of investors. The nearer the redemption date, the nearer the market price will be to par – held there by the so-called 'pull' of redemption.

INDEX-LINKED GILTS

Another very different type of gilt-edged stock is one that is linked to the Retail Prices Index (RPI) with the aim of protecting *both your capital and income* against inflation.

Index-linked stocks are shown each day in the *Financial Times*:

	Notes	...Yield... 1	2	Price £	+or –	...1995... High	Low
Index-Linked	(b)						
2pc '96	(67.9)	1.32	3.00	208 5/32	+7/32	208 5/32	201 1/16
4 5/8pc '98‡‡	(135.6)	2.55	3.41	109 7/32xd	.....	109 7/32	106 5/16
2 1/2pc '01	(78.3)	3.33	3.75	169 15/16	+5/32	169 15/16	165 25/32
2 1/2pc '03	(78.8)	3.43	3.76	166 1/32xd	+1/8	166 1/32	161 13/16
4 3/8pc '04‡‡	(135.6)	3.46	3.77	110 11/16xd	+1/16	110 11/16	108 3/32
2pc '06	(69.5)	3.52	3.76	173 1/8	+3/16	173 1/8	168 7/32
2 1/2pc '09	(78.8)	3.57	3.77	156 25/32xd	+1/32	156 25/32	152 3/32
2 1/2pc '11	(74.6)	3.60	3.78	162 1/8	+1/32	162 1/8	157 3/16
2 1/2pc '13	(89.2)	3.61	3.77	133 3/4	+1/16	133 3/4	129 9/32
2 1/2pc '16	(81.6)	3.64	3.80	142 11/32	+3/32	142 11/32	137 5/8
2 1/2pc '20	(83.0)	3.67	3.80	136 5/8xd	+1/16	136 5/8	131 27/32
2 1/2pc '24‡‡	(97.7)	3.66	3.78	113 5/8	+3/32	113 5/8	109 1/4
4 1/8pc '30‡‡	(135.1)	3.68	3.80	112 5/8	+1/8	112 5/8	108 9/32

Prospective real redemption rate on projected Inflation of (1) 10% and (2) 5%. (b) Figures in parentheses show RPI base for Indexing (ie 8 months prior to issue) and have been adjusted to reflect rebasing of RPI to 100 in February 1987. Conversion factor 3.945. RPI for August 1994: 144.7 and for March 1995: 147.5.

For example, 2% Treasury 2006 was issued at par of £100 in 1981. The Government promised to pay interest until the year 2006 at the rate of 2% per annum plus the rise in the RPI in each year. In 1981, the RPI base for indexing purposes was (after some very complicated adjustments) 69.5. The next two columns show the *real* redemption yields based on 10% inflation and 5% inflation. The price of the stock in April 1995 was £173⅛. The price rose £3/16, the day before, the 1995 high was £173⅛ and the low £168 7/32.

You will notice that the redemption yields are very low. The reason is that, in addition to annual interest being topped up each year by the RPI (with an eight-month time lag), *the capital sum repaid on redemption will also be increased by the full increase in the RPI over the whole period.* This capital gain can be enjoyed tax-free, because there is no capital gains tax on gilts. If, by the year 2006, the RPI over the period had risen by, say, 150%, the gilt would be redeemed in that year for £250. *Although the yield might have been relatively low, the purchasing power of the original £100 would have been protected.*

Obviously, it pays to buy index-linked gilts when there is a substantial risk of increased inflation. It can also be argued that it always pays to buy them in preference to conventional gilts, unless interest rates are about to fall sharply. When inflation is at a low level, other competitive interest rates will also be low. The key point about index-linked gilts is that your capital will be protected against the potentially ravaging effects of inflation.

There is no doubt that undated gilts like 3½% War Loan savagely reduced the capital of the investing public who subscribed. There is also no doubt that, even with dated gilts, although you will get your capital back with interest, that capital is very likely to have lost much of its purchasing power. No one can foretell the future but, if the past is anything to go by, your capital needs protecting against inflation. (I remember in my youth, fifty years ago, a daily newspaper cost a penny, against today's price of around 50p in new pennies. As new pennies are worth 2.4 times as much as old pennies, that means that the price has risen by 120 times. My father's house cost about £1,000; the same house today is worth £150,000.)

Equities are a practical solution to the problem of inflation, which will be dealt with in later chapters, but for people of a nervous disposition, who cannot accept an equity risk, index-linked gilts seem to me to be the first Government security that offers the investor a fair deal after allowing for inflation.

THE TAX BENEFITS OF GILTS

The main difference between gilts and other investments (apart from those which are tax-free) is that there is never capital gains tax (CGT) to pay on gilt profits and you do not even have to disclose any profits from selling gilts on your tax return. This has very obvious advantages to investors who regularly exceed their annual CGT allowance, but is of no consequence to those who do not earn enough to pay CGT in the first place.

If you buy a gilt when it is first issued and hold it to redemption, you will have paid out £100 and will receive back £100; there is no capital growth, so no CGT would arise. However, you *can* make capital gains from gilts. If you buy in the market at £95 and sell during the lifetime of the gilt at £110, you make a tax-free profit of £15.

You do, however, have to pay income tax on the interest you receive. Gilts bought through a stockbroker already have basic-rate tax deducted before the interest is paid out (apart from 3½% War Loan). Basic-rate taxpayers have no further tax to pay, but higher-rate taxpayers must settle the difference when making their tax returns. Non-taxpayers can reclaim the tax already paid.

When you buy through the National Savings Stock Register (NSSR), interest is paid gross. Non-taxpayers avoid the trouble of having to reclaim the money already deducted and taxpayers enjoy a delay until the tax bill arrives, but everyone must declare income from gilts to the Revenue.

The less interest you earn, the less income tax is payable, so higher-rate taxpayers should choose a gilt with a low interest rate, but with greater potential for capital gain on redemption. For example, in April 1995, Treasury 5½% 2008-12 at £75$^{13}/_{16}$ offers a capital gain of £24$^{3}/_{16}$ on redemption between 2008 and 2012. In the meantime, its yield is a lowish 7.25%. The same rules apply to index-linked gilts – the inflation-proofing element of the return of your capital is also free of CGT.

NEW RULES FOR TAXING GILTS AND CORPORATE BONDS

As we went to press in mid-1995, the Government issued a consultation paper on the taxation of gilts and bonds. A key proposal is to levy income tax on any gain on gilts and qualifying corporate bonds. You make a gain if you sell a gilt or bond for more than the price you paid for it, or if you hold it to redemption and receive more than you paid.

Under the old rules, you pay income tax only on the interest payment. Any gains are free of income tax and capital gains tax. Under the new plan, any gain would also be subject to income tax, although any losses you made would be set against your income.

However, it looks as though most private investors will not notice any difference. The Government has set a threshold of £200,000 of nominal value of all the gilts and bonds held. Anyone with holdings below the threshold will pay income tax only on the interest, not on any capital gains.

INFLUENCES ON GILT PRICES

Between issue and redemption, the prices of gilts fluctuate all the time as they react to external events such as the state of the economy.

Good for gilts
General interest rates are falling.
People think that interest rates are about to fall (markets look ahead).
Inflation is low (but bad news for index-linked gilts).
Other forms of investment are less attractive (for example, dividend yields are low).
Bonds in other countries are less attractive.
Sterling is strengthening (making gilts more attractive to overseas buyers).

Bad for gilts
General interest rates are about to rise.
People think that interest rates are about to rise (the longer the life of the gilt still left to run, the more the market takes a longer-term view of interest rates).
Inflation is high, or rising (apart from index-linked gilts).
Other investments are more attractive.
Foreign bonds are more attractive.
Sterling is weakening (frightening overseas buyers).

HOW TO BUY AND SELL GILTS

Gilts are very easy to buy and sell. The charges can be very low and there is no stamp duty. If you need advice on which gilts to buy, consult a stockbroker or investment adviser. These are the ways to buy them:

1. *New issues*

When you buy newly-issued gilts, there are no charges at all. Use an application form from a prospectus in a newspaper or contact the Bank of England at Threadneedle Street, London EC2R 8AH and ask for the appropriate form. The Bank's Registrar's department at Southgate House, Southgate Street, Gloucester GL1 1UW (Telephone: 01452 398000) maintains a mailing list of investors who are interested in hearing about new issues. The minimum amount you can buy is £1,000 worth of stock, but you might not have to pay for it all at once. For gilts which are issued partly-paid, you may have to pay only, say, half at the outset and then the balance a month or two later.

New gilts are often issued through auctions, but this does not make any difference to the small investor. You will have to buy a minimum £1,000 worth of stock, for which you will pay the average of the prices paid by the successful bidders, who will be professional investors such as pension funds, banks and insurance companies. You will pay more than some of the professionals and less than others for the same stock.

Occasionally, new issues come out through a tender. The Bank of England sets a minimum price but invites potential investors to bid higher. Once the bids are in, the Bank sets an allotment price, which is the same for everybody. Shortly after you have bought a new issue, you will receive a letter of allotment detailing the stock you hold.

2. National Savings Stock Register

The cheapest and simplest way to buy gilts which are already trading is through the National Savings Stock Register (NSSR). Application forms can be obtained from a post office.

You can buy up to £25,000 worth of any particular gilt each day through the NSSR. There is no minimum purchase requirement and no limit to the total amount you can hold, although you need a separate application form for each gilt you buy. The charge is 0.6% commission on the first £5,000 worth of gilts and 0.35% on any amount over £5,000 with a minimum charge of £5. Buying £1,000 worth of gilts will cost £6.

Once the deal has been done, you will receive an investment certificate and a statement detailing how much it has cost you.

Interest payments will be made through the Department for National Savings, either by cheque or direct into your bank or building society account.

To sell through the NSSR, simply pick up a sale application form from a post office and send it, together with the investment certificate, in the envelope provided. The cost for buying is the same as for selling, except that there is no minimum charge. Selling £1,000 worth of gilts will therefore also cost £6.

There are a few drawbacks to buying and selling gilts this way. You will not get any advice about which one you should buy. National Savings will buy and sell on your behalf as quickly as possible, and usually on the day they receive your instructions. However, they do not guarantee instant service, so the price you pay might not be the same as when you place the order.

3.   *Stockbrokers and banks*

Stockbrokers offer various levels of service (see Chapter 14). At the cheapest end, you can give instructions to an execution-only broker to buy the gilt of your choice. The commission will be about 1%, although you will probably find that there is a minimum charge of £20. If you want advice on which stock to buy, you need a full advisory stockbroking service, which is more expensive for people dealing in a small way (under, say, £5,000). The minimum charge could be much higher.

Alternatively, you can deal through your bank; some of them now have their own stockbroking subsidiaries but, if not, the bank staff will pass your instructions on to a stockbroker they use. Many people buy gilts and hold them to redemption, in which case there is no point in dealing other than through the NSSR.

Once you have decided exactly what you want to buy or sell (preferably with your broker's advice), give the necessary instructions. As soon as the deal is done, your broker will send you a contract note showing what you have bought, the price and the broker's commission. You will have to produce a cheque immediately because, unlike shares, gilts have to be paid for on the following day. A few days later, you will receive a stock certificate which confirms your ownership of the stock. The Bank of England will then begin to send you the half-yearly interest payments.

4. *Buying gilts through a unit trust*

Anyone who is sure that they want to have gilts as part of their portfolio, but is nervous about making buying and selling decisions at the right time, could invest in a specialist gilt or fixed-interest unit trust, some of which include foreign bonds as well as UK gilts. These trusts buy a wide range of gilts as and when the fund manager thinks the time is right.

There are, however, two major disadvantages. You have to pay an initial fee of between 3% and 5% and an annual management charge of between 0.75% and 1.5%. More importantly, any capital profits you might make on the units will suffer capital gains tax.

WHICH GILTS TO CHOOSE

If *you are a higher-rate taxpayer*
Select a low-coupon gilt standing at below par to minimise your income tax and maximise your tax-free capital gain on redemption.

If *you are worried that inflation is going to rise*
Buy index-linked gilts to maintain the spending power of your money.

If *you need a certain amount of money without fail in a few years' time*
Buy gilts at or below-par value. Gilts guarantee to pay back £100 face value on the redemption date. If you buy for less than £100 you will make a certain tax-free gain; if you pay more than par you will take a loss.

If *you need an income which will not fluctuate*
Interest on conventional gilts is fixed and will never vary. Choose a medium-coupon gilt priced at around £100.

If *you pay capital gains tax*
There is no capital gains tax to pay on gilts, however much profit you make. Do not buy a gilt unit trust because that would be subject to CGT.

If *you are a non-taxpayer*
Buy through the NSSR because interest is paid gross. Choose a high-coupon gilt for maximum income, although bear in mind that this will probably result in a capital loss at redemption.

If *you want a long-term investment you can put away and forget*
Dated gilts are very safe investments because they are backed by the
Government and, if you hold them to maturity, you always know how
much you will be paid back.

If *you are living outside the UK*
Non-residents can arrange for interest to be paid gross on certain gilts.

SUMMARY

1. A gilt is an IOU from the Government promising to pay you, the
    lender, interest at a fixed rate for a prescribed period at the end of
    which, if the gilt is dated, you will also receive back your capital.
    The names Treasury, Exchequer or Funding all mean the same
    thing – the Government stands behind the stock.

2. Gilts go up in times of falling interest rates when inflation is low,
    the economy is strong and the dividend yield on shares and other
    investments is less attractive. Gilts go down when the opposite
    conditions prevail.

3. Gilts are either redeemable (dated) or irredeemable (undated).
    With redeemable gilts, you will always receive the par value of
    your stock, if you wait for redemption. Undated gilts may never
    be repaid and, for that reason, can be a very unwise investment in
    inflationary times.

4. Dated gilts have a running yield and a redemption yield. If the gilt
    is purchased below par, the redemption yield will be higher than
    the running yield. If the gilt is purchased above par, the redemption
    yield will be lower. Dated gilts should be purchased when interest
    rates are falling sharply, but remember that inflation may
    substantially lessen the 'real' return.

5. Index-linked gilts are an excellent hedge against inflation,
    protecting both capital and income. There are arguments for
    buying index-linked gilts even in periods of low inflation, as all
    yields are low then. As soon as inflation resurges, index-linked
    gilts come into their own.

6. You pay extra for the accrued income of a gilt and you are entitled
    to it.

7. Unit holders in gilt unit trusts are not eligible for capital gains tax exemption on the capital profits made by selling their units. They also have to pay both initial and annual management charges.

8. Gilts can be bought through your stockbroker, bank or the National Savings Stock Register. New issues can be bought direct from the Bank of England. Gilts bought through the NSSR have interest paid gross.

9. All capital gains on gilts are at present tax-free. Income is taxed in the normal way. The Government issued a consultation paper in mid-1995. It proposes to levy income tax on any capital gains on gilts. However, most investors will be unaffected as the Government has set a threshold of £200,000 nominal value of all the gilts and corporate bonds held.

3

—

CORPORATE BONDS, PIBS AND GUARANTEED BONDS

You can obtain a higher yield than on gilts and you can obtain a tax-free yield from corporate bonds placed in a PEP. However, other securities are riskier and, in some cases, difficult to sell in an emergency.

Most safety-first investors are likely to settle for the tax-free benefits of TESSAs, the ease of access of deposit accounts or the peace of mind offered by Government securities. Apart from equity-based investments, however, there are a few other fixed-rate financial products that will be of interest to investors seeking a higher yield.

CORPORATE BONDS

We have seen how the Government borrows money by selling gilts to institutions and other investors. Companies borrow in a similar way by issuing loan stocks, also known as corporate bonds. They are very like dated gilts, with redemption dates and fixed rates of interest.

39

Loan stocks, like shares and gilts, are traded on the stock market. In order to buy them, you will need the services of a stockbroker (see Chapter 14) or your bank.

Specified corporate bonds, preference shares and convertibles can now be housed in a PEP and ringfenced from both capital gains tax and income tax. To qualify, corporate bonds must be denominated in sterling, issued at a fixed rate and have a minimum term to redemption of five years from the time they are bought. The qualifying companies in which you invest must not be financial companies (defined as institutions authorised under the 1987 Banking Act) and must be incorporated in the case of preference shares and convertible preference shares in any EC member State and in the case of corporate bonds and convertibles in the UK. The permanent interest bearing shares of building societies cannot be held in a PEP.

Almost invariably, loan stocks have a higher yield than shares, because they do not offer the prospect of rising dividends. If you buy loan stocks at their par value (usually the issue price and, as with gilts, always the redemption price) the most you can hope for is to have your money repaid on the redemption date and to receive a fixed rate of interest during the life of the stock. The interest on loan stocks is more certain than the dividends on shares. Interest falls due for payment whether or not the company makes a profit, whereas dividends on ordinary shares are payable at the directors' discretion. As a general classification, debentures, unsecured loan stocks and convertibles are often called bonds. Their characteristics and how they work in practice for an issuing company are explained in Chapter 12.

In just the same way that gilts are exempt from capital gains tax, so are all corporate bonds that are denominated and repayable in sterling. If interest rates are falling, bonds can be an excellent investment. All other things being equal, a bond yielding 10% seems very attractive if the base rate is only 6%. In such a case, the bond price quickly rises to remove the discrepancy, bringing the yield down closer to the base rate. Conversely, with a base rate of 10%, a bond yielding only 8% is unattractive and its price falls accordingly.

Unsecured loan stocks, or debentures with fixed redemption dates and fixed rates of interest, are in many ways very similar to gilts. However, the safety offered by any company is pale in comparison with a gilt, which is backed by the Government. Also, loan stocks are far less liquid (easy to sell) than gilts, which can always be sold instantly. As a result, bond yields tend to be higher than gilt yields.

Below are three typical bonds, with the prices they traded at in April 1995, together with their yields:

Bond	Price £	Yield %
Courtaulds 7¾%		
Unsecured Loan Stock 2000/05	91	8.5
BOC 12¼%		
Unsecured Loan Stock 2012/17	127¼	9.6
Trafalgar House 9½%		
Unsecured Loan Stock 2000/05	94	10.1

As you can see, two were quoted at a yield premium ranging from about 1% to 1.5% to the benchmark ten-year Government stock, which yielded about 8.5% in April 1995. Trafalgar House had a higher yield than the other two, because investors perceived that the risk was greater.

Obviously, a bond yielding as much as 15% would seem very attractive if the base rate was only 6–7%. However, a yield this high would almost certainly be a warning signal that the interest payment may not be met; any capital investment would also be at risk.

CONVERTIBLES

For investors who want their capital to be secure, to receive a fixed rate of interest and, at the same time, the hope of capital gain, convertible loan stocks are a possible answer. However, unlike other corporate bonds, convertibles are not exempt from capital gains tax (unless they qualify for inclusion and are used in a PEP). Usually they are very like a normal unsecured company loan stock, but the holder has the extra and important advantage of having the right (but not the obligation) to convert into shares in the company in question. The terms upon which the loan stock can be converted vary from one stock to another, but they are always set out in the company's Annual Report.

A conversion right into a company's shares is a valuable option, which the company charges you for by offering you a lower rate of interest than you would otherwise obtain. There would usually be at least a 2% gap, and possibly more, between a straight unsecured loan stock and a convertible in the same company.

If your primary concern is the security of your capital, you should only invest in the loan stocks of leading companies as they are issued or when they can be bought in the market near to par value or below it. The important point to bear in mind with a convertible is that its price tends to track the ordinary share. If a company's shares have risen by 50% since the date of issue, there is every possibility that the convertible will have risen by about 50% as well. In that event, the convertible would no longer offer a new purchaser the security of knowing that their investment would be repaid in full. If the share price fell, and the new purchaser waited until the redemption date, for every £150 invested only the par value of £100 would be paid back. The £50 of market froth would have disappeared, due to the fall in the share price.

Another factor in considering convertibles is the so-called conversion premium – the difference between a company's share price and the price at which conversion can be exercised. The share price at the time of the issue might be 120p, but the conversion price could easily be 150p, giving a conversion premium of 30p. In that event, it would be an uneconomic proposition to buy the convertible and convert it into ordinary shares. If you did so, you would lose the conversion premium immediately. When the conversion premium is very high, a loan stock is far more influenced by the factors that move fixed interest markets. For example, a change in interest rates could have a powerful effect. Once the conversion premium sinks to a low level and the shares start to move, the market price of the convertible will be mainly influenced by the performance of the shares. If a convertible has doubled in price to keep up with fast-moving ordinary shares, the original yield will have halved and be largely academic. At some point, however, it may pay to convert into ordinary shares because the dividends being paid by the company far outweigh the interest being paid on the convertible. A very nice problem to have – unfortunately it does not happen very often.

CORDIANT

Below is an example of a typical convertible share, issued by Cordiant, formerly called Saatchi & Saatchi, the advertising agency:

The Cordiant 6% Convertible Unsecured Loan Stock (2015), as its name suggests, pays a rate of £6 interest for every £100 (the par value) of the loan stock. It will do so until the year 2015, when it will be repaid at par or until conversion into ordinary shares. Conversion is at the rate of 25 ordinary shares for every £100 of loan stock.

In April 1995, the ordinary shares were trading at 92½p and the loan stock at £58. If you divide £58 by 25, the implied share price for the ordinaries is 232p. Clearly, it is not worth converting unless the share price rises considerably. The premium is high and the most important factor determining the price of the loan stock currently is the income available, not the pros and cons of conversion. At £58, the £6 annual coupon had a running yield of 10.3% (and a better redemption yield), higher than a long gilt because of the increased risk of investing in a company with a chequered past. However, 6% was cheap money when Saatchi & Saatchi (as Cordiant was called in its heyday) was riding high and the convertible was issued.

CABLE AND WIRELESS

An example of a more successful convertible is the Cable and Wireless 7% 2008. In April 1995, this stood at £201.50 against an issue price of £100 and carried the right to convert into 48.54 shares for every £100 worth of the loan stock's par value. The ordinary shares were priced at 422p, so the conversion premium had disappeared. The arithmetic is almost exact – an original investment of £100 in the loan stock now worth £201.50 would convert into 48.54 shares worth £204.83. So buying the loan stock would appear to be a cheap way of buying the shares. However, the yield on the ordinary shares is 2.7% against 3.5% on the convertible, so it does not yet pay to convert. It now looks as though the price of the convertible will track the ordinary shares. When and if the dividends rise by more than 30%, convertible holders will begin to convert into ordinary shares because it will then pay them to do so.

PREFERENCE SHARES

In addition to corporate bonds and convertible loan stocks, you should also be aware of preference shares and convertible preference shares, which are very similar securities. The only practical difference is that they are slightly less secure because preference shares rank behind loan stocks in a liquidation. They do, however, rank before all ordinary shareholders so, with really major companies, they are a secure investment. The characteristics of preference shares and convertible preference shares are set out in more detail in Chapter 12. As already explained, the preference and convertible preference shares of non-financial companies incorporated in any EC member State are now eligible for inclusion in PEP schemes.

PIBS

PIBS (Permanent Income Bearing Shares) are a new kind of investment first issued by building societies in 1991. They are never redeemable and, in essence, are loans to the building societies, who will pay you a fixed rate of interest twice a year *ad infinitum*. However, although PIBS sound safe, it is important to remember that your capital is at risk. The price of PIBS goes up and down according to supply and demand and there is no promise to repay a certain amount to investors. If a building society were to get into difficulties, it could pass the interest payment.

You buy PIBS through your stockbroker, who should charge you a relatively low commission, rather like dealing in a gilt. On smaller deals you would expect to pay about 1%, and less on larger ones. Halifax, Leeds Permanent and Cheltenham & Gloucester PIBS are sold only in lots of £50,000 nominal value; Bradford & Bingley and First National in £10,000 lots. You can invest as little as £1,000 in the rest.

The prices of PIBS fluctuate in the market according to market conditions. When interest rates are lower than at the time of issue, the price will rise above nominal (par) value. If interest rates go up sharply again, the price will fall back to nominal value and perhaps to a discount.

The Halifax has issued PIBS which had an initial yield of 12%. On every £100 of nominal value, you can therefore expect to receive £12 per annum in two equal instalments minus tax at the basic rate. Non-taxpayers can reclaim the tax deducted.

In April 1995, with the base rate at only 6.75%, the Halifax 12% PIBS were relatively attractive and the market value had risen from £100 to £118.50. To calculate the *effective* rate of interest if you were to buy at that price, multiply the 12% by £100 divided by the market price of £118.50 to give 10.1%.

In April 1995, most PIBS stood at a substantial premium to their nominal value. Investors had therefore made a capital profit and they are still enjoying a well above average return on their original investment.

Capital profits on PIBS (and losses for setting off against capital profits) are exempt from capital gains tax. In many ways, this means that PIBS are just like an irredeemable gilt. The main difference is that when PIBS were issued, very high interest rates were prevailing, whereas when 3½% War Loan and some other undated Government securities were issued, interest rates were very low. Be careful though, since future conditions are unlikely to be as favourable for PIBS as they were in the two years after they were first issued.

There are, of course, other risks with PIBS than just a drop in market value. The building society could fail, so you should obviously stick to leading ones. Below is a list of all the PIBS in issue, showing their yields and market prices in late April 1995:

Stock	Fixed Gross Coupon %	Buying Price £	Yield %
Birmingham Midshires	9.375	89.7	10.44
Bradford & Bingley	11.625	113.00	10.28
Bradford & Bingley	13.000	125.00	10.39
Bristol & West	13.375	127.00	10.52
Britannia	13.000	123.00	10.56
Chelt'ham & Gloucester	11.750	117.00	10.04
Coventry	12.125	115.00	10.52
First National	11.750	104.50	11.25
Halifax	8.750	88.00	9.94
Halifax	12.000	118.50	10.00
Leeds & Holbeck	13.375	126.75	10.54

Leeds Permanent	13.625	136.00	10.00
Newcastle	10.750	102.62	10.47
Newcastle	12.625	122.25	10.31
Northern Rock	12.625	121.25	10.41
Skipton	12.875	122.00	10.55

Source: Hoare Govett

In addition, First National and Cheshire have PIBS with floating rates, which may appeal to investors who believe that interest rates are headed north.

As you can see, the Halifax is the biggest and safest, so the yield on its PIBS is a little lower than the average, although there is not much to choose between them all.

PIBS are a possible answer if income is your main concern and you need a substantial yield that is relatively safe. But there are dangers:

1. PIBS are very interest-rate sensitive, so an upward movement in interest rates could adversely affect the prices of PIBS. Although this is not a serious problem for investors who need a predetermined level of income, it is very annoying to find that, if you had waited a few months, you could have bought much cheaper. It follows, therefore, that you should not invest in PIBS if you believe that interest rates are about to rise.

2. The building society is under no legal obligation to pay interest each year or make up any deficit in paying interest for previous years. Therefore, you should only invest in the PIBS of leading building societies where the risk of default is remote.

3. The building society might fail altogether. In that event, your PIBS would very likely become worthless. All other creditors and depositors would be repaid first and PIBS *are not covered by the building societies' compensation fund*. This risk is virtually removed if you only buy the PIBS of leading building societies.

GUARANTEED INCOME BONDS

Insurance companies issue fixed-rate bonds called guaranteed income bonds. They differ from the building societies' PIBS because they have a fixed life during which they are not tradeable. Investors are locked in for a given term, but have the security of knowing that their capital will be repaid.

Guaranteed growth bonds are much the same animal. The difference is that, instead of paying out an income, the fixed return comes in one lump sum at the end of the term.

Like other fixed-interest investments, guaranteed income bonds make sense if interest rates fall during the life of the bond. You retain the benefit of high income while the return on other products is falling. Conversely, if interest rates rise, because you are tied in you cannot take advantage of the higher interest being offered elsewhere.

If you need a certain level of income and want to lock it in, guaranteed income bonds can make sense, especially if interest rates are likely to fall. But remember:

1. The life of the bond will vary from one to ten years. Once you have paid the single lump-sum premium, your money is with the insurance company until the end of the bond's life. *It is not tradeable anywhere* and, although some insurance companies will allow you to cash in early, the terms for doing so are punitive.

2. Your money is not completely safe, as the insurance company might fail. In that event, you would be protected by the Policyholders Protection Act for 90% of your money. To minimise risk, choose a leading insurance company.

3. In April 1995, the interest rates offered by guaranteed income bonds were lower than short-dated gilts, which also offer the advantage of less risk and greater liquidity (ease of cashing them). However, interest rates on income bonds could become more attractive, so keep an eye on the Sunday newspapers. For most bonds £1,000 is the minimum investment, but to obtain the best rates, larger sums are necessary.

4. The basic tax rate deducted from a guaranteed income bond cannot be reclaimed. For non-taxpayers this is therefore a grave disadvantage. Higher-rate taxpayers would still have to pay further tax to bring the basic rate already paid up to their full rate.

For people over sixty-five there is a small extra advantage in investing in guaranteed income bonds. Unlike building society interest, the income from the bonds does not have to be grossed up for the purpose of calculating age-related tax allowances.

GUARANTEED EQUITY BONDS

Guaranteed equity bonds are very different from guaranteed income bonds and are probably proliferating because of the comfort offered by the word 'guarantee'. The appeal of guaranteed growth to safety-first investors goes without saying, but these products are not always as attractive as they seem.

There is a wide range of guaranteed products available from insurance companies and building societies. What they all profess to offer are the rewards of equity investment without the risk of capital loss. They do this by promising to return, for example, the percentage rise in the FT-SE 100 Index over five years. So, if you invested £1,000, and at the end of the five-year period the FT-SE 100 had risen by 40%, you would receive £1,400 at the end of the period. Some products even offer a lock-in facility, whereby you receive a given return if the index achieves a certain percentage rise at any point – even if it subsequently falls back before the end of the period.

This all sounds great, but think carefully before investing in one of these products. There are a number of points to consider:

1. If the FT-SE 100 Index falls during the life of the bond, your capital will be returned, but inflation will have eroded its value. Remember how the purchasing power of an investment in undated Government securities has been decimated.

2. Check the return you are promised if the FT-SE 100 Index rises. You may not get the whole of the increase, only a proportion of it, such as 90%.

3. Guaranteed equity products normally offer no income. The FT-SE 100 Index only reflects capital growth so, in effect, any dividend income is being pocketed by the issuer of the growth bond.

4. Most bonds have a fixed holding period and you may not receive the full value of your investment if you cash in early.

So, do not be taken in by the warm feeling given by the word 'guarantee'. There are no free lunches in investment.

Arguably, guaranteed products offer a poor deal in both bull and bear markets. If the stock market rises over the next five years, you would be better off investing in a unit trust that tracks the market. You would benefit from both capital gains and dividend income. If, on the other hand, the market falls, the real value of your capital would be better protected by the compounding effect of building society interest.

The subject of guaranteed income bonds and guaranteed equity bonds is complex so, if you are thinking of buying any, you should consider doing so through a financial adviser who fully understands your tax position. The adviser will usually receive a commission for selling the bonds, but this will not cost you anything extra. The commission is paid by the insurance company, who would charge you exactly the same premium if you dealt directly with them. Some advisers rebate part of their commission by giving a discount and insurance companies often offer one for applications received before a certain date.

FOREIGN BONDS

If you require a certain pay-out and a secure annual rate of interest, it is clear that you should invest in gilts, or sterling bonds of leading UK corporations like British Telecom and ICI. Companies can also raise fixed-interest money in the Euromarkets (markets which allow borrowers to raise money in currencies other than those of their own country). For example, an American company might raise a loan stock in Deutschmarks to finance expansion in Europe, and French, German and Japanese companies have turned to the Euromarkets when they needed to raise funds in currencies other than their own. The British Government borrowed in both dollars and Deutschmarks at the end of 1992 in order to support sterling. It issued $3bn of ten-year dollar Eurobonds and DM5.5bn of five-year Deutschmark Eurobonds.

Eurobonds are attractive if you believe that the value of sterling is about to fall against other currencies. Before you take a currency risk, however, you should take these factors into account:

1. Although sterling has fluctuated widely against other currencies during the last ten years, it has still been one of the best currency investments *if our relatively high interest rates are also taken into account.*

2. If you are resident in the UK, your expenses are in sterling. Any investment in a foreign stock exposes you to a currency risk. You can make a larger gain, but you also risk losing some of your money.

3. The currency markets are notoriously fickle and hard to predict.

4. Foreign bonds do not qualify for exemption from capital gains tax unless they are denominated and repayable in sterling.

In April 1995, the yield on Japanese Government ten-year bonds was only 4%, on American bonds 5.8%, and on German bonds 6.3%. UK gilts yielded 7%. Similar differentials also existed with the corporate bonds of the countries mentioned. The Japanese yen has been one of the strongest currencies in the world, but can you afford to sacrifice 3% per annum in the hope that the trend will continue?

Although it is sometimes very tempting to lay off the risk of sterling weakening, be aware that currency speculation is an expert's game and, as I have pointed out, most of your worries will already be in the price. With a tinge of regret, my advice is to leave foreign bonds alone, unless you are prepared to study the subject in much greater detail and acquire a degree of expertise.

SUMMARY

1. Corporate bonds in quoted UK companies offer higher yields than gilts, but companies can fail so the risk is greater.

2. Like gilts, corporate bonds that are denominated and repayable in sterling are exempt from capital gains tax. Income is taxed in the normal way. The Government issued a consultation paper in mid-1995. It proposes to levy income tax on any capital gains on bonds. However, most investors will be unaffected as the Government has set a threshold of £200,000 nominal value of all the gilts and corporate bonds held.

3. Unlike gilts, sterling denominated UK corporate and convertible bonds of non-financial companies, with a minimum of five years to redemption at the time of purchase, can now be held in a PEP. So too can the preference and convertible preference shares of non-financial companies incorporated in any EC member State.

4. Convertibles are an attractive halfway house between the safety of bonds and the prospect of capital gain, provided they are purchased at or near to par. You can then be reasonably certain of getting your money back at the end of the bond's life and receiving a worthwhile rate of interest in the meantime. You also have the added bonus of some capital gain, if the underlying shares

do well. Remember though, unlike other sterling bonds, convertibles are not exempt from capital gains tax.

5. PIBS are a relatively new and therefore untested form of fixed interest investment. They offer very attractive yields, but you should remember that interest rates have already fallen substantially since the first PIBS were issued. PIBS could be vulnerable if interest rates rise again. PIBS cannot be held in a PEP.

6. In mid-1995, guaranteed income bonds offered a lower rate of interest than a short-dated gilt. Income bonds are not marketable and are also more risky than Government securities. At times, the rates can be much more attractive, so they are worth keeping an eye on through the Sunday newspapers.

7. Although guaranteed equity bonds will return your capital to you in a few years' time, inflation may have eroded its value by then. You will also lose all the dividend income. A constructive alternative, for investors prepared to take some risk, is to invest in unit trusts which track the market. In extreme circumstances you might not receive back all of your capital, but the upside potential and flexibility is much greater as you are not 'paying' for the guarantee.

8. Foreign bonds carry the extra risk of currency fluctuations. They are also subject to capital gains tax unless they are denominated and repayable in sterling.

4

—

UNIT TRUSTS

On past evidence, unit trusts should protect your capital against inflation better than fixed-interest securities or deposits. However, very few unit trusts beat the market consistently, so consider investing in tracker funds. Use a savings plan to avoid being caught by a sharp fall in the market, and PEPs to avoid paying tax on capital gains and dividends.

A REAL RETURN

Deposits with a leading building society or bank are safe investments, and so are National Savings and dated gilts. You know that one day you will receive your money back with interest. There is a snag, though – you have no idea how much that money will be worth when you come to withdraw it.

Over ten years, during which inflation persists at 5% a year, the real value of an original investment of £10,000 would fall to £6,140. The purchasing power of cash would probably decline by more than the net interest received during the period. With inflation at a consistent 5%, capital is halved every fourteen years. At 10%, money halves in seven years.

To combat inflation, strive to obtain a real return on your money: you want there to be something left over after tax and after inflation. For example, with inflation at 2.2% per annum, a gilt or deposit yielding 7% would give a real return of 2% if your income was subject to tax at the full rate of 40%. The real return is computed as follows:

	£	%
Yield before tax on £10,000	700	7.0
Less tax at 40%	280	2.8
	420	4.2
Less inflation at 2.2%	220	2.2
Real annual return	200	2.0

If your tax rate is only 25%, the real return becomes £305 per annum, just over 3%. The important point is that your *real* income at the higher rate of tax is not 4.2%. The inflation element of 2.2% has to be added to your capital to protect its value. If, instead, you spend it each year, your original capital will quickly dwindle in value in real buying terms.

As you can see, it is very difficult to obtain a worthwhile real return on money, *especially with absolutely safe investments*. In Chapter 2, I explained the virtues of index-linked gilts which, in inflationary times, achieve this objective in a modest way.

A further constructive, and practical, alternative is to buy shares in quoted companies, either directly or through the medium of unit trusts or investment trusts. The long-term advantage of investing in the stock market is easy to see. If you had put £1,000 on deposit with the Halifax in May 1975 and reinvested the interest, by May 1995 this would have grown to £5,717 after basic-rate tax. This would have beaten inflation and maintained the purchasing power of your money.

In contrast, according to Micropal, the same money in the *average* UK Growth unit trust, with net dividends reinvested, would be worth £16,112; in the UK General sector it would have grown to £18,488, and in Equity Income, to £20,097. The best growth fund would be worth £30,450, the best general fund £34,651, and the best income fund £34,096. Even the worst general and income trusts fared much better than a building society deposit and only one of the twenty-five growth unit trusts marred the industry's record by falling below the deposit return of £5,717 to £4,040. This exception to the rule emphasises that unit trusts with share portfolios are equity investments *which can go down in value as well as up.*

THE WONDERS OF STATISTICS

Here is another example of the wonders of financial statistics, calculated by Micropal. Over the five years to 1 October 1992, the average unit trust fell by 5% but, during the five years to 1 November 1992, the same average unit trust rose by 40%.

The importance of shedding October 1987 from the calculations was due to that month's stock market crash. From November 1992 onwards, unit trust managers have been able to advertise very much better statistics for five-year investment than at any time during the preceding five years. Even with the better-looking figures, however, someone who had deposited £5,000 on a ninety-day basis with a leading building society would have enjoyed an overall return of 48%, beating the average unit trust during the period.

However, five-year figures do not cover a long enough period upon which to make a judgement. Taking a really long-term view, since 1919 the stock market (on a total-return basis) has out-performed deposits by an average of over 6% a year. This is a colossal difference, providing real protection against inflation.

The balance of probability is that the next decade will be a favourable one for investors in the UK stock market. However, there are no guarantees. Storm clouds can appear from nowhere and the investment outlook and share values might suddenly change for the worse.

In those circumstances, there is no substitute for cash and assets that can be easily converted into cash. However, the important point to grasp is that long-term equity investors should have a great deal to gain and very little to fear, provided they sit on their well-chosen shares or unit trusts through thick and thin. If their nerves are up to it, they should make even bigger profits if they continue to invest in bad times as well as good.

WHAT ARE UNIT TRUSTS?

A unit trust is a pooled investment in which thousands of small savers invest their money. You can invest as little as £20 a month or, for a lump-sum investment, £250. There is no ceiling on how much you can buy.

Unit trust fund managers invest the money coming into their funds from private and institutional investors. They use it to buy shares in British and overseas companies, gilts and corporate bonds. Exactly what the managers decide to buy depends on the investment criteria of the specific trust (there is a vast range on offer) and their view of the best opportunities. With the muscle of millions of pounds under their control, they have the advantage of being able to negotiate keen prices and competitive rates of commission.

Through a unit trust, an investor has an indirect share in its underlying investments, but with the advantage of a portfolio spread over many different companies and sectors. The better the shares perform in the portfolio, the more the units will be worth.

Usually, the shares are valued every working day and the total value of the unit trust portfolio is divided by the number of units in issue. Each investor buys a number of units and the value of each unit changes, either up or down, every time the portfolio is revalued. The value of the underlying portfolio is constantly changing and the managers will always sell units or buy them back from you at any time, because they can create or cancel units to meet demand.

You will usually receive dividends from your unit trust holding (unless you arrange for them to be reinvested) twice a year, although some income funds pay out more frequently. Dividends are paid with basic-rate income tax already deducted, but non-taxpayers can reclaim this from the Inland Revenue; higher-rate taxpayers will have to pay more. You also hope, when you sell your units, to make a profit over your original buying price. In this event, you will have to pay capital gains tax if you exceed your annual exemption limit (see Chapter 9). However, it is comforting to know that tax only has to be paid once, as the unit trust itself operates free of capital gains tax.

CHARGES

Not surprisingly, there is a price to pay for the advantages of size and spread offered by a unit trust. Your profits will be reduced by the charges paid to the management group to cover its expenses in running the fund. There are two types of charges: initial charges when you buy and an annual fee every year.

Charges vary from fund to fund, but the initial fee, or front-end load, is usually 5-6% and is included in the bid/offer spread, which is the difference between the buying and selling price of the units. The offer price is the one you pay when you buy and the bid price the one you receive when you sell – usually about 5% or 6% lower. About half of this goes to your financial adviser if you use one, but you usually still pay 5% even if you buy direct from the company.

Because of the bid/offer spread, if you bought units in the morning and sold them in the afternoon, you would receive 5% less than you paid. In other words, before you can start to make profits, the units must rise by more than 5%. It is a costly process dealing in and out of a unit trust, so bear this in mind. For example, if you bought units when the bid (selling) and offer (buying) prices were 100p and 106p, and sold when they were 127p and 133p, you would buy at 106p and sell at 127p. Your gain would, therefore, be only 21p (127p minus 106p). The performance figures of unit trusts allow for the spread between the bid and offer prices, which is one of the reasons that unit trusts do not, on average, keep level with the market as a whole.

Annual charges range between 0.75% and 1.5% and these are deducted from dividends, or from the capital, before they are paid out to you. Some types of funds have lower charges because they are cheaper for the management group to run. These include tracker funds, money funds, gilt funds and funds of funds.

SAFETY

There are two types of risk you face when buying unit trusts. One is that someone will run off with your money and the other that the value of the units will fall. Only the second is a real possibility.

Unit trusts are tightly controlled by law and all managers must be registered with the Securities and Investments Board (SIB), which most have done by joining its subsidiary watchdogs, IMRO and PIA. Even then, the manager does not hold your money. Outside trustees, which will be financial institutions such as banks, are responsible for the money and investments, and this is why they are called 'trusts'. In the very unlikely event that the unit trust manager or an adviser were to steal some money from the trust, a compensation scheme would pay out a maximum of £48,000 to each unit holder. This is made up of 100% of the first £30,000 and 90% of the next £20,000 of an individual's investment.

You cannot claim compensation if your investment simply loses value because of indifferent management or a fall in the market as a whole. However, as your money is spread over a vast range of different companies, there is less chance of a catastrophe than if you had bought individual shares.

Several unit trust groups run a share exchange scheme, which enables you to swap any existing shares you own into their units. Some will give you a better deal than if you had sold the shares on the market yourself. Others simply sell your shares for you and charge the appropriate commission. A generous scheme can be a cost-effective way of disposing of small parcels of shares, particularly from privatisation issues.

SHOULD YOU BUY UNIT TRUSTS?

There are three good reasons why so many people invest in unit trusts instead of investing in shares directly:

1. An individual may not have enough money to invest in a sufficiently wide spread of shares to reduce the risk to an acceptable level. However attractive an individual share may appear to be, there is always the danger that something totally unexpected might happen that could potentially cripple the company in question. For example, a leading company in the drugs industry might discover that some of its drugs had unfortunate side-effects and, as a result, could be sued by the patients who had suffered. Leading tobacco companies might find that legislation is passed one day to give people the right to sue for the damage caused by passive smoking. If all of your money was invested in companies like these, you could suffer sudden and sickening losses. However expert you are at investment, you need to spread your risk. A unit trust invests in a large number of shares and will achieve this important objective for you.

2. The cost of buying and selling shares in very small amounts is excessive. For a transaction involving only £100 worth of stock, you could find yourself paying a high minimum charge with a total cost of as much as 25% of your investment. It is only when you

begin to deal in sums of about £1,000 per share that charges fall to 1.5–2% and become at all reasonable.

3. Most unit trusts require a minimum investment of £500 but some allow investments of £250 and, with a regular savings plan, you can invest as little as £20 a month. It is not economic to invest such small amounts in the stock market directly.

I would like to be able to add a fourth reason for buying unit trusts – the advantage of obtaining professional management of your portfolio. But I am sad to report that unit trust managers have, in general, failed to beat the market. If it were possible to invest in the FT-SE A All-Share Index, the value of £1,000 investment would have grown to £3,538 with net dividends reinvested over the ten years to 1 May 1995. But according to Micropal, the same money invested in the average UK Equity Income trust would be worth £3,413, in the average UK General trust £3,087 and in the average UK Growth trust only £3,003. The five-year figures are worse, with the market returning 80%, against the three unit trust sectors averaging only 54%.

The key point is that, over the ten-year period, only 37 of the 174 unit trusts in those sectors beat the FT-SE A All-Share Index. Micropal have prepared the unit trust performance statistics on an offer-to-bid basis which is the accepted measure, albeit a harsh one, because it deducts all charges. If you were to buy shares directly there would also be some charges, so the comparison is not a totally fair one.

Needless to say, some funds performed considerably better and some much worse than the average. Many of them were specialist funds which sometimes do exceptionally well, but fare badly when their area of speciality is out of favour.

Keep your eyes open for articles in the weekend family finance pages highlighting the performance of unit trust management groups. The important quality to look for is *consistency* over a long period. A select few trusts have been in the top quartile (best 25%) of their sector over one, three, five and ten years. There is no guarantee that they will continue to perform so well in the future, but their past performance should give you confidence, and it is all you have to go on.

TRACKER FUNDS

There is a simple way of beating the performance of most unit trusts – a *tracker fund*, which is a unit trust that does no more than try to mirror the performance of a share index. Tracker fund managers trade only when shares are removed from the index and replaced by new constituents. This means they save costs by not switching their investments too frequently.

Tracker funds never match the index exactly; they have some expenses to pay, they do not always hold every share in the index and sometimes the funds have to sell shares to refund outgoing unit holders. But the time spent on management by the tracker funds is minuscule, so their charges are very much less than other fund managers. For example, Gartmore's UK Index Fund, which tracks the FT-SE A All-Share Index, has *no initial charge* and just an average 1% spread between the buying and selling prices. This is a tremendous advantage that saves investors from starting off with a 5–6% handicap. In addition, the Gartmore tracker fund's annual charge is only 0.5% a year, compared with double that or more for other types of funds.

Many tracker funds are more expensive than Gartmore, with initial charges of up to 5.25% and annual charges of 1% a year. Companies which offer tracker funds are Gartmore, Govett, HSBC, Legal & General, Morgan Grenfell, Norwich Union, Old Mutual, Royal Life, Schroder, Swiss Life and Virgin. There is also an investment trust, Malvern UK Index, and a building society, Newcastle, which have tracker funds. Between them they track the FT-SE A All-Share, FT-SE 100, the American S & P 500 and several other world indices. HSBC also tracks its own South East Asia and smaller companies indices.

It is important to realise that with a tracker fund there will be a small divergence, usually for the worse, from the index. In the case of Gartmore, over five years the difference was about 0.7% but, in spite of this, the fund was the second best performer out of eighty-three in the UK Equity General sector of the market. Several other tracker funds were in the top quartile. If reliability for keeping up with the market is your aim, tracker funds are your answer.

It may seem to be a modest objective simply to match the market. However, as you can see from the lamentable performance of many unit trusts, keeping up with the index is far easier said than done. One of the reasons for this is the high initial charges you pay when you subscribe to a conventional unit trust. The other is the way the indices are computed. Companies that fail to make the grade and shrink in size are automatically kicked out by the stock market's Review Panel, which meets once a quarter to review and decide upon the constituents. Their main criterion for selection is size, so most new entrants tend to be expanding companies. There is, therefore, a kind of automatic Darwin-like process which chops out companies that have faltered and replaces them with more vigorous ones. In addition, when changes are made, there is no deduction for commission or stamp duty. This means that unit trust managers are competing against excellent portfolio management operating without cost.

Research, conducted by the *Observer* newspaper, showed that in 1993 the FT-SE 100 Index, the market's most popular measure, was 500 points higher than it would have been had it stuck with its original constituents (the index was first compiled in 1984). In other words, 25% of the index's 2,000 point rise since it started life at a base figure of 1,000 had been achieved by switching into companies as they entered the index and selling shares in those companies that were demoted. If you think about it, the outperformance is very logical and is another compelling argument in favour of indexed funds.

RANGE OF FUNDS

If, in spite of the foregoing, you still want to have a shot at beating the UK market by investing in a unit trust, you can choose from a vast selection of 1,500 authorised unit trusts. There are twenty-two different categories, ranging from the very general, International Balanced, to the very specific, Commodity and Energy. Some concentrate their investments in particular parts of the world, such as the Far East or North America.

The complete list of categories shows the range:

UK funds
UK General
UK Equity Income
UK Growth
UK Gilt and Fixed Interest
UK Balanced
UK Smaller Companies

International funds
International Equity Income
International Growth
International Fixed Interest
International Balanced
Japan
Far East including Japan
Far East excluding Japan
Australasia
North America
Europe

Other funds
Commodity and Energy
Financial and Property
Investment Trust Units
Funds of Funds
Money Market
Convertibles

Rather like being presented with too large a menu at a restaurant, you are spoilt for choice. You cannot avoid having to make difficult decisions about the parts of the world and sectors you want to invest in and the degree of risk you are prepared to take. There is little doubt that an alien landing on earth for the first time would not have his entire portfolio invested in the UK or, for that matter, in Europe. Looking at the world as a whole, our alien might prefer the prospects of America or the Far East. China's Gross Domestic Product has, for example, been expanding at over 9% per annum during the last decade. The whole Far Eastern region could be the engine for the world's growth in the early part of the next century. A range of unit trusts are on offer investing in all of these areas.

There are also good arguments for having a small percentage of any portfolio invested in a unit trust that specialises in gold shares, as a kind of insurance policy against hyper-inflation. I explain a little more about gold in Chapter 22. There are also a few trusts that invest up to 60% of their funds in convertibles. In rising markets, they will not fare so well as full-blooded equity funds, but they will be much more defensive if markets turn down.

I am not allowed to suggest specific unit trusts or even recommend particular sectors to you. You have to decide for yourself. The Association of Unit Trusts and Investment Funds Information Unit, 65 Kingsway, London WC2B 6TD (Telephone: 0181-207 1361) will be pleased to supply you with a free list of all unit trusts offered by its member companies, together with a booklet giving advice on how to buy and sell them.

Details of new unit trusts are given regularly in the financial press; in particular the *Financial Times* and *Investors Chronicle*. There is also an excellent monthly magazine, *Money Management*, which you should buy occasionally or you might find in your local library. *Every issue charts the progress of all unit trusts and lists the best and worst. Money Management* shows how £1,000 would have fared in each trust over periods ranging from six months to ten years.

If you decide to concentrate upon the UK market, you will have to choose between the following main categories:

UK General Funds
Over 80% of their assets are in the UK market, primarily in larger companies. They invest for income as well as growth. Very strong performance over the last fifteen years.

UK Equity Income
Over 80% of their assets are in the UK. They aim to provide regular and growing income with a yield at least 10% higher than the market as a whole. Another very strong performer over the last fifteen years.

UK Growth Funds
Over 80% of their assets are in UK equities with the main objective being capital and income growth. This category also includes recovery and special situation funds. The income is much lower so the yield will be below the average. The performance can be volatile.

UK Balanced

A mix of fixed interest and equity investment with no more than 80% in either category. Very popular with conservative investors but, in my view, neither fish nor fowl.

UK Smaller Companies

At least 80% of their funds are invested in much smaller UK companies. The basic idea is excellent if there is sufficient evidence that the management is exceptionally capable.

To have a chance of beating the performance of both the UK market as a whole and tracker funds, I would suggest a UK General Fund or UK Equity Income Fund. You should choose one that *regularly* appears in the top 25% of the *Money Management* league tables. Even then, though, you cannot be absolutely sure that the team of managers responsible for the superior prior performance has not moved on elsewhere or lost its touch.

At all costs avoid picking the very best-performing fund from any one year. Those that produce exceptionally high returns are nearly always the very specialist funds and, because they are by definition the riskiest, they stand a good chance of being near the bottom of the table in the following year. For example, during the year to 2 May 1994 the two best performing trusts were:

Waverley Australasian Gold	+93%
Mercury Gold & General	+83%

This is how they performed in the following year:

Waverley Australasian Gold	-24%
Mercury Gold & General	-3.6%

As you can see, the performance of these trusts reflects the volatile nature of gold shares. But other high-flyers also flopped the following year; Old Mutual European tumbled from third place to 1108 out of 1331 trusts and Hill Samuel UK Emerging Companies fell from fifth place to 817.

SAVINGS PLANS

Timing is another vital ingredient for successful investment. It is comforting to realise that even full-time professionals find timing difficult. I have already demonstrated that, if you had invested your full quota in unit trusts on 1 October 1987 instead of 1 November 1987, over the following five years you would have been about 45% worse off. You can easily avoid buying at exactly the wrong time by using a regular savings plan, investing £20, £50, £100, or whatever you can afford, each month.

Most unit trust managers run regular savings schemes and will set up the paperwork for you. Dividends are reinvested in the plan, but you can withdraw money whenever you want. You can switch to a different fund in the same management group and make occasional lump sum contributions as well.

If you had set up a savings scheme even in the month of the 1987 crash, the October and November instalments would already have given you an average gain of 17.5% by early 1993. When prices are low, you receive more units for the same amount of money, so further subsequent instalments quickly minimise the adverse effect of one very bad month.

With a savings plan you will never hit the highspots of perfect and lucky timing. However, the technique of pound/cost averaging, investing a set amount each month, ensures that your overall cost is never extreme. Your money buys more units when the price is low than in months when it is high, so the average price works out well over a year. Here is an example:

Month	Offer price	Units bought by £10
Month 1	50p	20
Month 2	25p	40
Month 3	10p	100
Month 4	25p	40

You have bought a total of 200 units for £40, at an average price of 20p, but during those four months the average price was 27.5p.

More importantly, you minimise the potentially catastrophic effect of another stock market crash. Bear in mind too that, on the past performance of markets, *with average timing*, you would have succeeded admirably in protecting your capital against inflation.

INCOME SHORTFALL

In 1995, UK interest rates are much lower than they were at their peak in the 1980s. This means that the returns available on deposit accounts are now lower than before, which is one of the reasons why sales of unit trusts have been boosted. Currently, the *average dividend yield* (the percentage annual income you would obtain before tax by investing in the average share) is 4.1% (April 1995), which is higher than the headline inflation rate of 3.4% and the underlying (retail price index excluding mortgage costs) inflation rate of 2.6%.

In April 1995, the average dividend yield is 1.9% short of the yield of about 6% currently obtainable on a fixed-term deposit. It is also 4.4% less than the yield of 8.5% available on a ten-year gilt. If you need income, this gap is a substantial one.

To minimise the income shortfall, you could invest in equity *income* unit trusts, which offer a slightly higher yield than the average unit trust together with the prospect of significant capital growth. You could also consider the more specialist investment trusts that will be explained in the next chapter.

There is, however, another way of bridging the income gap. Investors seeking the long-term protection against inflation provided by equity investment could still invest in unit trusts or shares and sell sufficient unit trusts or shares each year to lift their income to the required level. This is not my idea – it first occurred to me when reading Peter Lynch's excellent new book, *Beating the Street*. He makes exactly the same suggestion to small investors in America, where their problem is identical.

The main difficulty of this simple approach is psychological, especially if, in the first year or so, the share or unit trust investments do not perform so well because of a weak stock market. There is no doubt that, statistically, *on past performance*, it would pay an investor to invest in shares or unit trusts instead of deposits and conventional gilts, selling sufficient equities each year to make up any income shortfall. Since 1919, the total return on shares has out-performed deposits by an average of 6% a year. To make the approach work even better, a phased programme of investment in shares or unit trusts would lower the risk of investing your capital at the wrong time.

If you are confident that you can stand the strain of a possible bear market, you could try this idea in a small way. Read the rest of this book first, however, and consult a financial adviser.

HOW TO BUY UNIT TRUSTS

Unit trusts are provided by specialist unit trust investment groups, insurance companies, banks, stockbrokers and building societies.

There are various ways to buy unit trusts, so you might as well choose the most convenient:

Direct from the management group by writing or telephoning

From a salesman who works for the group

By answering an advertisement in a newspaper or magazine

Through a financial adviser or stockbroker

Over-the-counter at a bank or (occasionally) a building society

Managers are very happy to take investors' orders on the telephone and many investors buy and sell this way. The telephone numbers are published in most of the daily and Sunday newspapers. However, the person you speak to may not be qualified to advise whether or not you are doing the right thing. You can ask to see a company salesman who can run through the pros and cons of unit trust investment, but that person can only sell the funds managed by his company. He will be very keen to make a sale, so be on your guard.

Unit trusts are regularly advertised in the press, especially when the stock market is booming, because that is a time when investors are more likely to buy. Management groups are not deterred by the fact that this could be the worst moment for the public to invest in the stock market. They also advertise when they launch a new fund and usually give a discount of between 1% and 3% on the price of units for a fixed initial period. Do not be tempted into buying just because of the discount; look on it as a bonus if you would buy the units anyway.

Once you have picked your unit trust, place your order with its management group. When your order has been received, the company immediately sends you a contract note which sets out the unit price paid, the number of units bought and the amount paid. About three weeks later, you will, in some cases, receive a registration certificate. It is important to keep these documents safe because they are your only proof of ownership. Every six months you will also receive a report from the investment managers reviewing progress, highlighting the main investments and advising you about the asset value.

If you want advice, you can ask your stockbroker or an independent financial adviser. They will then buy the units for you. Banks and building societies also sell unit trusts, sometimes through a financial advisory subsidiary, but increasingly over-the-counter.

HOW TO SELL UNIT TRUSTS

Practice on the selling of unit trusts varies from company to company. You may have to send instructions by post but, in most cases, they can be given over the telephone provided you can establish your identity. You will not normally be sent the proceeds until the company has received written confirmation of your order and the registration certificate. Your money will usually arrive after about five working days.

Many stockbrokers will sell unit trusts for you without charging a commission, provided the units were purchased through them in the first place. If the stockbroker insists on a commission, you can instead deal direct with the unit trust management group.

PERSONAL EQUITY PLANS

You should also consider using Personal Equity Plans (PEPs) to minimise your tax liability. PEPs are explained in detail in Chapter 9. You and your spouse can each invest £6,000 a year in unit trusts investing at least 50% of their funds in UK or EC shares or qualifying corporate bonds. The limit for unit trusts which do not meet the 50% rate is £1,500. By holding your unit trusts in a PEP you will pay no capital gains tax when you cash in your units and no income tax on any dividends. PEPs are a very attractive extra incentive, although you should avoid those with high charges.

SUMMARY

1. Unit trusts are a hassle-free method of investing in shares and the stock market without the risk of buying individual shares.

2. On the basis of past performance, long-term investment in unit trusts (and the stock market) has protected capital against the ravages of inflation far better than fixed interest securities or deposits.

3. If you have an annual income requirement that is more than the average yield obtainable on unit trusts, still consider the possibility of investing in them and selling a small number of units each year to bridge the shortfall. You should also consider equity income unit trusts which are higher yielding than the average, and examine some of the more specialist investment trusts that you will read about in the next chapter.

4. There are sound arguments for building a portfolio of unit trusts covering UK and European investments, America, the Far East and a small insurance policy in gold.

5. Over the past ten years, only 21% of unit trusts investing in the main UK sectors have beaten the market as a whole. If you want to match the market's performance as nearly as possible, consider investing in a tracker fund with the lowest possible initial and annual management charges.

6. If you are determined to try to improve on the performance of the market and tracker funds, choose a unit trust that *regularly* appears in the top 25% of the *Money Management* league tables.

7. The timing of stock market purchases is very difficult, even for experts. Use a savings plan to spread your unit trust investment over the highs and lows.

8. For unit trusts investing in the UK and the EC, use a PEP for up to £6,000 to save both capital gains tax and the income tax on dividends. A superb extra incentive to invest in equities.

5

—

INVESTMENT TRUSTS

**Investment trusts are an ideal way to invest in and learn about the stock market without the risk of buying individual shares. They are more flexible than unit trusts and more able to meet the differing needs and tax requirements of investors. Unlike unit trusts, they can often be bought at a discount to their underlying net asset value.
Use savings plans to lessen the risk of being caught by a market fall and PEPs to avoid tax on capital gains and dividends.**

WHAT IS AN INVESTMENT TRUST?

Investment trusts are the ideal vehicle for people who want to invest in equities, but do not want to risk committing all of their money to just a few shares. They are another form of pooled investment, with the savings of thousands of private investors collected and managed by professional fund managers who invest on a large scale. Like unit trusts, they are also tax efficient. Investors pay capital gains tax on any profits made by buying and selling an investment trust share, but the key point is that tax only has to be paid once. The trust itself can operate free of capital gains tax, provided the managers comply with a few simple Inland Revenue regulations. For example, the trust's articles must prohibit the distribution as dividend of surpluses arising from the realisation of investments.

Investment trusts are far more flexible than unit trusts. Above all they have the power to borrow, thereby improving performance if market conditions are favourable. They can also invest in unquoted companies, which can sometimes be an advantage. An additional factor in favour of investment trusts is that they are more structured. Unit trusts can suddenly face heavy withdrawals by unit holders, forcing their managers to sell investments at what may be an inopportune time. Conversely, if market conditions are bullish, unit trusts may receive a sudden influx of funds to be invested. Investment trusts have a *fixed* amount of money under management, so they are not subject to violent swings in investor sentiment, which are likely to happen at just the wrong time.

Each investment trust is a separate publicly-quoted company and, despite its name, not a trust in any legal sense. One investment trust group might manage several different investment trust companies, but every company will have its own board of directors, who keep an eye on the managers and are answerable to shareholders. The managers make the day-to-day investment decisions. Only a few investment trusts, such as Alliance Trust and Scottish Investment Trust, are self-managed, which means all the administration and investment decisions are taken in-house rather than by an outside management group.

Investment trust companies are quoted on the London Stock Exchange in exactly the same way as, for example, Marks & Spencer or British Telecom. When you invest in an investment trust you are buying shares in the company, which gives you the right to attend annual meetings and to vote. Unlike Marks & Spencer and British Telecom, the business of investment trust companies is buying and selling shares to make a profit. The fund manager decides what to buy and when to deal, subject to the objectives of the fund.

Investment trust managers look after portfolios of shares which, according to the stated intention of the fund, may be UK and/or foreign, quoted or unquoted, and range in size from around £2m to over £1bn. The managers collect the dividends paid out by the companies in the trust's portfolio. The total of these dividends, after management expenses, forms the profits of a conventional investment trust which, in turn, are paid out to its own shareholders. Usually, dividend payments are made twice a year, but some income funds pay quarterly. The size of dividends and the degree of capital growth depend on the manager's skill and success in selecting good shares. However, some investment trusts concentrate on capital growth and provide little or no income.

Unlike a unit trust, each investment trust company has a fixed number of shares, so you can buy only if another investor is willing to sell and you can sell only when there is a willing buyer. As with any other quoted company, a market is made in the shares by one or more market-makers in the stock market. Like all quoted shares, they can go up and down for a number of reasons. The main influence on the share price is supply and demand, which is affected by market sentiment, the management's performance and reputation, and the net asset value of the trust (which, in turn, is determined by the value of the shares in the underlying portfolio).

ASSOCIATION OF INVESTMENT TRUST COMPANIES

There are a number of important characteristics of investment trusts and there are many different types available. You can relax, however, because the Association of Investment Trust Companies (AITC), based at Durrant House, 8–13 Chiswell Street, London EC1Y 4YY (Telephone: 0171-588 5347), has done excellent work promoting them and is anxious to clarify the information that is currently available. The AITC offers a number of services to the private investor, including:

1. A range of eight free fact sheets explaining how investment trusts work, savings schemes, and how different investment trusts can be used for specific purposes.

2. Monthly statistics, which show the share price, performance data, net asset values, gearing, discounts, premiums and total returns. These invaluable statistics cost £28 a year (£40 for overseas investors). One set of statistics is sent free with each information pack. As an alternative to the monthly statistics, you could opt for receiving them four times a year, in which case the charge would be £15 for UK residents and £22 for overseas investors.

CHARACTERISTICS OF INVESTMENT TRUSTS

Investment trusts are different from unit trusts because, as public companies, their shares are quoted on the London Stock Exchange. There are also three further distinguishing characteristics to which you should pay particular attention:

1. The discount or premium to net asset value.

2. The possibility of a takeover.

3. The level of gearing (borrowing).

Discount to net asset value

Invariably, the price of shares in an investment trust differs from the value of the investments held in the portfolio and usually the share price is lower than the net asset value (NAV); the shares are then said to be trading at a 'discount'. The NAV is the value of all the shares and assets in the portfolio, minus any loans outstanding, divided by the number of shares in issue and expressed in terms of pence per share. Dunedin Worldwide, for example, traded at 693p in March 1995. Its net asset value was 802p, a discount of 14%.

It seems to me to be more a matter of convention than reason for investors to expect investment trusts to stand at a discount to their underlying NAV. Investors seem to share my view as, during the last ten years, the average discount has been narrowing; since 1985 it has fallen from a staggering 24.25% to 8% in early 1995, after a low of

6% in 1994. Certainly, any conventional investment trust standing at a very large discount to its NAV merits very close attention and could be an outstanding bargain.

Very occasionally, the share price stands at a premium to NAV. You pay, say, 106p to buy a share of a portfolio worth perhaps only 96p a share. There is no point in doing this when you can buy other investment trust shares at a discount. An obvious way of making money by investing in investment trusts is to buy when the discount is large and sell after it has narrowed and the underlying portfolio has risen in value.

This kind of approach was well illustrated in August 1993 when Sir John Templeton, the dean of international investment, sold all of his shares in the publicly-traded Templeton Emerging Markets Fund. When asked to explain, he said that he could invest for a lot less money in another of his funds, with the same manager and very nearly the same portfolio. He went on to say that he had spent eighty years searching for bargains and he could not think of a stock being a bargain at 32% above liquidation value. Learn from the master!

The discounts vary widely. In March 1995, taking just high income trusts as an example, they ranged from 6% to a premium of 24%. Shares in conventional trusts standing at a 20% discount could be the bargain buy of the year but, usually, there is a very good reason why they are so out of favour with investors. The AITC gives details of discounts to NAV in its monthly statistics – while you want to buy at a discount, always seek an explanation for the very large ones.

By studying the monthly AITC statistics, you will be able to tell whether the discounts are widening or narrowing. Where economic conditions are worrying, discounts are likely to widen. Where market sentiment is improving, such as in some of the emerging markets and among smaller companies, discounts could narrow.

Be on the lookout for trusts standing at large discounts, but specialising in markets which could be on the brink of improving. For example, in April 1995 this was the case with some trusts specialising in Europe – it is conceivable that investor sentiment could improve and the trusts could become all the rage for a while. Investors would then benefit from the uplift in the prices of the shares in the trust's portfolios and from the narrowing of the discounts of the trust's own shares in relation to their NAVs.

Takeovers

Like other public companies, investment trust companies sometimes make or receive takeover bids, which can be friendly or hostile. Whether shareholders accept the takeover terms they are offered depends on many factors current at the time.

The possibility of takeover is an added inducement for buying an investment trust rather than a unit trust and a further reason for buying an investment trust with a share price at a discount to net asset value. Occasionally, managers become very anxious about a widening discount and, fearing a takeover, *unitise* the trust (turn it into a unit trust). When this happens, or when there is a takeover, shareholders can sit back to enjoy the fun and hope to make a substantial capital gain.

For small investors in receipt of a takeover bid, a major consideration may well be tax. They may be forced to sell shares and take a capital gain in a year when they would prefer to hold on, because other gains have already pushed them beyond their free capital gains tax allowance. However, it is quite common for a bidding company, which needs to win shareholders' votes, to devise an investment package which switches old shares into an interest in the new company; this avoids realising any capital gain. Usually, the best line of action is inaction – wait until the last possible moment in the hope of a higher offer or a bid from elsewhere.

The cut and thrust of a contested bid for an investment trust was colourfully demonstrated in March 1993 when EFM Dragon, a trust specialising in Far Eastern stock markets, successfully bid for its bigger rival, Drayton Asia Trust. Drayton, managed by Invesco MIM, had fallen to a discount to net assets of nearly 30%, making it vulnerable to a bid. EFM Dragon, in contrast, had at times been trading at a small premium to its underlying net worth, and was able to take advantage of this by offering its own shares for Drayton rather than cash.

As part of its attempt to fight off Dragon, Drayton offered shareholders a choice between swapping their shares for units in a new unit trust or accepting more valuable split-capital shares. However, voted down by the Coal Board pension fund (which had a big stake in both trusts), Drayton abandoned its scheme and threw in the towel. Investors who spotted the vulnerability of Drayton when it traded at a 30% discount to assets made a substantial profit in a short time.

One of the most interesting claims during the bid came from the beleagured Drayton managers. They complained that Dragon's superior performance over the previous year was nothing to do with better share selection, but simply reflected the fact that the trust had borrowed more money to give it a greater exposure to a rising market. Dragon defended its actions, saying that 'Gearing is part of management. We took a bullish view of markets and it worked.'

This brings me to the third difference between unit and investment trusts.

Gearing

An important difference between investment and unit trusts is the ability of investment trust managers to borrow extra money in an effort to maximise the performance of the assets under their control. They borrow money to purchase more shares and other securities in the hope that the extra dividends earned, plus capital growth on the securities, will offset the cost of borrowing. When the fund manager's judgement is right, the additional securities purchased rise in price and the fund's performance benefits. Conversely, if share prices fall, the fund's loss is magnified.

A highly-geared investment trust will have substantial borrowings, which will need to be repaid at a predetermined date or when the company is wound up. Repayment of borrowings ranks ahead of shareholders, so it is conceivable that if the manager's judgement has been poor, very little will be left over for them. This makes highly-geared investment trusts far more risky than lowly-geared ones, so it is important to know the extent of the gearing before you invest. The AITC monthly statistics will give you the necessary details.

Gearing is a two-sided coin – if the manager's judgement is excellent, the capital growth of a highly-geared trust will massively outperform lowly-geared ones, and vice versa. It follows that the proven ability of the managers and your view of the market outlook are two key factors in determining whether or not to choose an investment trust that is highly-geared or lowly-geared.

To illustrate the principle of gearing simply, imagine a hypothetical investment trust company with assets of only £100,000. If it invested in shares which quadrupled over a ten-year period, the £100,000 would become worth £400,000. If the managers had borrowed £50,000 and invested the total of £150,000, the funds would then be worth £600,000. After repaying the £50,000 of borrowings, shareholders in the trust would have £550,000 instead of only £400,000 from the ungeared trust.

If, on the other hand, the market had halved during the same ten-year period, the trust without the gearing would be worth £50,000, while the highly-geared one would be worth only £25,000. The managers would have invested the original £100,000 plus the £50,000 of borrowed money, and the total of £150,000 would have halved in value to £75,000. The borrowings of £50,000 would then need to be repaid, leaving only £25,000. It is also possible that during the ten years income would have been less, as the cost of borrowings might have exceeded the extra income from the additional investments purchased with the borrowings.

In the monthly statistics provided by the AITC, gearing is expressed as a percentage figure; broadly speaking, the higher that figure, the higher the risk/reward profile of the fund. The gearing factor shows the percentage amount by which the net asset value per share would rise or fall in excess of the rise or fall in the value of the total assets of the trust. A gearing factor of 100 means that the company has no gearing, while a highly-geared fund could have a gearing factor of 190: if total assets were to rise or fall, shareholders' funds rise or fall by 90% *more*.

Foreign & Colonial's International trust, which had a gearing factor of 116 in March 1995, is a good example. If the value of the shares in which it had invested were to rise, the trust's NAV would rise by 16% more than if the trust had no borrowings. The important thing to realise about gearing is that a high gearing factor places a greater emphasis on the skill of a trust's managers. Their mistakes and successes will be magnified by their trust's gearing.

High gearing also means that your skill in choosing the right trust will be more severely tested. As with the Dragon fund managers, if your gamble on, say, Far Eastern shares pays off, your return will be enhanced. But so will your losses if you pick the wrong market or sector in which to invest.

It is difficult to give precise guidance, but I suggest that in general you should avoid conventional trusts with a gearing factor of over 125, unless the management has proved itself over a very long period or you are prepared for a bumpy ride.

DIFFERENT CLASSES OF INVESTMENT TRUST SHARES

There are several different types of investment trust shares. Each class has its own attributes and their diversity enables investors to organise sophisticated tax and investment planning to suit their own purposes.

The most widely used shares are:

ORDINARY SHARES

SPLIT CAPITAL SHARES, which include:
  Income shares
  Capital shares
  Zero dividend preference shares
  Stepped preference shares
  Ordinary income shares (called highly-geared ordinary shares by
  the AITC)

ORDINARY SHARES

These are the standard form of shares in conventional investment trusts. You buy them, earn dividends and hope that the price will have risen by the time you want to sell. Ordinary shareholders can turn up at annual meetings, cross-question the directors, and vote on resolutions.

SPLIT CAPITAL SHARES

Split capital investment trusts have become popular in recent years and many new split capital funds were launched in the early 1990s. As they became increasingly complex, doubts began to surface. Many investors did not really understand what they were buying, which is why they can be dangerous. In fact, some offer low-risk investments.

Income and capital shares

To help you understand the principle of splits, I will explain the broad framework first. At its very simplest, a split capital investment trust has two classes of shares: *income shares and capital shares.* Shareholders choose which type to buy, depending on whether they want income or capital growth.

The two types of investors share a single portfolio, but all the dividends from the underlying shares are given to the income shareholders. Income shareholders, representing half the share register, receive 100% of the income; no income goes to capital shareholders. However, the capital shareholders receive all the capital growth, so again half the shareholders receive 100% of the benefit, which in this case is the growth in the value of the shares.

Split trusts also give scope for tax planning. If, for example, a wife pays no income tax, she can hold the income shares without having to pay tax on the dividends, while her husband holds the capital shares, which are subject only to capital gains tax.

All split capital funds have a limited life, usually seven or ten years, although the shares can be sold on the stock market in the meantime. At the end of the specified period, unless shareholders as a body decide to prolong the life of their company, the proceeds from the sale of the underlying portfolio are distributed according to the trust's articles of association. With capital and income trusts, the first to be paid are income shareholders, who receive an amount agreed at the outset; typically, they will get back their original investment.

Capital shares are suitable for investors who do not need income. They aim to achieve the maximum possible capital growth, albeit at the risk of losing more if the managers make capital losses. Income shares are for investors who are primarily interested in income. There are three main types:

1. The income share that receives all income from the company's assets and receives a predetermined price at the wind-up date of the trust.

2. The income share that receives the income from the assets, with at least a predetermined price at the end of the trust's life, plus a share of any capital appreciation.

3. The income share which receives a high income, but only a nominal payout at redemption. This is suitable for investors who want a high income for a specified period, perhaps during the years they are paying school fees.

Simple splitting between capital and income is easy to understand, but in recent years a number of more complicated innovations and hybrids have been spawned.

Zero dividend preference shares

Zeros are similar in many ways to capital shares. They have no entitlement to dividends of any kind and, on winding-up, are paid an almost guaranteed predetermined return. I say 'almost' because they would not be paid the guaranteed return if there were insufficient funds in the trust when the time came for repayment.

Zeros are safer than ordinary capital shares because they rank ahead of them on liquidation. They have a fixed redemption date (the day you will be paid out) and a fixed redemption value (the amount you will receive). The monthly statistics from the AITC provided information on the thirty-seven zero dividend preference shares available in March 1995. As well as their share prices and NAVs, the monthly tables also show the annual percentage rise in the trust's assets required to guarantee payment of the predetermined redemption price. This is called the 'hurdle-rate'. In March 1995, twenty-six of the thirty-seven had a negative hurdle-rate, meaning that the trusts already had more than enough assets to honour their redemption prices.

For example, Fleming International High Income zeros traded at 103p and had one year and seven months to run before redemption at 117.6p. They offered a redemption yield of 9.1% and had a hurdle rate of -14.7, suggesting that they were a pretty safe short-term investment with a good yield.

Investment in zeros is a way of investing for a lower-risk predetermined capital return. They are suitable, for example, for an investor who needs a certain capital sum on a specified future date (perhaps for school fees) and who cannot afford to take a risk. They are also suitable for higher-rate taxpayers because no income tax is payable.

Stepped preference shares

Like zeros, these shares rank ahead of other classes of capital and are relatively safe. Again, there is a fixed redemption date and value but, in addition, they pay a six-monthly dividend which is increased each year (stepped up) by a fixed amount. They are a kind of priority income share.

In March 1995, there were five of this type of share available. One of them, offered by Scottish National, was priced at 152p, had a 5.8% gross yield and three years and six months still to run. A redemption price of 171p was promised and in the meantime income would grow at 5% a year. If the share was held to maturity it would give a gross redemption yield of 9.6% and, with a hurdle rate of -35.2%, also looked likely to be able to honour its payout commitments.

Stepped preference shares are suitable for investors who need a steadily rising income and pre-set capital growth, which is paid out on winding up. They are, therefore, ideal for nervous investors who are not seeking exceptional capital gains.

Ordinary income shares

These hybrids are called highly-geared ordinary shares by the AITC. They combine the characteristics of highly-geared capital and income shares. They have a high yield because they receive all the income and they also benefit from capital growth if the performance of the fund managers is good. If the capital growth of the fund is insufficient, they could easily become worthless.

Highly-geared ordinary shares meet the objectives of investors who want high income and are prepared to take a risk to receive some capital growth as well.

WARRANTS

No analysis of the different classes of investment trust shares would be complete without a review of warrants, which are becoming increasingly popular with trusts and can be very rewarding investments. Warrants are transferable certificates giving the owner the right, but not the obligation, to buy shares in a company at a fixed price on a specific date or during a specific period in the future. The exact terms of each warrant are set out when it is issued.

Warrants usually cost very little to buy in comparison with the ordinary shares of the company in question, and you can either make a great deal of money if the shares rise dramatically or lose all of your money if the shares fail to reach the *exercise price* (the price at which you have the right to buy the ordinary shares). Before warrants expire, they can be bought and sold in the stock market at prices which go up and down like ordinary shares. However, because of their *gearing* (a small outlay for the prospect of a large percentage gain or loss), they are much more risky and volatile than ordinary shares.

Before investing in a warrant, you first need to determine whether or not you would like to invest in the investment trust in question. Normal criteria apply – how successful has the management been in increasing assets per share, what is the discount to net asset value, the gearing and the area of speciality, if any. Then you need to consider the relationship between the warrant and the share price and a number of other important factors:

1. *The conversion premium*
    A warrant almost invariably costs more to buy than its *intrinsic worth*. For example, in March 1995 a Fleming Japanese warrant

to buy one ordinary share at 192p until February 1999 traded at 101p, while the ordinary share was 220p. The intrinsic worth of the warrant was therefore 28p (220p minus 192p) and the *conversion premium* (or warrant premium) was 73p (101p minus 28p). In relation to the share price the conversion premium was just over 33% – $\frac{73p}{220p} \times 100$.

The higher the conversion premium, the dearer the warrant; the lower the premium the cheaper the warrant. There is a very wide variance between conversion premiums, so it is always worthwhile examining them carefully.

2. *The life of the warrant*
    The longer the life of a warrant, the greater its value. This is because there is longer for the magic of the market to do its work and for the shares to climb well above the exercise price. As the warrant's life begins to expire, so the *time value* diminishes. At the end of the warrant's life, the time value becomes worthless and the value of the warrant is determined by simple arithmetic. For example, if in February 1999 (the final month of exercise) the Fleming Japanese shares were 300p, the warrant would then be worth 108p (300p minus the exercise price of 192p).

3. *Volatility*
    All other things being equal, a warrant in a China fund, for example, would tend to be worth more than a warrant in a European trust. China is growing at an extremely rapid rate and is subject, therefore, to the dangers that usually accompany great speed. The more volatile a trust's share price, the more valuable the warrant, especially if it also has a considerable time value. There is then greater scope for larger capital profits, but be careful as there is also greater potential for larger losses – the value of your warrant could fall to next to nothing.

4. *Warrant gearing*
    There is a complicated calculation that can be made to establish a warrant's *Capital Fulcrum Point* (CFP). This is the annual percentage rate of growth at which an investment in the shares of the trust or the warrants would be equally successful. Over the CFP, the warrants would be more attractive than the shares.
    For most investors, a much simpler approach is to look at the

warrant's gearing. In the case of Fleming Japanese, this was 2.2. The calculation is easily made – the share price of 220p is simply divided by the warrant price of 101p.

The higher a warrant's gearing, the more chance there is of a profit *if all goes well*. However, warrant gearing at an exceptionally high level usually indicates that there is little chance of the shares reaching the exercise price. If a warrant is nearing its final exercise date at a time when the ordinary share price is well under the exercise price, there may be little chance of the ordinary share price rising enough to make the warrant worth buying. In such a case, warrants can be trading at just a few pence and this would make their gearing exceptionally high.

5. *Exercising warrants*
   You buy a warrant because you hope to make an exceptional profit if the underlying share performs well. You make your profit by selling in the market while the warrant still has some time value before expiry or you wait until the last exercise date and subscribe for the shares. Clearly, you only exercise a warrant at expiry if it is '*in the money*' (the exercise price is below the share price) and you write off the loss to experience when the warrant is '*out of the money*' (the exercise price is above the share price).

6. *Full Dilution*
   Investment trusts show their NAV in a number of ways, but warrant holders should concentrate their attention on the *fully diluted* NAV, which shows the net assets per share if all warrants and convertibles are exercised. The AITC monthly returns show NAVs in this way and so does the *Financial Times*.

Reasons for buying warrants

Warrants can be a good investment for children under eighteen, who are entitled to a full capital gains tax allowance. Except in a very few instances, there are no dividends from warrants which would otherwise have to be aggregated with the income of donor parents.

Warrants are also interesting for more speculative investors who are attracted by their gearing and the exaggerated gains that can sometimes be produced. Sometimes, investment trust warrants can rise dramatically over a short period if the stock markets in which they specialise show a sharp rise.

The other attraction of warrants is for balancing a very safe portfolio with their strong upside potential. Investors could put a portion of the money they would normally invest in the shares of the company in question into a long-term warrant and then invest the remainder of the money in a completely safe security like a low-coupon redeemable gilt.

The AITC has written an excellent explanatory leaflet on warrants and their monthly statistics include details of all investment trust warrants currently in issue. They also give details of final month of exercise, exercise price (sometimes called subscription terms), the warrant and share prices, the conversion premium and the warrant's gearing. In addition to the AITC monthly information service, *Investment Trusts*, a quarterly investment magazine (Telephone: 0181-646 1031), includes information on warrants in every issue.

Investors who want to become very active in warrants should consider *Warrants Alert*, which in April 1995 cost £99.95 a year. This monthly newsletter gives detailed recommendations on warrants that are over- and under-priced and also draws attention to new warrants being issued. The founder, Andrew McHattie, has also written an excellent handbook, *An Introductory Guide to Warrants*, which is free to subscribers but sold separately for £6. The telephone number of the McHattie Group is 01275 855558.

I cannot stress too strongly that warrants are complicated and risky so, if you are interested in them, you should consult your stockbroker or financial adviser.

SPECIALIST TRUSTS AND GEOGRAPHICAL SPREAD

Investment trusts differ widely in their aims from the very general and comparatively safe to the very specific and highly risky; they can be (almost) all things to investors. As well as providing a range of different types of shares to choose from, there is a selection of geographical and specialist categories.

The AITC divides companies into nineteen different sectors:
International: General
International: Capital Growth
International: Income Growth
UK: General
UK: Capital Growth
UK: Income Growth
High Income

North America
Far East: including Japan
Far East: excluding Japan
Japan
Continental Europe
Pan Europe
Emerging Markets
Property
Commodity and Energy
Smaller Companies
Venture and Development Capital
Closed-end Funds

The more progressive investment trust managers are very keen to talk to potential investors on the telephone or send them information through the post. Many are now very marketing-minded, especially those which have set up savings schemes for investors to buy shares direct, and they have staff ready to talk to potential investors.

The AITC will supply you with the telephone numbers of its members – the vast majority of investment trust companies. For investors who would like to meet them and ask questions face to face, the AITC runs a regular series of roadshows around the country. A few management groups, including Fleming, send their own staff to talk either to individuals or to clubs and groups of potential investors.

The AITC fact sheets explain exactly how savings schemes work and how investment trusts can be used for specific investment purposes, such as funding school fees or investing for children.

PERFORMANCE

Investment trust shares vary widely in their performance record and, not surprisingly, the more specialist the fund the more variable its performance. Most management groups have very good reputations, although this does not necessarily mean that every investment trust company under their control does well.

For investment trusts that specialise in overseas shares, currency movements can be just as important as investment policy. During the past ten years, sterling has tended to weaken against other major currencies, but that does not mean that sterling investors can ignore currency risks in future. Funds specialising in Japan have enjoyed massive currency gains due to the strength of the yen and this may well continue. But for funds investing in Latin America, the currency outlook might be very different.

The past performance of management groups is the best indication we have of their likely future performance. As with unit trusts, you should be wary about drawing any conclusions from just one year's exceptional performance of a specialist trust. Year-in-year-out performance should be your main criterion.

As a general rule, the big, well-known groups with excellent long-term records take a lot of beating. For example, during the past ten years an investment of £1,000 in the best-performing UK General Trust, with net income reinvested, would have grown to £4,863 compared with £3,416 for the average trust in the sector.

MONTHLY STATISTICS

As you can see, there is a wide variety of split-trust capital structures and possible securities from which to make your choice. The good news is that AITC provides monthly statistics giving you full details of discounts and premiums to NAV, gearing, geographical spread, hurdle-rates, yield and total return on both the share price and NAV over one, three, five and ten years. These statistics are invaluable for choosing investment trusts and monitoring their subsequent performance.

CHOOSING AN INVESTMENT TRUST

Choosing an investment trust to meet your personal objectives and tax position is a complex process. Most people need professional advice, but there is a great deal to be said for understanding the investment criteria to be considered and how to weigh up the various factors involved. The key points to bear in mind are:

1. Geographical spread or specialist activity.

2. Financial structure of the trust and the exact nature of the particular security that suits your tax position and objectives. To give a simple example – is the trust a conventional one or split for capital and income?

3. Performance of the management group over recent years and consistency over the long term.

4. The discount to NAV compared with the discount available in the investment trust market as a whole.

5. The level of gearing.

As with most other investments, you have to decide first if you are looking for a safe investment that can be put away and nearly forgotten, or an exciting one that will need watching very closely.

For a first investment, and a safe long-term proposition, I would suggest one of the large international general funds. When you begin to learn a little more about investment trusts, you can start differentiating between, say, international funds which are strong in the Far East and those which are more evenly spread; or capital funds which still provide reasonable income against those which concentrate solely on capital growth.

It is difficult to give precise guidance on how to weigh up all the various factors that should be considered when selecting an investment trust. You (and your adviser) have to decide upon the geographical or specialist area of activity, and select the class of share that suits your objectives – capital, income and tax-wise. You then need to concentrate upon the performance statistics, the discount to NAV and the gearing. The ideal combination of criteria for a conventional investment trust is a *consistently* high total return over the years, a moderate gearing factor and a substantial discount to NAV. Unfortunately, life is not always so kind – if the growth record is excellent, the discount to NAV will almost certainly be negligible.

There is a great deal to be said for buying shares in investment trusts at a substantial discount to NAV. The bargain you have struck is instantly measurable and the greater the discount the more the chance that it will be closed by market forces, a takeover or unitisation. However, a large discount may be justified in a venture capital trust (full of unquoted shares) or one that has very poor management. My inclination would be to go for the discount, but I can see the attractions of a consistent performance, provided you do not pay too much for it. Even if performance is your main criterion, I would never pay a premium over NAV for management and I would make sure that the discount is in line with the market as a whole or not too far away from it.

SAFETY

All investment trust managers must register with the Securities and Investments Board, the financial watchdog, or with SIB's subsidiary self-regulatory organisation, IMRO. However, if the company fails, unless the managers have been dishonest you have no recourse to the Investors' Compensation Scheme. Investment trusts are quoted companies and shareholdings are excluded from the Financial Services Act, which provides protection for other types of investment. The directors are regulated by company law and, while this gives shareholders rights, they have to go to court to exercise them. In extreme circumstances, they can sack the directors and the managers and sue the auditors.

If the managers have been dishonest, investors will have recourse to the Investors' Compensation Scheme, which will pay up to £48,000. This covers all of the first £30,000 invested in one company and 90% of the next £20,000.

However, there is another type of risk which an inexperienced investor is far more likely to face, and for which compensation is not available – losing money through a bad investment decision. This is very possible with high-risk trusts such as those in the venture capital and single-country fund categories. If your objective is to minimise your risk, buy large, well-spread UK or international investment trusts from well-established management groups with a good track record.

HOW TO BUY AND SELL

Investment trust shares can be bought in three ways: by applying for newly-issued shares; through a stockbroker; or direct through a management company's savings scheme (if one is available). For inexperienced investors, buying direct through a savings scheme is the best way.

New issues

Each new investment trust is a new company and investors who buy when the company is launched pay no stockbroker's fees or other charges. This makes investing cheaper, but there is a strong likelihood that the shares will drop to a discount immediately they start to trade on the stock market. You should therefore wait a week or two and try to buy the shares more cheaply in the market.

Stockbrokers

Do not waste your time with the large institutional stockbrokers because they are not interested in dealing with small parcels of shares and their charges are high. Instead, look for a private client stockbroker who specialises in analysing investment trust companies. The Association of Private Client Investment Managers and Stockbrokers (APCIMS) sends out a free brochure about private client stockbrokers with a complete list of members. Write to: APCIMS, 112 Middlesex Street, London E1 7HY.

The one advantage of dealing through a stockbroker is that you receive advice about which particular investment trust is most suitable for your needs. The variety of sophisticated capital structures of investment trusts makes it worthwhile to pay a little extra in commission to receive expert advice.

Savings schemes

Savings schemes are often the cheapest and simplest way of buying investment trust shares. They were invented in the early 1980s by Foreign & Colonial and have since been copied by many other management groups. The managers realised that having to use a stockbroker was a barrier to many potential investors, particularly those who had never had contact with a broker before.

The name 'savings scheme' is slightly misleading, because it can be used for both regular investments, with minimum monthly payments ranging from £20 to £50 per month, and for one-off lump sum investments. The managers make their own arrangements with stockbrokers to buy on behalf of their investors; they can negotiate low commission rates because they are dealing in bulk. Investors need only fill out an application form and send off a cheque; all the rest is done by the management company. Some groups pick up the bill for the charges within the fund and, while this obviously adds to the attraction of the fund, it should not be the only criterion because a good investment performance can more than make up for the higher charges.

With a regular payment scheme there is the added advantage of minimising the risk of entering the market at just the wrong moment. Investing a set amount every month ensures that your overall cost is never extreme and works in a very similar way to a savings plan with a unit trust.

Investment trusts are not allowed to advertise to the public because Stock Exchange rules forbid companies from recommending their own shares. However, they can advertise the savings schemes and this has made them more accessible.

You would do better to obtain a list of all the savings schemes that are available rather than leave it to the chance of seeing an advertisement about an investment trust that appears to be a good buy. The AITC will send you one of their explanatory fact sheets and a list of addresses for all the management groups with the companies they manage, together with the names of the people to contact.

CHARGES

How much you pay to put money into investment trust companies depends on the method used but, as a guideline, if you buy through a stockbroker you will usually pay about 3% of your investment. This is made up of the difference between the bid and offer prices, usually around 1.5% for investment trust shares, stamp duty of 0.5% and stockbroker's commission of, say, 1%. Commission can be as high as 1.85% and, of great importance to buyers of small parcels of shares, the minimum commission can be as much as £50 each time you deal.

Buying through a savings scheme can be much cheaper; charges vary from as little as nothing except stamp duty to as much as 3%. The full details are set out clearly in the AITC monthly information service. Annual management charges vary from 0.3% with some of the larger trusts to 1.5% or more.

Although it is unpleasant paying high charges, your main criteria should be the suitability of the investment trust for your purposes and the quality and record of the management.

PEPS

You pay income tax on the dividends you receive from an investment trust and, if you make enough profit in the year that you sell, as with any other share, you may have to pay capital gains tax as well. Basic-rate tax is deducted from dividends before you receive them, but non-taxpayers can reclaim the credit. Higher-rate taxpayers have to pay more. Zero dividend shares pay no dividends, so there is no income tax to pay on them.

Investment trust shares can be put into General PEPs so the dividends are free from income tax and any gains free from capital gains tax. To qualify for the maximum £6,000 annual General PEP investment, the investment trust must have at least half its portfolio invested in UK or European shares or qualifying corporate bonds, convertibles and preference shares. If it fails to meet this criterion, then only £1,500 a year can go into that fund, although investors can top up to £6,000 with qualifying investment trust shares (or other shares and qualifying unit trusts).

This still leaves scope for a significant holding in shares from further afield and an investment trust PEP can provide a very cost-effective international portfolio, especially if it is combined with a savings scheme. Watch the level of charges, though.

PEPs allow you to receive both dividends and capital gains tax-free. If you are a smallish investor, who does not breach the current £6,000 CGT exemption, the only benefit you will receive is to save tax on your dividends and the charges could outweigh the benefit.

Regular monthly contributions can be paid into most investment trust PEPs, although investors must be careful not to exceed the annual £6,000 limit.

USES FOR INVESTMENT TRUST SHARES

Inheritance tax planning
To avoid inheritance tax, people can give away their assets during their lifetime and, provided they live for another seven years, there will be no tax to pay. One drawback to this scheme is that any gift must be made outright with no strings attached. You cannot give away your capital and retain the interest – except with investment trust shares. To do this, buy both income and capital shares and then give away the capital shares to your beneficiaries. From that date, any growth in the capital shares goes to them and not to your estate and all growth is immediately free of inheritance tax because it did not form part of the original gift. You continue to hold the income shares, which provide you with what may be a necessary income stream but, when you die, may be worth comparatively little.

Planning for school fees
Buy zero dividend shares which promise (provided funds are available) to pay a fixed sum on a certain date, at which time the money can be used for any purpose. Investment trusts provide complete flexibility because, unlike specialist school-fee plans, you are not committed to paying for education, nor are you buying expensive life insurance.

Avoiding income tax

Zero dividend preference shares pay no dividends so there is no income tax to pay on them.

Retirement planning

Zeros and capital shares provide virtually no income now but concentrate on maximising capital growth for later, when you can sell them to buy income-producing investments. Unlike pension contributions, your money is not locked in and, if they are sheltered within a PEP, you avoid income tax and capital gains tax as well (but you do lose the tax relief on your investment, which is one of the main attractions of pension contributions).

Self-invested Personal Pensions

Investment trusts are ideal investments to use in your own pension fund.

Maximising income

If you desperately need income at any cost, you can buy investment trust shares which provide high dividends but no capital growth, or even eat into your capital to maintain a high income stream.

INVESTMENT TRUST V. UNIT TRUST

Investment trusts and unit trusts are often compared in the financial press. Below is a summary of some of the main distinguishing features:

Investment trusts	Unit trusts
Public companies ruled by company law and the Stock Exchange.	Governed by trust deed.
Closed-end funds with fixed number of shares, making fund management an easier task.	Open-ended funds with units which can be created or cancelled (sometimes resulting in substantial influxes of money or major withdrawals).

Can have different classes of shares.	All units are identical.
Able to invest in unquoted companies.	Cannot invest in unquoted companies.
Allowed to borrow.	Cannot borrow.
Charges vary from nil to 3% of initial investment plus 0.3 to 1.5% or more annually.	Charges vary from nil (tracker funds) to over 5% of initial investment plus up to 1.5% annually.

RELATIVE PERFORMANCE OF UNIT AND INVESTMENT TRUSTS

The performance of unit against investment trusts was measured by the *Investors Chronicle* in July 1993. The statistics are as follows:

1. SECTOR PERFORMANCE COMPARED

		Value of £100 invested*			
	Trust type	1 yr	3 yrs	5 yrs	10 yrs
UK TRUSTS					
General	Unit	103	121	151	391
	Investment	108	125	140	347
Capital growth	Unit	104	119	142	368
	Investment	102	128	149	545
Income	Unit	106	121	146	463
	Investment	109	143	201	563
INTERNATIONAL					
Growth	Unit	117	116	163	295
	Investment	119	124	197	405
Income	Unit	116	127	167	314
	Investment	115	137	199	474
SPECIALIST					
Europe	Unit	107	94	176	424
	Investment	106	79	177	391
N America	Unit	128	141	213	231
	Investment	131	148	226	307
Japan	Unit	151	107	128	455
	Investment	137	118	147	474
Far East	Unit	135	120	168	443
(inc Japan)	Investment	149	128	191	542
Far East	Unit	134	149	278	456
(ex Japan)	Investment	145	124	210	–

*Unit trusts on offer to bid price basis. Investment trusts include allowance for dealing costs, both with net income reinvested.
Source: AITC and Micropal.   1/6/93

2. OVERALL PERFORMANCE COMPARED

	Value of £100 invested*			
	1 yr	3 yrs	5 yrs	10 yrs
Unit trusts	115.8	120.7	159.3	349.4
Investment trusts	115.8	127.3	185.7	447.1
Building society				
Highest rate account	105.6	126.0	152.5	228.6

*Unit trusts on offer to bid price basis. Investment trusts include allowance for dealing costs, both with net income reinvested.
Source: AITC and Micropal.   1/6/93

As you can see, investment trusts have outperformed unit trusts, which is not surprising bearing in mind their capacity to borrow in what have been rising markets and their lower average charges. However, it is very important to take into account that the average investment trust discount to NAV has narrowed from 26.7% to 9.7% during the ten-year period. Unit trust prices rise and fall with the underlying value of their portfolios, but the prices of investment trust shares depend upon market forces. The 17% closing of the discount to asset value of investment trusts accounts for a large part of the difference in performance. This once again emphasises the importance of buying investment trust shares that stand at a hefty discount to NAV.

As the *Investors Chronicle* article concludes, the right answer is to make the most of what is on offer from the two industries. Both investment trusts and unit trusts have some star performers and a range of products designed for very specific purposes that might suit your requirements to a nicety.

SUMMARY

1. Investment trusts are an ideal way of investing in shares and the stock market without the risk of buying individual shares.

2. Investment trusts are more flexible than unit trusts. They can borrow and invest in unquoted securities.

3. Investment trusts have a fixed amount of money under management, so they are not embarrassed by sudden swings in investment sentiment causing substantial influxes of money or major withdrawals.

4. The charges of the best investment trusts are cheaper than most unit trusts. However, some unit trusts, such as tracker funds, have very low charges.

5. Over the last ten years, the average investment trust has performed somewhat better than the average unit trust, even after allowing for the narrowing of the average investment trust discount to NAV. This is not surprising bearing in mind investment trusts' capacity to borrow (in what have been rising markets) and the extra charges of most unit trusts.

6. Most people need the help of a professional adviser when selecting an investment trust. There is a large variety of investment trusts available to meet the differing needs of investors. In particular:

    a) **Conventional trusts** – offer a fund spread over a large number of securities with the clear objective of and the entitlement to both capital growth and increasing dividends. Suitable for investors who are prepared to take an equity risk and want expert management with a spread of general investments or investments in a specialised field such as the Far East or gold shares.

    b) **Capital shares** – offer all the capital growth at the risk of losing more if the management make losses. Suitable for more experienced investors who do not need income and accept the extra risk for the extra possible reward of superior capital growth.

    c) **Income shares** – offer a higher and growing income, but no prospect of capital growth and a negligible chance of making a capital loss. Suitable for investors who need a high and growing income and are not concerned about making a capital gain.

    d) **Zero dividend preference shares** – offer a predetermined capital growth when the time comes for redemption. There is no income, however, and therefore no income tax. There will, of course, be tax on capital profits. Ideal for investors who need a lump sum at a future date for a specific purpose and, in particular, for higher-rate taxpayers because no income tax is payable.

e) **Stepped preference shares** – offer a predetermined capital growth rate and a dividend increasing a little each year at a fixed rate. Ideal for investors prepared to settle for low but relatively certain capital growth together with growing income.

f) **Ordinary income shares** – these hybrids combine the characteristics of highly-geared capital and income shares, offering a high yield and capital growth if the performance of the fund is good. Only suitable for very experienced investors who want a high income and are prepared to take a risk for capital growth as well.

7. Warrants in investment trusts can also be purchased. They are highly-geared to capital growth and, in the main, are only suitable for speculators.

8. The special additional factors to consider when choosing a conventional investment trust are the *long-term* performance record, the level of gearing and the discount to NAV. The ideal but unlikely combination is excellent performance, moderate gearing and a substantial discount to NAV.

   In making a choice, you usually need to balance performance against the discount. The better the performance, the nearer to NAV you should be prepared to pay. Avoid buying any trust at a premium to NAV.

9. Savings schemes are often the cheapest and simplest way of buying investment trust shares. They also offer a very effective method of averaging your costs to minimise the risk of entering the market at just the wrong moment.

10. Up to £6,000 per annum per person can be invested in investment trusts through a General PEP to avoid both capital gains and income tax. However, the charges levied by plan managers can outweigh the benefits for investors with very small portfolios.

11. The Association of Investment Trust Companies (AITC), which publishes a wide range of fact sheets and statistics, is anxious to help prospective and existing investors in investment trusts. Investment magazines like *Money Management* and *Investment Trusts* also regularly provide details of performance, together with discounts and premiums to NAV.

6

—

LIFE INSURANCE AND PENSIONS

Pensions and life insurance are key elements of financial planning. They can be very tax-efficient, but they are also complex and long-term, so you will almost certainly need professional advice. Be in no hurry to sign up.

For most people, securing an income for when they retire and making provision for their family in case they die are very high financial priorities. After our homes, life insurance* and pensions probably represent the biggest single investments most of us ever make.

It is worrying, then, that so many people sign up for contracts, costing thousands of pounds over many years, that they do not properly understand and are not necessarily suitable for them. Worrying but

---

*The word 'insurance' has been used rather than 'assurance'. In fact, 'assurance' describes covering a risk that is bound to happen – such as dying; whereas 'insurance' refers to risks that may or may not happen – like burglary. However, 'insurance' is becoming a more accepted general description, so I have used it throughout.

not surprising, given the complexity of both pensions and life insurance and the pressure on salesmen, who earn their living through commission, to get your signature on the dotted line. They have far more experience of doing that than you have of saying no.

Not everybody needs life insurance and some people need a different type of product from the one that is sold to them. Do not be rushed into buying something you do not feel completely happy about, and remember that, while pension contributions have tax advantages, they are not the only way of providing an income for later life.

One thing is certain – everyone who lives long enough needs an income during their retirement. Most people who rely on the basic state pension, and any earnings-related addition for which they qualify, will find it difficult to make ends meet. Extra provision of some kind is therefore vital.

LIFE INSURANCE

The point of life insurance is for a sum of money to be paid, when you die, to the people who are financially dependent on you. The younger you die, the more likely you are to have a family which needs your income and relies on your support. Without the breadwinner, a family's income can be decimated. Without the person bringing up the children and taking care of the home, family expenses can rocket. In both situations, there is a case for life insurance as a means of looking after dependants.

This type of protection is provided comparatively cheaply by term insurance (a specified period of life cover) and has nothing to do with investment. As with insuring your car, you pay a regular premium in return for the promise of a larger repayment if disaster strikes. If, at the end of the agreed term, all is well, you breathe a sigh of relief but forfeit the premium you have paid. You should be very clear about the difference between buying protection for your family in case you die unexpectedly and buying insurance as an investment.

If you decide to take out a life insurance policy, ask the company representative how you can put the proceeds in trust. It is usually simply arranged and means that when you die the insured sum will avoid inheritance tax and can be quickly paid out to your dependants. Also remember to make your will if you have not already done so.

Endowments

The type of insurance used for *investment* is mostly endowment, which pays out at least a guaranteed sum of money on maturity, or on your death if you die before then. On top of the guarantee, the amount you receive may increase year by year as bonuses are added.

Some policies have two different guarantees. The first is the guaranteed payment on maturity, known as the basic sum assured; initially this might be quite low, though it increases as bonuses are added. The second is the guaranteed payment to your dependants if you die before the policy reaches maturity. This is often higher and depends on how much life cover you require.

Different policies have different divisions between the amount of premium used to buy life cover and the amount allocated to investment. Because this form of investment includes life insurance, the old and unhealthy will find it much more costly than the young and healthy.

The money you pay in premiums for a with-profits policy is invested by the insurance company in a wide spread of investments. The performance of that portfolio determines the level of bonuses added each year to your guarantee. An alternative is to link your policy (without a guarantee) to the performance of one or more funds from under the umbrella of funds managed by the insurance company.

Policies can last for any period although, *to qualify for tax advantages, regular premiums must be paid whether they be monthly, quarterly or annually*. Since March 1984, the premiums paid on new policies no longer qualify for tax relief. However, basic-rate taxpayers do not pay tax on the proceeds (when the policy matures) and higher-rate taxpayers are exempt if the policy is allowed to run for at least ten years (seven and a half years in the case of a ten-year policy). This is no real advantage for basic-rate taxpayers because the investment returns in the fund have already been subjected to basic-rate tax.

Endowments are long-term policies and you should only take one out if you are reasonably confident of seeing it through and have carefully examined more tax-efficient alternatives.

With-profits policies

For years, the mainstay of endowment insurance was the 'with-profits' policy. With these schemes, a minimum sum is guaranteed to be paid on maturity and, in addition, the policy earns annual or regular bonuses. When the policy matures, it also earns a terminal bonus, but that is not decided until the final year. In order to leave their options open, some insurance companies pay as much in the terminal bonus as in all the annual bonuses combined. Once declared, a bonus is guaranteed for the rest of the life of the policy. The aim of the with-profits structure is to smooth out some of the sharp rises and falls in share prices, so that investors receive a steadily increasing, but unspectacular, return on their money.

When you buy a with-profits policy, you can only get a rough idea of how much of your money is going in fees to the insurance company because the charges are hidden within the premiums you pay.

Unit-linked policies

Unit-linked insurance works differently. Your premiums, after a sum has been deducted for charges, buy units in a fund of investments. As with unit trusts, each unit reflects a small proportion of the value of the underlying fund. The value of the final pay-out depends on the value of your units on the day the policy matures.

Unit-linked life insurance has a higher risk/reward ratio than with-profits policies, because the size of your final payout depends on the level of the stock market at the end of the policy's life. For example, if your policy had matured the day after the 1987 crash you would have received around 20% less than the day before.

Charges are calculated in several different ways and they all reduce the return from your investment. Typically, there will be an initial charge of around 5%, a policy fee of about £2 a month and an annual charge of around 0.75%, but charges vary from company to company.

Unitised with-profits policies

A with-profits pay-out is guaranteed and topped up by annual bonuses, so insurance companies must ensure they have enough resources put aside to meet their commitment when it arises. This is onerous for them, so in recent years they have produced the unitised with-profits policy, a hybrid combining the elements of both basic types of policy. Your premiums are divided into units, and each year you earn bonuses in the form of extra units (or by way of an increase in the value of your existing units). Like with-profits bonuses, these cannot be taken away from the policy once they have been added to it. This is more manageable for the insurance companies because their guarantee only creeps forward gradually.

EARLY SURRENDER VALUE OF LONG-TERM ENDOWMENT POLICIES

You will always be offered a poor deal if you cash in an endowment policy after only two or three years; you are unlikely to get back even the premiums you have already paid. *Every year around half a million investors lose between £100 million and £200 million by doing just this.*

Very often, people will cash in one policy to buy another when they move house and take out a new mortgage. This is completely unnecessary because the existing policy can be used to support the new mortgage. If you take advantage of a special offer loan which compels you to buy a new insurance policy, you can keep the old policy going on its own.

Surrender values are low because of the high charges which the policyholder has to pay to buy the policy in the first place. A salesman can earn from £700–£1,000 by selling you a twenty-five-year policy with premiums of £100 a month. You pay £100 a month for the next twenty-five years, but the salesman's commission is paid in full over the first one to two years. The insurer deducts this and the start-up costs at the outset, so it is not until the policy has been running for some time that any of the money starts working for you.

If you have a with-profits policy that has run for seven to ten years and you need to surrender it, bear in mind that there is an alternative to accepting the official surrender value. You could sell the policy in the second-hand endowment policy market, which usually offers much better prices.

SINGLE PREMIUM BONDS

These are lump-sum investments which do not have the same tax advantages as qualifying regular premium policies. Nowadays they tend to be unit-linked and give the right to switch into different funds, including those that are unitised with-profits.

Basic-rate taxpayers have no tax to pay on the ultimate proceeds, because basic-rate tax has already been paid within the fund on investment income and capital gains during the life of the policy. Higher-rate taxpayers have to pay the difference, unless they can organise their affairs to become basic-rate payers in the year they cash in the policy.

Anyone can withdraw up to 5% of the original investment each year for twenty years without paying tax; withdrawals missed out in one year can be carried forward until the twentieth year. If you are a higher-rate taxpayer when the bond is cashed in, or after you have taken your 5% income over twenty years, higher-rate tax will be due on all the income withdrawn.

LIFE INSURANCE AS AN INVESTMENT

The days when investment-based life insurance offered significant tax advantages are long gone. Tax relief on new life insurance policies was abolished ten years ago. Only higher-rate taxpayers who also use up their capital gains tax allowance can obtain any tax benefit from this kind of investment. All insurance-based funds pay the equivalent of basic-rate tax on investment income and they also pay capital gains tax, so there is no real advantage for basic-rate taxpayers in obtaining a 'tax-free' pay-out, since tax has already been paid. But for qualifying regular premium policies, there is no higher-rate tax to pay, which is an obvious advantage for higher-rate taxpayers.

For everyone else, there is no logical reason to confuse investment with insurance. They are separate issues and, in any case, investment-based life insurance is much more inflexible than most other forms of investment. You cannot cash in a policy early without being penalised. Pooled funds such as unit trusts and investment trusts are much more flexible and the tax advantage now lies with this kind of investment, which can be held in PEPs free of tax on both income and capital gains. PEPs cost very little to set up compared with insurance-based investments, which carry heavy commissions.

Defenders of regular premium life insurance claim that it imposes a discipline on savers. They have to keep up payments for the full term of the policy in order to benefit. It is an argument which fails in practice because only a minority of savers manage to keep their policies going for the full term.

If you need life insurance, buy a cheap protection-only policy. Of course, you will not get any of your premiums back if you survive the term of the policy. You will, however, probably be very pleased still to be around.

If you want to make an equity investment, do so through unit trusts, investment trusts or directly in shares. It will be far less expensive and more flexible than an endowment and also, if you use a PEP, much more tax-efficient.

Insurance companies have a vested interest in perpetuating the myth of endowment policies as a good investment. You do not have to believe it.

PENSIONS

Anyone who works for the same company with a good pension scheme all their working life will retire on a maximum of two-thirds the salary they earned in their last few working years. However, some people have a nasty surprise when they discover that, for one reason or another, they fall far short of the maximum. They may not have been with the same employer for long enough to qualify for the maximum pension, or the scheme's rules may be drawn up in a way that excludes part of their pay, such as regular overtime. Some employees will not have a pay-related pension at all. 'Money purchase' schemes depend on how well the contributions you pay into the fund are invested, and on what sort of annuity your pension pot will buy when you retire. It is obviously well worth the time and effort to find out exactly how your pension scheme works and how much pension you will receive on retirement.

For most people, cradle-to-grave employment is a thing of the past and they are likely to have several employers during their careers. If you have changed jobs a few times, even if you have had a company pension throughout your career, you may have eroded your pension already and may need to make separate arrangements to top up your retirement income. People without a company pension definitely need to make their own arrangements.

Retirement planning becomes crucial once you turn fifty; it is important long before then, but most people ignore the subject until they see retirement looming. The earlier you start the better; a delay of a few years can be very costly in terms of your final pension fund.

IMPROVING A COMPANY PENSION

Anyone who is in a company pension scheme will be told how much of their earnings will be taken out for pension payments and often the employer will make extra contributions. If you want to pay more than the firm's scheme allows, you can make Additional Voluntary Contributions (AVCs), which allow you to top up to the statutory maximum contributions of 15% of net earnings. The AVCs can be supplied through your employer's scheme or they may be provided by a different financial institution.

Employees who want to choose their own AVC arrangements can pick their own Free Standing AVC from an insurance company of their choice. They do not have to use the one provided by their employer. However, you will not know in advance how well the company you have chosen will perform with your money and any illustration it provides will assume investment returns set down by the City watchdog, the Personal Investment Authority.

PERSONAL PENSIONS

You obtain tax relief at your highest rate of tax on contributions to company and personal pension plans. The funds are also allowed to grow free of income and capital gains tax and you can draw a tax-free lump sum when you retire. In terms of tax-efficiency alone, pensions are unbeatable.

Anyone who does not have a company pension, or who elects not to join the company scheme, can buy a personal pension. The choice of personal pensions is as varied as with any other type of investment. You can have a with-profits personal pension, or a unit-linked one that is invested in a broad managed fund or a specific fund such as North American shares, Far Eastern shares or property. Most people rightly play safe with their pension contributions and stick with a widely-based fund, particularly when they are close to retirement.

If you have chosen a specific fund early in your pension planning, it is sensible to transfer a proportion of this to a cash fund once you are within five years of retirement. You might miss out on some spectacular stock market gains in those last couple of years, but you will not risk losing a lot of money. If you have to retire on a certain date, and cannot carry on working to earn more money, you cannot afford to take risks with your pension.

People who are confident of their own investing ability, and have the time to take care of their pension, can buy a self-invested personal pension. You make all the decisions about where your contributions are invested, subject to the Inland Revenue regulations, but the pension must still be organised through an authorised pension provider.

ANNUITIES

When you finally take your pension, the insurance company provides the cash to buy an annuity. You have the option to take up to 25% as a tax-free cash lump sum and spend this money on whatever you like, *but usually AVC money cannot form part of the lump sum payment.* Also, if you have used a plan to contract out of the state earnings-related pension scheme (SERPS), the part of the fund replacing SERPS cannot be taken as a lump sum.

New rules, which came into force in 1995, allow you to take a lump sum on retirement but to postpone until you are seventy-five (or earlier at your option) buying an annuity with the rest of the fund. Postponement of the annuity may be a sensible option if annuity rates are currently low. In the meantime, and within limits, you can draw an investment income from your pension fund.

Obviously, the more you take out as a lump sum, the less there will be to provide your retirement income. The annuity can be with the same company as your pension or a completely different one. *It is worth checking around because annuity rates vary widely* and, whatever rate you begin with, you will receive for the remainder of your life unless you choose an annuity with predetermined or inflation-linked increases.

You can either telephone a number of insurance companies and ask for their annuity rates or check with a specialist magazine such as *Pensions Management*, which publishes the rates available each month. This will not tell you how much you would personally receive because rates are tailored to each individual, depending upon your age and interest rates on the date you start. It will, however, allow you to compare different companies.

You need to calculate the sums carefully to ensure that you will have enough money to live on for the rest of your life. You might be quite comfortable when you first stop work, but retirement can last twenty or thirty years, during which time inflation will erode your income. You can buy an annuity which will increase each year, but a fully index-linked pension is very expensive and the high cost means you will start off with a pension very much lower than it would otherwise have been.

The later you start to draw your pension, the better the value you will obtain from an annuity. However, against this you must balance the fact that the pension pot you receive from the insurance company could be less a year or so later if its investments have performed badly. The final bonus for a with-profits policy might be cut or, if you have a unit-linked one, share prices could have fallen. General annuity rates might also be lower.

Personal pensions can be written as a cluster of policies, enabling you to activate one part of your pension and leave the balance to continue earning money. This is sometimes called *staggered vesting* and gives flexibility to people who can afford not to take all their pension at the same time. If you are in this happy position, the ideal solution is to phase in your pension over a period of years, waiting for it to increase in value. As and when it does, you will have more funds available to buy a larger annuity and you will also be able to obtain better annuity rates then as you will be that much older.

HOW TO INVEST IN LIFE INSURANCE AND PENSIONS

These are not investments to buy on the spur of the moment, because they are very long-term commitments which have severe penalties if you change your mind. Indeed, in most cases, with pension contributions you cannot get your money back until you reach at least fifty. You can switch your investment between different funds within the same scheme and you can, if you are extremely unhappy, move to a different pension provider, although you will have to pay exit charges and commission all over again.

New rules introduced in 1995 mean that life insurance and pensions salesmen have to disclose much more information about the actual costs associated with a plan. You will be told how much, if any, commission the salesman receives. But commission is just one of many costs associated with these kinds of investments. Now, life and pensions companies have to take account of all their running costs and charges and show how these would affect the ultimate pay-out, based on standard levels of return laid down by the regulators.

You should be shown how much your policy could be worth at various stages in its life taking account of a company's own charges.

Bear in mind that the figures cannot predict actual investment returns, but they are a way of comparing costs. High-charging companies may claim that their superior investment performance will more than make up for higher charges, but the higher the charges the harder it will be for them to beat the competition.

Because of the variety and complexity of ways in which charges are deducted, some companies may look better after just a few years, while others will more than catch up after the full term of a policy. At first sight, it may be better to select a company which charges less overall. In practice, companies which charge less in the first five years or so could be a better option. Many people's circumstances change and they often fail to keep up a plan for the full period originally intended.

If you know which insurance company you want to deal with, you should arrange for a meeting with a salesman who will be able to explain all the company's products. If you do not have a specific company in mind, you can search through the personal finance pages of your newspapers, although it is most unlikely that they will be writing about this particular subject the day you want to know. Monthly personal finance magazines are more likely to cover the subject in detail and they often produce performance tables to show how various companies have fared. But bear in mind that there are so many different products to choose from that obtaining a complete picture can be difficult.

This leaves you with independent financial advisers, who are unlikely to know every single product from every insurance company. However, they have a wide range of knowledge and should concentrate on the companies which they believe will produce the best results for you. A few advisers will charge you a fee for their advice, but most rely on earning commission from selling you life insurance or a pension, so be warned that they have a strong incentive to encourage you to sign up. In Chapter 11, I give much more detailed advice on how to find and appoint a financial adviser.

SUMMARY

1. Pensions and life insurance are vital elements of financial planning, but they are complex, long-term and often aggressively sold. Do not sign up until you fully understand exactly what you are buying, have made sure that it suits your requirements and have slept on the proposal overnight. You will almost certainly need expert (and preferably independent) professional advice.

2. The cheapest way to provide for your family in case you die is to buy term insurance. However, if you are still alive at the end of the policy's term you will lose your premium. Most people would prefer this to the alternative.

3. Most investment-based life insurance products are endowments. These either add yearly bonuses to your regular payments or buy units in a fund. Unit-linked products can go up or down in value, which makes them slightly riskier.

4. Endowments can offer an advantage to higher-rate taxpayers. For everyone else there is no logical reason to mix up investment with insurance. Investment through a PEP, in unit trusts, investment trusts or shares, is cheaper, more flexible and far more tax-effective.

5. If you already have an endowment policy, or sign up for one, bear in mind that they are long-term investments. If you cash in early, you will receive a poor surrender value. If at all possible, keep up payments until maturity.

6. For people who often job-hop, company pensions may not provide a decent retirement income. Either make Additional Voluntary Contributions to top up a company scheme or take out a personal pension.

7. Unlike company pensions, personal pension plans are wholly portable.

8. Pensions are very tax-efficient savings vehicles because you obtain tax relief on the payments you make and the funds in which they are invested are allowed to grow free of income and capital gains tax. This is a very substantial benefit and far outweighs the disadvantage of their relative inflexibility.

9. *You should check the rules of your personal pension plan* to find out when you have to use it to buy an annuity and when you have to decide whether or not to take up to 25% as a tax-free lump sum. Some plans allow a lot of flexibility within the Inland Revenue rules, but others are far more rigid.

7

BUYING YOUR OWN HOME

There are strong financial arguments in favour of owning your own home if you believe that high inflation is likely to return. PEP and pension mortgages seem to be the most tax-efficient ways of borrowing to fund a house or flat purchase. Endowment mortgages are much less attractive.

No one compels you to buy your home. These days, renting is a practical alternative with some real advantages. It gives you much more flexibility and avoids the worry of a fall in house prices or unexpected expenditure in the event of subsidence or major roof repairs.

Whether you buy or rent is entirely optional and is not just a question of arithmetic. You cannot simply analyse financially the difference between buying and renting a house and come to a rational conclusion. Some people cannot stand the hassle of ownership, whereas others are driven by the territorial imperative and are lost without the warm feeling that is part of the pride and pleasure of owning your own home. For many people, an Englishman's home is still his castle.

If you decide to buy your home, you are likely to tie up so much of your money that you will be compelled to look upon the house or flat as an investment as well as a place to live.

THE ARGUMENTS FOR HOME OWNERSHIP

I believe that owning a house or flat is, from an investment point of view, to be preferred to renting. As with any other investment, you need first to study past performance. Here is a graph showing what has happened to house prices and retail prices between 1956 and 1992:

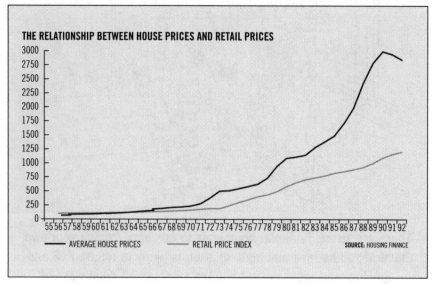

As you can see, it was only in the early 1970s that property took off in earnest. Inflation also rocketed, and this is reflected in the steep rise in retail prices.

A typical London house might have risen in price from about £15,000 in 1973 to £180,000 in late 1992. Since then, prices may have firmed a little, but they are still below their peak at the top of the boom in the late 1980s. £15,000 to £180,000 in twenty years compares very favourably with most other investments. In fact, the percentage gain could be even better, as most people would have arranged a mortgage to finance, say, two-thirds of the original cost. In this instance, the net outlay would have been as little as £5,000 with a resultant capital profit of £165,000 after paying back the mortgage.

In addition, for much of the period, the interest on the £10,000 mortgage could have been charged against income for taxation purposes. In contrast, rent would have had to be paid out of net income. As if this was not enough, the capital gain of £165,000 would have been free of tax. No wonder so many British people have been enriched by home ownership during the last two decades.

The question now is whether or not property will continue to be such a rewarding investment in the years ahead. No one can tell the future, but I believe that there are reasons for being positive. Inflation is very likely to return now that sterling has left the ERM and, although the present Government has begun to tinker with the tax privileges of home ownership, it is unlikely that any future Government will do away with them entirely.

The effects of inflation are insidious for savers but the value of houses in Britain has largely kept pace with rising prices. If the value of a house costing £100,000 grows in line with inflation of, say, 5% per annum, at the end of an average man's lifetime of seventy years it will be worth a staggering figure of over £3m. Even with underlying inflation at the April 1995 rate of only 2.6%, the house would still become worth £600,000. As you can see, there is a colossal difference between a high and low rate of inflation, but bitter experience tells us that the former remains a threat.

FREEHOLD OR LEASEHOLD

In England and Wales, buying a house freehold means you own outright the building and the land on which it stands. With a leasehold, you pay a lump sum for the right to occupy the house for an agreed period of years, subject to paying a small ground rent, which can range from £20 a year to a few hundred pounds. At the end of that time, the land and buildings revert to the landlord.

In England and Wales, flats are invariably leasehold, but there is no need to worry about this provided the lease is long. Over eighty years would be regarded by valuers almost as a freehold. If the lease is less than twenty years, then you should begin to regard it as a wasting asset and expect the value in real terms to decline a little each year. Obtaining a loan will also be more difficult. To be on the safe side, you should make sure that the lease of any flat you buy has well over fifty years to run, and preferably over eighty years, unless you can afford to write off some of the value year by year, or have a special reason for buying a very short lease.

In 1993, the Leasehold Reform, Housing and Urban Development Act was passed by Parliament, giving English and Welsh leaseholders, with leases with an original term of over twenty-one years, the right (subject to a large number of caveats) to extend those leases or purchase the freehold. In the case of a block of flats, this might be arranged on a collective basis by all of the tenants.

In Scotland, leasehold flats and houses are few and far between. Some properties have a feu duty attached, but these now have to be bought out when houses and flats are sold, so they are gradually disappearing.

FUTURE OUTLOOK FOR HOUSE PRICES

In April 1995, the outlook for house prices is uncertain. We are a long way removed from the mood that prevailed at the height of the residential property boom. I remember being impressed by my younger son when, during a spell between school and university, he was working in the dealing room of a commodity broker. He came home one evening in 1988 and announced confidently that we were almost at the end of the residential property boom in the UK. 'They are all talking about getting their feet on the property ladder and how much they have made so far,' he said. 'They cannot even imagine property going the other way.' His feeling, that the property market was near the top, proved to be correct.

Now the mood is very different. People can easily imagine their property falling in value, with the result that they might become saddled, like many others, with a mortgage larger than the value of their property – the so-called negative equity trap. Property is no longer thought to be a sure thing. As a result, it is more affordable in relation to earnings than for much of the last fifteen years. The house price/earnings ratio was 3.15 in early 1994.

Also, with lower interest rates than in the 1980s, the cost of a mortgage now compares very favourably with rents. However, owners have to pay for repairs and with flats there are often substantial service charges. Another important caveat to bear in mind is that interest rates might increase again, so if you are buying it is important to lock in at least a substantial part of any mortgage at a rate of interest that you can afford on a long-term basis.

114

IMPORTANCE OF POSITION

The most important criterion when buying a property is position. The Americans put this better; they say that there are *three* important things to consider – location, location and location. The words 'position' and 'location' in this context embrace the whole ambience of a property. For a large country house, most people would seek a house on high ground, surrounded by its own land, with a long drive and panoramic views. The essence of all these points is that most buyers are looking for peace and quiet and control over their own immediate environment. Exactly the same principle applies to buying flats and smaller houses.

A CHECKLIST FOR BUYERS

Over the years, I have been in the business of buying residential property in a substantial way. I have also consulted my elder son and two friends, all of whom are very active in buying flats and houses today. We have put together a number of things to remember, some of which may be obvious. However, I hope that our list will include one or two points that might not have occurred to you and will provide a useful checklist:

1. Attractive views from the windows and garden, if any, are an obvious major plus.

2. South and west-facing is usually preferred, as the living rooms enjoy more hours in the sun.

3. Winter light is very different from summer light. This is particularly important for houses or flats overlooked by large buildings, or country houses with hills nearby. (A friend of mine quizzed the owner of a house in a valley on whether his sitting room, basking in the July sun, ever enjoyed the winter light. He admitted that it did not and also mentioned that no other prospective purchaser had asked that question.)

4. An attractive garden is a major plus, especially in a block of flats where only yours has access to and responsibility for the garden. Similarly, a balcony to catch the sun is also very desirable.

5. In major cities parking is becoming increasingly difficult, so a good garage or easy parking for residents is a major advantage.

6. A top flat can be the most attractive in a block, provided there is a lift. Otherwise, too many steps are only for the young and athletic, restricting the number of potential buyers when you come to sell.

7. In cities, avoid basement flats (usually described by estate agents as lower ground floor). They are bad for security, dark and often suffer from damp problems.

With a basement flat one must expect a bit of damp

8. Check whether or not the house or flat is on a flight path or likely to be on one. Similarly, your survey (see later) should check if any roads are likely to be diverted your way or new ones built nearby. A tube line running underneath your house or flat can also be a big minus.

9. *Always* inspect the property at night as well as during the day. Many neighbours will be home from work then and you can assess the noise level better. The road may be busier with night lorries or, if the houses have no garages, you may find that there are too many parked cars in the road. You may also notice the smell of someone cooking curry or a meal heavily laden with garlic. I like curry – but not other people's.

10. Bad neighbours, who make a lot of noise and are inconsiderate, are to be avoided like the plague. Not only will they annoy you, but they will also make it far more difficult for you to sell advantageously when the time comes.

Checking up on future neighbours can be done in two ways. First have a good look at their garden and the state of repair of their house or flat. Then knock on their door and tell them that you are thinking of buying the house or flat nearby, would like to meet them and wonder if they have any advice to offer. If they are going to be the right neighbours, they will welcome your initiative. If not, far better to find out before signing the contract.

11. It is usually bad news to be near a pub, restaurant, massage parlour or youth hostel or *too near* a railway station. All are prone to extra activity with the risk of rowdiness, often late at night.

12. Access to good schools, shops, a railway station and buses are excellent selling points.

13. A big additional plus is having sufficient space to expand. Bear in mind, too, that there are additional restrictions for listed buildings and for those in a conservation area. In a few years' time, the possibility of adding an extra room to your house might make all the difference to your family.

14. Storage space is important, so welcome walk-in cupboards and built-in wardrobes.

15. Gas central heating and cooking facilities are usually to be preferred. They are cheaper, more efficient and easier to control.

16. With houses in particular, watch out for large trees that might be too near the house. The first danger is from the roots and the second from storm damage.

17. Houses near to rivers are to be avoided if the lie of the land makes flooding a possibility, but access to good trout fishing at a safe distance can be a big selling point.

18. The porter in a block of flats can be a very helpful source of information about other tenants and possible problems. With a country house, a visit to the village pub can often be very informative.

A COMMON-SENSE SURVEY

If you decide to buy a house or flat, you will need to arrange for a professional survey. However, to save money, first do a common-sense survey of your own to eliminate any prospect that has obvious faults.

For a start, visit the property at least twice. You will often find that it is not quite as good as you first thought, especially if you make the second visit at night.

It is important to keep your objective firmly in mind. Try not to be distracted by side-issues like the seductive smell of coffee being ground or bread baking or, for example, by minor architectural features like attractive cornices or special brass door fittings. Concentrate instead upon how you will use the property you buy. Consider the number of floors and the practicalities of the layout. Check the essentials and make sure that the rooms are the right size, the property is in good condition and will meet your family's requirements. Here is a further check-list of some more mundane points to concentrate upon during your common-sense survey:

1. Make sure that all the bathrooms, toilets and kitchens have proper ventilation.

2. Look, not only at eye level, for damp patches, stains, peeling wallpaper, flaking plaster and mould.

3. Check beams, doors and other woodwork for woodworm holes. They are usually easy to see.

4. Check the outside walls for cracks and make sure that the roof appears to be level and is not sagging. Also, keep an eye open for holes in the guttering and slipped slates.

5. A musty smell could be caused by dry rot, which can be very expensive and messy to deal with.

6. Remember that furniture and pictures that have been in place for some time may have caused discoloration, making redecoration necessary. If the previous owner is a heavy smoker, there will usually be yellow stains.

7. Remember that furniture often hides carpet stains and both large and small pieces of furniture can sometimes dramatically alter your perception of a room. Much of the charm and atmosphere of a property may be due to the contents and the way they are arranged. Once they are taken away, substantial redecoration may be required and much of the charm lost.

8. Imagine your own furniture positioned throughout the flat or house. In particular, check the kitchen area to make sure there is

enough room for your washing machine, dishwasher, fridge, freezer, microwave and the like.

9. Check the measurements of each room. Not to the inch, but make sure that they are broadly in line with the sales particulars.

10. Rotten window frames are quite common and easy to see from the outside. Curtains can hide the condition of inside windows, so pull them back to have a good look and make sure that they work properly.

11. Lead pipes and tanks are undesirable following a health scare a few years ago.

12. Ask about insulation, especially in the roof. This can save a great deal of money in heating bills.

13. Check the main fuse board and sockets and make sure that they appear to be modern. Sockets should be 13 amp, preferably with more than one in each room. Lead-covered cables and old cord wiring are bad news.

14. Subsidence is usually evidenced by cracks, leaning doors and frames and sloping floors.

15. In a block of flats, check the outgoings and management charges in detail. The management only has the right to charge reasonable fees for running the building. Check if there is a sinking fund to cover common repairs and renovations – if not you might suddenly be asked to contribute a large sum. Also, ask about common repair bills.

    If you are buying a top flat, you should make sure that you do not have sole or disproportionate responsibility for roof repairs. If the flat is on the ground floor, check that no contribution is made to maintenance of the lift.

NEGOTIATING THE PRICE

Once you have finished your common-sense survey, you have to decide whether or not to proceed to a full survey. To have gone this far, you obviously like many features of the property. However, the unsatisfactory points that you discovered during your common-sense survey may outweigh the plus points. If you still feel on balance that you want the property, you should use the list of negative points to negotiate a reduced price.

Remember that most people have been hardened by the recession and almost everyone is prepared to negotiate. If, to take two examples, the asking price was £62,500 (or £625,000), I suggest you should shake your head sorrowfully and tell the agent that a lot of work needs doing. You should then list the problems one by one and end up offering, say, £57,500 (or £575,000). The agent may then suggest £61,000 (or £610,000) and you could eventually settle at £60,000 (or £600,000) after a little more ritual to-ing and fro-ing.

Now comes the most important single point – your offer should always be made *subject to contract and survey*, and these important words must appear on any letters originating from you. This will ensure that you cannot be held to the deal if your surveyor finds a hidden problem. If the owner accepts your offer, you may be asked to make a small deposit to show good faith. There is no harm in this provided the deposit is made with the estate agent or the owner's solicitor. Make sure, too, that the receipt clearly indicates that the deposit is refundable if, for any reason, you decide not to proceed. (The law is different in Scotland – you should get legal advice if you are unsure about the practice there.)

At this point, you will see that you have not yet had to use and pay for any professional services. You will have kept these to an absolute minimum by doing the common-sense survey yourself and the negotiation. You may have to look closely at a large number of houses or flats before you make a final choice, so do not waste money on professional fees for prospects that fail to meet your requirements.

APPOINTING A SOLICITOR

If you do not have a solicitor of your own, I suggest that you ask close friends or able business associates to recommend theirs. There is no better introduction than a strong recommendation from someone you know well and respect. Ask the solicitor to give you a written estimate of likely charges – if they seem exorbitant, you can cross-check with other solicitors. The written estimate will also help to pin down the charges when your solicitor presents his final bill.

Your solicitor will conduct a search on likely developments in the area, such as new roads and housing estates. He will also arrange for land registration, payment of stamp duty of 1% on the whole of the purchase price (if over £60,000), exchange of final contracts and completion, which is usually a month afterwards. You do not have to be present during completion. Your solicitor can pass over your cheque, exchange documents and obtain the keys for you to move in.

APPOINTING A SURVEYOR

You should also try to find your surveyor by personal recommendation. You want a member of the Royal Institution of Chartered Surveyors with an FRICS or an ARICS after his or her name. Another equally acceptable alternative is a member of the Incorporated Society of Valuers and Auctioneers – an ISVA.

You can ask your surveyor to supply you with a valuation, a house buyer's report or a full structural survey. A valuation, which costs from less than 0.1% to 0.25% according to the value, will be required by the lender of any money you may borrow (explained later). A house buyer's report costs about double, and will highlight any major defects in the house or flat, stopping short of structural problems, drains, brickwork and woodwork. It is more elaborate and can be carried out by your surveyor at the same time as your valuation.

You get what you pay for; the only completely satisfactory answer with an old house or flat is a full structural survey incorporating the valuation. This way you obtain a definite fix on any work that may need doing, together with full details of any structural defects. The cost is about 0.5% of the value, but nowadays all fees are negotiable, especially for larger houses.

Be sure to ask the lender or your mortgage broker if the surveyor you use is on the lender's panel of approved surveyors. You should be able to negotiate a discount if your survey is done at the same time as the compulsory valuation for mortgage purposes.

FURTHER PRICE NEGOTIATION

Let us return to the hypothetical house we were buying for the agreed price of, say, £60,000 and assume that you had just paid £300 for a full structural survey. The surveyor's report might show that the roof was in a terrible state of repair and needed £1,500 to be spent to make it safe and rainproof. You should now use the surveyor's report like a chisel to chip at least £1,500 off the £60,000 you had previously agreed *subject to survey and subject to contract*.

The surveyor's report can and usually does pay for itself and will also give you a firm idea of the repairs you will need to do if you proceed with the purchase. In the unlikely event that the house is given a clean bill of health, look upon the surveyor's fee as a kind of insurance policy. Great news to find that you are buying a completely sound house.

My suggestions for negotiating the price are given in 1995, in the aftermath of the recession when the housing market is still sluggish. Gazumping (sellers accepting a higher price from another buyer after having agreed a price with you first) is a symptom of a frenetic and rising market. If there is a sudden resurgence of demand for property, you might well find that your negotiating powers are severely curtailed. Needless to say, you should adapt to the prevailing climate, but meanwhile make the most of the buyers' market.

MORTGAGES

A mortgage is a long-term loan which is paid back over a period of time, usually by monthly instalments which include both capital and interest. On mortgages of up to £30,000, there is tax relief on the interest paid, at a rate of 15% from April 1995. Your house or flat is pledged as security for the loan and if you fail to repay it, there is a substantial possibility that the building society or bank that lent you the money will sell your house and use the proceeds to effect repayment. In that event, you would still be left owing any deficit or would be entitled to any surplus proceeds after full repayment of the lending institution's capital, interest and costs.

Borrowing money in the 1990s is a very different proposition from ten years ago. Today, provided you earn enough and have no bad debt record, you will be offered a wide range of deals from a variety of lenders keen to make you a loan.

Today, there are two other certainties: special offers that cut costs on one side may take money back (often more) on the other, and your choice of home loan will be unimaginably difficult. One lender alone may offer you as many as fifteen different options, including fixed rates for differing periods and various first-time buyer and large loan discounts. The main methods of repaying a mortgage, and some of the special terms offered by lenders, are:

Methods of repaying a mortgage:

Capital repayment
Full with-profits endowment
Low-cost with-profits endowment
Low-start endowment
Unit-linked endowment
Unitised with-profits
Pension-linked
PEP
Interest-only

Lenders' special terms:

Fixed rate
Capped
Cap and collar
First-time buyer's discount

You need a very broad understanding of what is on offer and how much you can afford before approaching a bank or building society. There are two elements to a mortgage – the interest and the capital. Both have to be repaid, but you can treat them separately.

YOUR CHOICES

Few people can afford to buy a property outright; most need to borrow some of the money. Banks and building societies will lend it to you, but they want security: if you fail to keep up the payments, they have the right to take your house. Mortgages today are dressed up in various guises, but they are all based on two basic types, capital repayment and interest-only.

Capital repayment

The first mortgages were simple repayment ones. Each month you paid interest and repaid a small part of the capital until, after twenty-five years or so, you had paid back the entire sum.

Full with-profits endowment

In the 1970s, with-profits endowment life insurance policies started to be sold with mortgages. Each month, you repay the interest element to the lender and premiums on the life policy to an insurance company; the policy pays out on death or the date the loan is due to be repaid.

Lenders prefer endowment mortgages because they earn commission selling them on behalf of insurance companies. However, since 1984, there has been no tax relief on life insurance premiums, so the attractions for borrowers are very limited.

Low-cost with-profits endowment mortgage

Full with-profits endowment mortgages were expensive, so the next stage was the low-cost and/or low-start with-profits endowment mortgages, which are still widely sold today. Because the final payout on a full with-profits endowment mortgage was usually far more than was needed to meet the debt, lenders began to allow borrowers to insure for less than the loan. The assumption was that the annual bonuses and terminal bonus added to the basic sum assured would be more than enough to repay the debt.

In the past year or two, with-profits bonuses have fallen. There is just a possibility that someone who has taken out a low-cost with-profits endowment during the last few years might not receive enough money from the policy when the mortgage is due to be repaid. In that event, they could anticipate the problem by increasing their premiums; otherwise they would have to find the balance elsewhere.

Low-start endowment mortgage

Low-start policies are another kind of add-on option to the range of endowment policies on offer. They were designed to enable borrowers to pay back less in the early years, generally working on the basis of increasing premiums by 10-20% per annum for a fixed period. Like low-cost policies, they can be either with-profits or unit-linked.

Unit-linked endowment

During the 1980s, unit-linked life insurance policies became more widely used for repaying mortgages. Unit-linked policies relate directly to movements in the stock market, so they are riskier as, over the years, the value of your investment can go down as well as up.

When you invest for the very long-term with a unit-linked policy, *provided you do not cash it in early,* you can be reasonably confident that your money will grow substantially and the proceeds should be more than enough to pay off your mortgage. However, there is no certainty of this, and another stock market crash might give you some very worrying moments.

Over the period of a unit-linked policy, you will usually be best advised to invest in a general 'managed' fund. If you want to be more adventurous, you do have the choice of more specific funds such as those that specialise in European, American or Far Eastern markets. If the fund has enjoyed substantial capital growth when you are a few years away from needing the money, you should lock in the gains already made by switching to a with-profits fund within the same policy. The worst that could happen to you then would be to lose out on any spectacular rise in the stock market in those last few years. However, you will not live in fear of losing the capital growth already established.

Unitised with-profits

More recently, with-profits policies have become less available as the insurance companies have converted to selling unitised with-profits policies, a hybrid between the two which is less expensive for the insurer. They are less risky than traditional unit-linked policies because the value of the units cannot go down as bonuses are locked in each year.

SHOULD YOU USE LIFE INSURANCE TO PAY OFF A MORTGAGE?

To my mind, all these different kinds of endowment policy only confuse the main issue, which is quite simple. If you are borrowing a large amount of money to buy a home, you want to pay as much as you can reasonably afford each month to be sure of repaying the capital sum on the due date. Meanwhile, if you have any dependants, you will almost certainly want to insure your life, so that if you die prematurely, the mortgage will be paid off in full. I do not like or recommend the idea of paying substantial commission to insurance salesmen for endowment policies, which may or may not provide future capital profits. These kinds of policies are a completely separate issue from buying a home, which can be financed by a simple, straightforward arrangement like a capital repayment mortgage. There are also two relatively new ways of saving tax, which are worth very serious consideration.

MODERN MORE TAX-EFFICIENT METHODS

Pension-linked mortgages

During the house price boom, lenders became more relaxed about accepting life policies as collateral because they could always sell the property for a profit to reclaim their money. They started allowing borrowers to save up the money to repay the loan in personal pension schemes, even though these cannot be assigned to the lender.

A pension-linked mortgage is very tax-efficient because it gives tax relief on both the mortgage interest and pension contributions. As a consequence, the net monthly payments you need to make are lower than for a comparable endowment policy. Also, pension fund investments can grow faster than endowment policies, because they pay no tax on income or capital gains – another reason for lower monthly premiums.

But there are drawbacks. You will not receive such a large lump sum from your pension arrangement on retirement. You will have to use much or all of it to pay off your mortgage. Furthermore, you may have to take a bigger lump sum than you would otherwise choose, and that will result in a lower pension income.

If you are young, you could end up paying interest on the mortgage for a great deal longer than twenty-five years. Also, you should not rule out the possibility that, at a later stage in your career, you may want to join a company pension scheme. That could be complicated and, in that event, you would need to obtain expert advice.

PEP mortgages

In recent years, personal equity plans (PEPs) have become acceptable as tax-efficient savings schemes linked to mortgages. A PEP can be very tax-efficient; there is no tax on investments within the plan. In addition, PEPs are more flexible than other interest-only mortgage repayment methods as you are not locked in for a set period.

PEP mortgages pay a very small commission compared with unit-linked endowments, with-profits endowments and pension-linked mortgages, so do not expect commission-based advisers to be wildly enthusiastic about them.

INTEREST-ONLY MORTGAGES

With interest-only mortgages you just pay the interest to the lender, who leaves it entirely up to you to find the money at some future date to repay the debt (typically by saving in a unit or investment trust or from an inheritance). Not many building societies or banks offer this option.

FIXED-RATE LOANS

At present, lenders are competing very hard for business and there is a plethora of fixed-rate low-priced deals. With all of them, the fixed-rate period lasts for a limited time, sometimes only one or two years, and there are always conditions attached, such as penalties for early redemption. *Also, borrowers may have to take out other insurance policies (sometimes general and sometimes life) with the lender and pay higher than usual arrangement fees before they are allowed a special-offer loan.*

In April 1995, the basic mortgage cost around 8.4% and the cheapest fixed-rate loan from a larger building society was 2.75% from the Yorkshire. However, the fixed rate lasted only until the end of March 1996. There was a £250 arrangement fee, but the potential savings could still be substantial. One drawback was that borrowers would be locked into the Yorkshire, with redemption penalties of six months' interest in the first two years of the loan and three months' interest in the next two years.

At the same time, longer term fixed rates for periods of five years or more were around the 8.8% to 9.9% mark. That could be expensive if rates, which were rising in early 1995, peaked at these levels and then fell back. You have to make your own decision about the kind of mortgage you prefer. To help overcome this uncertainty, some lenders offer capped mortgages where the interest rate is variable, but guaranteed not to rise above a certain figure; and also offer cap-and-collar loans, where the interest rate can move but must stay within a certain range for a specified period. Barclays, for example, offered a capped rate in April 1995 at 6.99% for two years. You should always check the exact terms; a cap may mean that interest above a certain level is simply deferred and added to the outstanding capital you owe.

OBTAINING A LOAN

As I have explained, straightforward repayment, PEP and pension mortgages seem preferable to endowment mortgages. The difficulty is finding a building society or bank which can meet your requirements. Most of the big ones are already tied to an insurance company and will try to sell you an endowment, often coupled with an attractive fixed-rate loan. However, if you want a straightforward capital repayment mortgage, *insist* on it. You may encounter considerable resistance and will almost certainly lose the benefit of any special rates on offer.

The whole subject of mortgages is a very complex one, so most people need expert professional advice. In my view, there is a lot to be said for seeing an *independent* adviser who knows all the products on offer and can shop around on your behalf for the most competitive and suitable one. However, you should always find out how much the advice will cost you.

If you are prepared to put in the groundwork yourself, you can go straight to your bank and/or nearest building society and find out what they have to offer. As I explain in Chapter 11, you should also establish early in the proceedings how they are remunerated and if they have products that meet your requirements. If, for example, they cannot offer repayment or PEP mortgages, you might have to go elsewhere.

SUMMARY ON MORTGAGES

1. Lenders want your business. Remember that special deals are often not so special when you examine them more closely.

2. Mortgages linked to endowment policies, whether with-profits or unit-linked, are not attractive as they offer minimal tax advantages for higher-rate taxpayers only. Salesmen receive large commissions for selling these kinds of policies. One way or another, the borrower ends up paying, so there is less money available to repay your mortgage.

3. There are substantial tax advantages with pension mortgages. They usually result in lower monthly payments than for endowment policies.

4. PEP mortgages are very tax-efficient. They may provide more than enough to repay a mortgage at the end of the period, but there is also a possibility that they may provide less.

5. If you cannot afford to pay much in the early years, you may have to consider a low-start and/or a low-cost mortgage. Remember though, you will have to pay more in the later years and if it is linked to an endowment policy, hefty commissions will be involved.

6. With a capital repayment mortgage, you know exactly where you stand and, provided you can keep up your monthly payments, you know for certain that your mortgage will be repaid at the end of the period. If you have dependants, you should also consider insuring your life to fully repay the mortgage in the event of your death. A simple term insurance will suffice – an endowment policy is not necessary.

8

ALTERNATIVE INVESTMENT

Although the main objective of collecting should be fun, collectables are also a form of investment. As with other investments, it pays to specialise, master your subject and buy the best you can afford.

You do not need to be wealthy to start a collection. Most works of art, apart from paintings and fine furniture, are auctioned for less than £500 and many can be bought in out-of-the-way antique shops for even smaller sums.

You might decide to collect anything from vintage radios to old pens, dolls, Dinky toys, cigarette cards or matchboxes. Collectability usually depends on nostalgia and scarcity. When deciding what to collect, I suggest choosing things that are well within your price range, appeal to you and encapsulate the style of a generation. The humblest objects get thrown away or destroyed, their design considered out-of-date and unfashionable. You would not shop at Dixons today to buy a pocket-calculator manufactured ten years ago. It would seem clumsy and unsophisticated. But in twenty years time the same calculator, kept neatly in its original package, could be worth a small fortune. In 1993, for example, a 1934 Bakelite wireless surprised everyone by fetching £17,500. At an auction, 'It only takes two to tango.'

Everyone knows that paintings and antiques can become extraordinarily valuable but, fifty years ago, who would have thought that a Hollywood poster of the *Phantom of the Opera* would have an estimated sale price of $20,000-$30,000 and that a selection of toy dolls would sell at prices ranging up to £20,000 each. Even collections of old comics or Dinky toys can become surprisingly valuable.

Old master paintings are obviously only for the very rich, but watercolours and prints, coins, rare books, stamps, cigarette cards and memorabilia are well within the reach of most people. Some excellent collections have been built from small beginnings.

Inflation, coupled with shortage of supply due to museum purchasing, has increased the prices of many collectables to levels that only twenty years ago would have been thought absurd. A well-chosen collection with a few lucky finds can quickly grow in value and, as a result, become a significant part of the collector's net personal wealth.

The main objective of any collector should be to have fun and to enjoy the chase and the pleasure of building and owning a worthwhile collection. However, there is no denying that collectables are also a form of investment and, although books and cigarette cards, dolls and paintings could not be more different, there are a few common guidelines that apply to the building of any collection:

1. *Buy only those works that give you pleasure*

Your only dividend from owning a work of art may be a lifetime's enjoyment, so make sure that you are happy to live with whatever you select.

2. *Specialise in a relatively narrow area of your chosen field*

I called my last book *The Zulu Principle* because my wife once read a four-page article on Zulus in *Reader's Digest*. From that moment onwards she knew more than I did about Zulus. If she had then borrowed all the available books on the subject from the local library and read them carefully, she would have known more about Zulus than most people in Surrey. If she had decided subsequently to visit South Africa, live for six months in a Zulu kraal and study all the available literature on Zulus at a South African University, she would have become one of the leading authorities in Great Britain and, possibly, the world. The key point is that the history of Zulus and their habits and customs today is a clearly defined and narrow area of knowledge into which my wife would have invested a disproportionate amount of her time and effort, with the result that she would have become an acknowledged expert. The study of this noble people might not have been profitable, but there are many other very specialised subjects that would have been very rewarding financially.

So it is with investment in collectables. By specialising in a particular period or style, or the works of a limited number of artists, you will develop extra knowledge in your area of interest that should enable you to buy well and to keep fully abreast of events. For example, it would make very little sense to try to accumulate a worldwide collection of stamps. Far better to concentrate upon one or two countries. That way you might be able to build a worthwhile collection and dealers would then find it more difficult to arbitrage your ignorance. Over a long period, you will grow to know more about your speciality than many of the dealers and you will probably start dealing yourself to upgrade and help to finance your own collection.

3.   *Understand your subject*

The most important general point is to learn as much as possible about, as Magnus Magnusson would say, 'your chosen subject'. There are hundreds of books written on fine art, furniture and ceramics but, even on more obscure subjects like scientific instruments and toys, you should be able to find a few worthwhile and instructive books.

4.   *Learn how to deal with dealers*

When you begin to collect, you would be best advised to try to establish a relationship with a dealer who has an excellent reputation and has been recommended to you. Failing that, the *Guide to Antique Shops of Great Britain*, published yearly by the Antique Collectors' Club, includes a large selection. You can be reassured if dealers belong to either The British Antique Dealers Association (BADA) or the London and Provincial Antique Dealers Association (LAPADA). At least you will know that they have been approved for fair trading and, if there is a problem, you can appeal to the relevant association.

Make no mistake that your dealer is out to make a profit on any works he has purchased. If he has bought well, his mark-up might be as much as 100%. Your objective is to buy as keenly as possible so, in that sense, you are in conflict. However, dealers do not always win – I remember about five years ago buying a Gothic lantern from a dealer in Petworth for £1,850. Three years later I sold it for £12,500. I am sorry to say that I can also recall a number of other purchases that did not work out so well.

On balance, I recommend taking a well-chosen dealer into your confidence, explaining your objectives and trying to establish a personal rapport. More often than not, you will find that you will be treated fairly.

Try to find a dealer without massive overheads. Many dealers work from home and go to antique fairs. Their profits are not supporting shops in Bond Street or St James's and, as they have fewer clients, they are delighted to help any new ones.

Some dealers will allow you to take home pictures or pieces of furniture so that you can try them out; others will give you a buy-back agreement on more expensive items. A buy-back is an excellent idea even if there is no allowance for growth in the agreement and you lose interest on capital employed. Never rely upon a verbal promise for a buy-back – ask for it to be set out clearly in writing. There may be a time limit of three to five years before you can ask for the item to be bought back, and you may never want to sell, but far better to have the option just in case you change your mind. Of course, when the time comes to sell the item in question, it may be worth far more than the buy-back, in which event you sell to the highest bidder.

5.   Buy the best within your means

The market in collectables and works of art can be very illiquid at times. However, there is always a market for the best. This does not mean that you have to buy a Rembrandt – it simply means that you should buy the best you can afford within the period and style in which you are interested. You may, for example, specialise in the works of much lesser artists and, in that case, you should pay a little more to buy their best works.

In the 1970s, I was interested in the paintings of Frederick William Watts, who followed the style of Constable. A fine painting by Watts seemed to me to be a far more attractive proposition than a poor work by Constable. At the time, the paintings of Watts were readily available at prices ranging from £1,000 to about £5,000. I felt that he was much underestimated and bought his paintings almost indiscriminately. As soon as one became available, I snapped it up.

I did not realise that Watts was such a prolific artist and that the quality of his work varied a great deal. A lesser painting that cost £1,000 in 1973 might today sell for £4,000–£5,000. A greater work, which sold for £5,000, could now be worth as much as £125,000.

I was right about Watts being underestimated, but I should have concentrated upon his *finest* works. The best works of a lesser artist can often be a far more rewarding investment than the lesser works of a better artist.

6.   Buy works of art with an interesting provenance

The history of the ownership of a work of art is called its provenance; it is similar in many ways to the CV of an individual. A work that has had an interesting and proven history is always worth more than one with an undistinguished past. You may have seen in catalogues the term 'property of a gentleman'. There are too many gentlemen around, so try to obtain more precise details.

7. *Condition*

Works of art and collectables in prime condition are always worth a colossal premium over those that are slightly damaged. A book with a page torn out, or with an inscription (other than the author's), is worth much less than a mint copy. A stamp with a heavy postmark, a painting with a small hole in the canvas and chipped porcelain are all to be avoided.

8. *Maintenance*

Learn how to look after your collectables. I am sure you are aware that oriental carpets, watercolours and rare books should not be exposed to harsh sunlight, but did you know that books can also suffer from bookworm? It is important to find out exactly how to store your collectables and how to maintain them in good condition. Otherwise they will lose their value rapidly.

9. *Cataloguing*

Catalogue the date of purchase, source, provenance, cost and every other relevant detail of each and every purchase. This record will be very useful for tax purposes, insurance and for future reference.

10. *Insurance*

Make absolutely sure that your collection is regularly revalued (if only by you) and fully insured. Also make sure that the policy covers collectables in transit or at a dealer's premises. You may be able to reduce your insurance bill by taking an initial element of the risk yourself or by beefing up your security arrangements (by, for example, having locks on your windows or doors and putting more valuable items in a safe or at your bank when you are on holiday).

11. *Try not to let the rare ones get away*

For rare works that you really have a yen for, I recommend being prepared to bid a little beyond the estimated saleroom prices as shown in catalogues. These estimates are often conservative and you will usually regret the ones that get away. Speak to the auctioneer before the sale to ask him about the interest shown in your lot and how much he thinks it will fetch. Most well-known auctioneers are prepared to help the novice collector.

If a work is available that will fill a hole in your collection – reach for it. Of course, you should not pay an unlimited price, but be prepared to go that little bit further to save yourself years of regret. Remember that collecting should be fun and the best fun is to build a really satisfying collection.

12. *Time your purchases well*

The prices of collectables go up and down, usually in sympathy with the stock market, but also with fashion. Try to buy when the market is depressed and, if you have anything to sell, do so when the market is buoyant. It is, of course, hard to know exactly when any market is at a top, but there are usually a few telltale signs. Salerooms are full, record prices are being established and everyone agrees that things are a far better investment than cash.

13. *Remember that safety is directly linked to wideness of appeal*

The most stable areas of investment in art and collectables are those with a long history and a large number of dealers, all of whom have a vested interest in keeping the market alive and well. Good examples are old master paintings, porcelain and rare books.

West Indian or Nigerian modern paintings might be very interesting, but their appeal could be limited, especially in difficult times. In contrast, Chinese paintings might become much more valuable if China continues to grow rapidly and prosper. The safest, and possibly the most profitable collections, will always reflect the economy of the country of origin. For example, thirty years ago no one could have imagined the prices now fetched by works of art, books and pictures about the Middle East. When an emerging economy takes off, you can be sure its art market will not be far behind.

I do not particularly recommend stamp collecting as a way of making money, as dealers take such a high percentage and the market in stamps can be very illiquid. I remember that my two sons were horrified when they came to sell their prized collection of Australian mint stamps. Leading dealers were only prepared to offer 20% of the original cost – the albums held their value better. If you are keen on collecting stamps and enjoy doing so, I suggest that you specialise in countries with a very strong economy and a prosperous middle class. They are the people most likely to be interested in the stamps of their country, if and when you come to sell.

14. *Join the club*

For most collectables, there are clubs or associations which are well worth joining, if only to find out what is going on in your area of interest. For example, the Antique Collectors' Club offers both buying and selling opportunities through its monthly magazine, *Antique Collecting*. An added bonus of subscribing is that you will see the reviews of specialist books that may be of particular interest to you.

15. *Keep in mind tax considerations*

Since 1982, you have been allowed to make a deduction from capital profits to take inflation into account, so you are only taxed nowadays on any 'real' capital gains you might make in excess of your overall £6,000 annual personal capital gains tax exemption. Also any work of art sold for under £6,000 in value is completely exempt from capital gains tax. A fuller explanation is given in Chapter 9.

To end on a more convivial note, let us turn to wine. It is one of the few attractive investments that enjoys a double benefit from the passage of time. The taste improves and there is less of each vintage around.

The generally accepted advice, if you are building up a cellar of good wine, is to buy young through a wine merchant. You should buy a little more than you need, with a view to selling some after a few years and reinvesting the proceeds in new young wine. Unlike most investments, there is a very simple remedy if you find it difficult to sell – drink a little more or have a party.

SUMMARY

An excellent general book on the subject of collecting is *Alternative Investment* by Jackie Wullschläger (Financial Times Business Information). I found myself agreeing with almost all of the conclusions and strongly recommend this excellent book to you.

Whatever you decide to collect, investment should be a secondary consideration. Far more important is the thrill of the chase, whether it be in antique shops, country houses or at auction. The satisfaction of finding a rare piece that you have been searching for and adding it to your collection; the pleasure of showing your collection to friends, or just simply browsing over it on a winter's night; all of these pleasures are in store.

9

TAXATION

There are a number of simple and legitimate ways to save tax on investments. It will pay you to know them, so that you can plan ahead and minimise your family's tax bill.

The word 'taxation' always gives me the chilly feeling that I am about to be asked to part with a substantial sum of money. The feeling is well-based, as usually both income and capital gains are taxed and, one way or another, I always seem to end up paying more money than I would like to the Collector of Taxes.

The key point to grasp is that you can reduce your tax bill by perfectly legitimate means. To do so effectively, you need to understand how the taxation system works and the concessions that are available to you, so that you can plan ahead.

The two taxes that will concern you most are income tax and capital gains tax. The former is levied on income, which, as well as your salary, includes interest received and dividends from investments. The latter is charged on profits made on the disposal of unit and investment trusts, shares, property other than a main home and chattels, including pictures, antiques, silverware, gold coins and stamps, and other forms of alternative investment.

Since 1982, you have been allowed to make a deduction from capital profits to take inflation into account. This 'indexation allowance' means that you are now only taxed on any 'real' capital gain you have made. To work out the amount of indexation, take the RPI on the month of purchase of the asset (say 104) and deduct it from the RPI on the month of sale (say 130). The difference (26) divided by the starting value (104) indicates how much prices have risen since the purchase of the asset. In this case prices have risen a quarter ($^{26}/_{104}$), and the purchase price of your asset is inflated by this amount *before* your gain is calculated. (See Appendix IV on p.332 for the monthly RPI figures.)

So, for example, if you bought shares for £10,000 when the RPI was 104 and sold them for £25,000 when the RPI was 130, the Inland Revenue would let you take the first £2,500 (£10,000 x ¼) of the gain tax-free. Your tax liability would be limited to the profit above inflation of £12,500. Remember though, in the 1995-6 tax year, the first £6,000 of any one year's capital gains come free of tax so you would only be taxed on the excess. At one time it was possible to turn a gain into a loss by adding the indexation allowance. Now you can only use indexation to eliminate or reduce a gain.

To save you the trouble of calculating the rise in the RPI, tables published in both the *Investors Chronicle* and *Moneyfacts* do it for you. The tables are very easy to use. If an asset was acquired before 31 March 1982, then, if advantageous, you can use its value at that date as your base rather than original cost.

Indexation of capital gains is just one way of improving your tax position and there are many others that should be given active consideration. Most of these have been dealt with in detail in other chapters, but I will summarise the main points again.

INDEPENDENT TAXATION

We have Nigel Lawson to thank for the changes in legislation which introduced independent taxation for married women. This is a great boon for married couples who have investment income and differing levels of earned income that do not use up all of the combined tax allowances available to them.

In the 1995-6 tax year, personal allowance is £3,525, so no tax is payable on the first £3,525 of income. The lower rate band of tax (20%) is the first £3,200 of *taxable* income and the basic rate band (25%) is the next £21,100. This means that you can enjoy an income of up to £27,825 before you become liable to tax at the highest rate of 40%. For someone paying the top rate of tax, therefore, there is a big incentive to transfer some of their income to a non-taxpaying or lower-rate-taxed spouse. The total potential tax savings available for a higher-rate taxpayer are calculated as follows:

	£	£
Personal allowance	3,525 x 40% =	1,410
Lower rate band	3,200 x 20% =	640
Basic rate band	21,100 x 15% =	3,165
	27,825	5,215

The personal allowance is a complete saving of the entire 40% that would otherwise be paid in tax by high-income earners; the lower rate band of 20% saves 20% compared with the full rate of 40% and the basic rate band of 25% is 15% less than the full rate.

Let us assume that one spouse is in employment and has sufficient taxable income to use the personal allowance and both the lower rate and basic rate bands while their partner does not work and has no income at all. If the couple also have investment income of anything up to £27,825, it would clearly pay them to put the investments generating the income into the name of the spouse who had no earned income. In this way, they would save up to £5,215 per annum – a tidy sum that might otherwise have to be paid over in tax. Once both spouses' allowances have been used up, it makes no difference for tax purposes which of them owns the investment; tax is then payable at 40%.

An important caveat for husbands and wives transferring their money to each other is to be as certain as possible that their marriage is likely to remain a long-term proposition. If not, some difficult legal arguments on the subject of who owns what are likely to ensue.

CAPITAL GAINS TAX EXEMPTION

Annual capital gains of less than £6,000 per person are exempt from capital gains tax, which is paid on the excess over that figure. This means that, if one spouse in a marriage had made no capital gains in a particular tax year, and the other spouse had investments pregnant with gains, the investments in question could be transferred at original cost from one spouse to the other in order to minimise the tax bill. When the capital gains were realised, they would then use up the £6,000 free limit of the spouse who would otherwise have had no capital gains. If the transfer of investments was not made, and the investments were realised before the end of the tax year, the spouse with the capital gains and the pregnant capital profits might otherwise exceed his or her personal limit of £6,000. In that event, a sum of up to £2,400 (40% of £6,000) would be paid over to the Collector of Taxes quite unnecessarily.

Taxpayers who do not use their annual capital gains tax exemption to the full should consider investments which offer the prospect of capital growth at the expense of income. As we have seen in Chapter 5, some investment trusts have been devised with this end in mind. These kinds of investments are complicated, so I would recommend the use of a professional adviser.

BED AND BREAKFAST

You should review your portfolio at least once a month and, in particular, a month or so before the end of the fiscal year on 5 April. You might find that you have substantial potential capital gains but, unless you take action, you will not use up your £6,000 capital gains free annual allowance. If you have any shares pregnant with gains that you want to sell, you should obviously give instructions to do so, to ensure that you reach at least the £6,000 limit. You should also consider realising losses to bring your gains down within the limit or to offset other gains.

If you are satisfied with your portfolio, a constructive alternative is to *bed and breakfast* sufficient shares or unit trusts to use up your £6,000 limit. This means selling some shares one day and buying them back the next, in order to crystallise a gain or loss. Your broker or bank will arrange this for you. Remember, too, that for a married couple the £6,000 free limit is available for both spouses.

PEPS

Personal Equity Plans (PEPs) are a tax-break for investors who regularly exceed the annual capital gains tax exemption limit or who pay income tax on their investment returns. Private investors can invest tax-free up to £9,000 every year. Over a few years, it is possible for them to build up a really meaningful tax-free portfolio.

What is a PEP?

Basically a PEP is a tax-free suitcase into which you can pack investments costing up to £9,000 every year. These can be:

Ordinary shares incorporated in the EC and listed on any EC Stock Exchange

Specified corporate bonds and convertibles

Specified preference shares and convertible preference shares

Unit trusts

Investment trusts

To qualify, corporate bonds and convertibles must be in non-financial UK companies, denominated in sterling and with more than five years to run to redemption from the time of purchase. Preference shares and convertible preference shares must also be in non-financial companies incorporated in any EC member State.

There is a £6,000 annual General PEP limit for any or all of the above. A further £3,000 can also be put into a single company PEP, which invests in the shares of just one company. These limits apply to individuals, so a married couple can invest up to £18,000 a year in PEPs.

Unit and investment trusts are divided into qualifying and non-qualifying trusts. To qualify, a trust must be at least 50% invested in UK and EC shares and qualifying corporate bonds and preference shares. Only £1,500 of the £6,000 general allowance can be invested in non-qualifying trusts.

What are the tax advantages of a PEP?

The attraction of PEPs is that all capital gains and dividend income are tax-free. For investors who regularly make substantial capital gains this has obvious attractions. But even for smaller investors who are unlikely to breach the £6,000 capital gains tax exemption, PEPs can be used advantageously as long-term savings vehicles. It is possible, for example, to use PEPs as the savings mechanism for paying off an interest-only mortgage. Endowments are more popular, probably because salesmen receive bigger commissions, but they are much less tax-efficient than PEPs.

Flexibility

Another advantage of PEPs is that they can be closed at any time. This makes them much more flexible as a long-term savings vehicle than either endowments or pensions, which have poor early surrender values.

Restrictions

There are very few restrictions on the investments General PEPs can hold. They can be used to make an investment in one company or in a pooled investment to spread risk. However, the charges levied by the PEP plan manager will reflect how much work he has to do and the fund management costs he incurs. Self-select plans, with you making the final decision on the shares to buy, are cheapest but they are only for experienced investors.

PEP charges

Of course, the flexibility and tax efficiency of PEPs comes at a price and the charges levied by PEP managers can, in some circumstances, outweigh much of the tax advantage.

A PEP normally has two types of charge, one up-front payment when you take out the plan and an annual fee for as long as you hold it. Both are normally levied as a percentage of your investment, but some plan managers offer a fixed fee, which can be cheaper. Thanks to increased competition, initial charges have fallen in recent years and some plan managers make no initial charge, although they may levy an exit charge if you withdraw in the five years, although some plans still charge as much as 6%. Obviously, if you plan to invest the maximum £6,000 in a general PEP, a flat fee is more attractive than if you are only able to invest, say £3,000. Flat fees (typically £25 or £30) can be as little as 0.5% of your investment, if you invest the maximum amount.

The day-to-day administration of your PEP is paid for by the annual charge, usually a percentage but sometimes a fixed charge. Annual fees are typically between 0.75% and 1.5% of the value of the PEP. Again, if you have invested the maximum allowance of £6,000 in a General PEP, a fixed fee can be attractive, although these usually apply to single company PEPs which require less active management.

Caveat emptor

PEPs are very attractive to higher-rate taxpayers who regularly exceed their £6,000 CGT exemption and investors in this position should definitely use PEPs to the full. The benefits will far outweigh the cost. However, if you are a basic-rate taxpayer who fails to use up the gains tax allowance, you need to weigh up charges more carefully. If, for example, the shares invested in your PEP pay a dividend yield of 4% (the current average), your *income* tax saving from the PEP will be just 0.8% of the value of your fund (20% – the basic tax rate for investment income – of your 4% yield). If the income tax saving is the only attraction of the PEP, then you should steer clear of any plan which, after adding VAT, charges more than 0.8% in annual fees.

Finally, remember that a PEP will only perform as well as its underlying investments. You should never buy a financial product just for the tax breaks. A PEP will enhance the performance of a good investment, but it will not rescue a bad one.

My new book, *PEP Up Your Wealth*, explains the advantages of PEPs and also gives details of a very attractive and successful system for investing in high-yielding stocks.

A full list of PEPs and their charges, costing £12.95, is published by Chase De Vere (Telephone: 0800 526 091).

TESSAS

Taxpayers with cash on long-term deposit should use a TESSA to the maximum possible level of £9,000. A married couple once again have separate allowances, which should both be used to the full. See Chapter 1 for fuller details.

PENSION CONTRIBUTIONS

If you are in employment and in a company pension scheme, you should consider increasing your eventual pension by making AVCs (additional voluntary contributions). You are allowed to use AVCs to top up your existing contributions to 15% of your annual earnings. This is a particularly tax-efficient way of saving for people who have income to spare and are nearing retirement.

If your employer does not have a pension scheme, or you are self-employed, you should consider contributing to a personal pension plan. For people under thirty-five, the limit is 17.5% of relevant earnings up to an earnings cap of £78,600. The permissible contribution rises gradually with age, from 17.5% of earnings to 40% for people of sixty-one and over.

Personal pension plans offer one of the most efficient ways of saving tax. The contributions are charged against taxable income, so for high earners the tax saving is at the top rate of 40%. For example, someone aged thirty-five or less with taxable income of £40,000 per annum could contribute £7,000 per annum and save £2,800 per annum in tax (40% of £7,000). Once your money is in the pension scheme it enjoys tax-free capital gains and income is also untaxed. The different kinds of pension plans that are available are outlined more fully in Chapter 6.

BUYING YOUR OWN HOME

Any capital profit on your main home is free of capital gains tax and there is tax relief on the interest on the first £30,000 of a mortgage. In the 1995-6 tax year, relief will be restricted to 15% of interest paid.

In the highly inflationary mid- and late-1980s, freedom from capital gains tax made house-buying a very lucrative pastime. Many people parlayed their winnings to bigger and bigger houses, accumulating large tax-free gains. In recessionary times of low inflation, this is no longer such an attractive game. However, the tax concessions for house-buying are too large to ignore and, although inflation is lying low at the moment, it is still lurking there under the surface ready to rise again. It seems to me that owning your own house or flat is hard to beat as an investment, especially if the annual cost of paying off a mortgage, together with the interest, is less than the rental charge for a similar property.

NATIONAL SAVINGS CERTIFICATES

Higher-rate taxpayers should buy their maximum allowance of National Savings Certificates. See Chapter 1 for further details.

GILTS AND BONDS

Gilts and qualifying corporate bonds bought below par offer a tax-free capital gain if held to redemption. For the proposed new rules, issued in a consultation paper in mid-1995, for taxing gilts and corporate bonds, see pages 32–33.

Bear in mind the great attraction of index-linked gilts is that the inflation element, as measured by the RPI index, will be paid to you tax-free on maturity. If inflation resurges, this capital payment could be very substantial.

An important point for non-taxpayers investing in gilts is to purchase them through the National Savings Stock Register, so that the interest will be paid gross.

Remember that an investment in a unit trust specialising in bonds and gilts is not eligible for capital gains tax exemption. You also have to pay both initial and annual management charges.

Non-taxpayers should also remember that the basic-rate tax deducted from a guaranteed income bond cannot be reclaimed. Higher-rate taxpayers have to pay further tax to bring the basic rate already paid up to their full rate.

PICTURES, ANTIQUES AND OTHER COLLECTABLES

There is no capital gains tax on chattels which, when first acquired, have a likely life of less than fifty years. You will not need to pay tax on any profit you might make by selling your car or pedigree dog. But the rules are not clear cut. For instance, an investment in a long-lasting piece of furniture would probably be considered to have a life of more than fifty years, so any gain could lead to a tax bill. For chattels with an undoubted life expectancy of over fifty years, whether or not tax is payable depends upon the selling price. The magic number is £6,000. A modest work of art bought for £2,000 and sold for £4,000 would fall outside the tax net simply because the selling price is less than £6,000. If it were more, you would be taxed on the lower of either the actual gain you make or on five-thirds of the excess over £6,000.

Here is how it works in practice. Say you bought a painting for £4,000 and sold it for £8,000. Your actual gain would be £4,000 and the proceeds in excess of £6,000 would be £2,000. Multiply the £2,000 by five thirds and the result is £3,333. This is less than £4,000, so you would be taxed on £3,333 not £4,000. Also, before arriving at your taxable gain, you are able to add your indexation allowance to the original acquisition cost or value.

INHERITANCE TAX

In addition to income and capital gains tax, there is also inheritance tax to worry about. I hasten to reassure you that it is far less worrying than the other two, because it only comes into effect when you are no longer around. However, while you are alive and in a planning mood, it obviously makes sense to ensure that when you die your worldly wealth is not eaten up by the Inland Revenue and that you pass on as much as possible to your chosen heirs.

If your total assets, including the value of your house and the value of certain gifts made in the seven years before you die, are below £154,000, no inheritance tax is payable. Also, no tax is payable on anything that passes to your spouse or is given to charity. Remember, though, that most gifts made by you in the seven years prior to your death are added back for the purpose of inheritance tax calculations. Gifts must be made without any form of conditions, otherwise they will be added back, even if made over seven years before your death. You should not, for instance, give an asset away and retain the income from it. Marginal relief does apply if you die more than three years after making the gift. For example, after five years only 40% of the total tax liability would be charged.

There are other inheritance tax reliefs available which are worth taking advantage of, if you can spare the money. For instance, every year you can give away £3,000 and as many gifts as you like of under £250 to different people. You can also take out life insurance in trust for your beneficiaries. The policy has to be assigned to trustees so that it does not become part of your estate when you die. If you fail to achieve your objective within a reasonable time, you will at least have the consolation of still being alive.

Investments in business or agricultural property qualify for generous inheritance tax reliefs. For instance, an interest in a business, as a sole trader or partner, qualifies for 100% relief in the same way as a farm with vacant possession. Also, a shareholding of up to 25% in an unquoted trading company qualifies for 50% relief.

This is a complicated subject, so if you have sufficient assets to make it worthwhile, you should enlist the help of a professional adviser to lessen the potential inheritance tax liability of your estate.

SUMMARY

In this chapter, I have not tried to do more than highlight the main areas in which tax implications are likely to be significant and may call for action by you. If you want to understand more fully the framework of how the whole tax system works, I recommend you read the *New Penguin Guide to Personal Finance* by Alison Mitchell, the co-presenter of 'MoneyBox' on Radio Four. This excellent book will explain in simple language the intricacies of the tax system, and it also has chapters on such important subjects as making a will, divorce, widowhood, insurance, pensions and life insurance.

10

—

READING ABOUT INVESTMENT

The more books, magazines and newspaper articles you read on investment, the nearer you will be to mastering the subject that is so germane to your financial health.

If you intend to take an active interest in your money, whether it be on deposit or invested in a unit or investment trust or in gilts, you will need to know what is happening to the British economy in particular and to the world in general.

A daily newspaper is a must. In purely financial terms, there is no substitute for the *Financial Times*. If you only want to keep in touch with your investments on a weekly basis, Saturday's *Financial Times* is particularly good value. There is an extensive weekend supplement, including coverage of events in world markets during the preceding week, detailed quotations of most unit trust and investment trust prices, interest rates obtainable on deposits and a range of different securities, and the prices of individual shares.

Most of the other quality dailies also have extensive and well-informed City pages, as well as providing a backcloth of general news. Whichever of these newspapers you take, make sure that you read the City pages thoroughly.

The City columns of the Sunday papers are also well worth reading and they have extensive family finance supplements, which review unit and investments trusts, and give details of leading share prices and the interest rates available on a range of possible investments. ProShare has produced an excellent free publication for its members – *A Guide to Information Sources for the Private Investor*. In this, they rank each daily and Sunday newspaper, according to simplicity of language, value for money, up-to-date coverage and ease of use. Below is an extract covering just the Sunday newspapers to give an idea of the kind of information that you can obtain from ProShare.

NEWSPAPERS: SUNDAY, REGIONAL, INTERNATIONAL

INFORMATION SOURCE	COST & AVAILABILITY	CONTENT	PROSHARE COMMENT	Simple Language	Value for Money	Up-to-Date	Ease of Use
SUNDAY TELEGRAPH	70p "Business and Family Finance" – separate supplement.	City, economics and Wall Street comment columns. General corporate and economic features and news stories. Business personality profiles. City Diary.	Respected for its accuracy and judgements. Wide range of share recommendations and extensive family finance section.	■■■■■	■■■	■■■	■■■
SUNDAY TIMES	£1.00p "Business" and "Personal Finance" – separate supplements.	Three comment columns and "PRUFROCK" to give personality news. Diary and share recommendations and news columns. Corporate news. Personal finance.	Widely read and by far the leader in the business field. "Popular" approach to financial news – editorial "Agenda" is influential. Strong investigative journalism.	■■■■	■■■	■■■	■■■
THE OBSERVER	90p "Business" – separate supplement.	Business news, "Second Opinion" for share commentary, "THROG STREET" for share updates. Comment columns. Profiles. Personal Finance section.	Strong investigative bent and industry/economics slant. Well-regarded shares and comment columns.	■■■	■■■	■■■	■■■
INDEPENDENT ON SUNDAY	£1.00p "Business" – separate supplement.	"Bunhill" diary column. Two comment columns. Business news – "Your Money" – personal finance section.	Strong features slant. Works hard at news breaking. Good share commentary and international coverage.	■■■	■■■	■■■	■■■
MAIL ON SUNDAY	65p "Financial Mail on Sunday" covering 40 or more pages – separate supplement.	Business news. Comment columns. Personal finance pages.	Re-launched supplement is hitting high standards. Investigative but sometimes tangential coverage. A range of features for private investors including the "Midas" column and "Mrs. Cohen's Diary".	■■■■	■■■	■■■	■■■

SUNDAY EXPRESS	65p "Express Money" section usually covering 10/12 pages.	Business news covering personalities, economics and business. Personal finance.	An easy-to-read business section with some personal financial advice.	▉▉▉ ▉▉▉ ▉
SUNDAY MIRROR	50p Usually 2/4 pages but occasional supplement.	Mainly personal finance.	Usually personal finance "hints". Expanded coverage in recent times.	▉▉▉ ▉▉▉ ▉
THE PEOPLE	50p "Money Matters" – two pages.	Personal finance.	Mainly family finance.	▉▉▉ ▉▉▉ ▉

The *Investors Chronicle* is a weekly must for the serious private investor. There are extensive sections on business, investment and personal finance (including unit and investment trusts), companies and Europe. It also often has special supplements and features on a range of topics from personal financial planning to property. In April 1995, the annual UK subscription, including postage, was very good value for £84.

The *Economist* is also a very worthwhile publication, but a much heavier read, more international and not so essential for the small investor.

In Chapter 23, I give details of the extra reading you should consider if you are interested in investing directly in shares. In this chapter, I am more concerned with reading to help you with deposits, unit trusts, investment trusts, gilts and the like. Below is a list of the best magazines, in no particular order:

Moneywise offers complete personal finance coverage with in-depth articles on such subjects as mortgages, pensions and PEPs. The Monitor section gives a monthly round-up of financial facts and figures from savings to tax rates and gives details of the best rates of interest available, the top performing unit and investment trusts, National Savings, guaranteed income bonds and TESSAs. Detailed prices and performance statistics of all unit and investment trusts are not supplied. (£2.40 monthly; Telephone: 0800 181 151)

Moneyfacts is an excellent monthly publication with comprehensive tables of bank and building society deposit rates, information on National Savings and TESSAs, credit card and mortgage rates, and historic data on base rates, inflation and the level of the stock market.

The annual subscription rate in April 1995 was £38.50, but Moneyfacts will send you an introductory copy on request. Address: Moneyfacts Subscription Dept., Laundry Loke, North Walsham, Norfolk, NR28 0BD. Telephone: 01692 500677.

Money Management is mainly for professional advisers. There are detailed articles on a wide range of personal finance subjects, but its main attraction is the very detailed review of the performance of unit trusts, investment trusts and insurance funds. Performance in the preceding month is shown, together with the longer term record over ten, five, three and two years and over the last twelve and six months. (£4.50 monthly; Telephone: 0181-680 3786)

Planned Savings is, like *Money Management*, very much geared towards the professional. Each issue contains a number of articles focusing on a particular aspect of personal finance. There are also performance tables on unit trusts, investment trusts, life funds, pension funds and broker funds. (£5.50 monthly; Telephone: 0181-868 4499)

Investment Trusts gives a very similar review of the results of all investment trusts together with in-depth articles on managers, new products, PEPs and the like. (£3.70 quarterly; £12 per annum or £10 if you pay by direct debit; Telephone: 0181-646 1031)

Another source of investment trust details is the Association of Investment Trust Companies. The cost for very comprehensive monthly performance details is £28 per annum, but you can elect to receive them quarterly for £15 per annum.

What Investment? gives comprehensive monthly details of prices and performance of both unit and investment trusts together with a large number of articles on all aspects of personal finance. (£2.50 monthly; Telephone: 01732 770823)

Money Observer is last but by no means least. As well as a wide range of features on subjects from investment strategy to company profiles and tax tips, there is a comprehensive 'Databank', detailing the performance of all listed shares, unit and investment trusts. (£2.50 monthly; Telephone: 01424 755 755)

Several specialist magazines aimed at the home buyer are published monthly and can be found in the magazine racks of newsagents. For example, *What Mortgage?* (£1.95), *Your Mortgage* (£1.95) and *Which Mortgage?* (£1.95) all carry details of current mortgage offers.

I should make it clear that some of this information is available from time to time in your daily newspapers, but you may prefer to receive a regular comprehensive guide, which will prompt you to double-check your investments systematically. An obvious alternative is to set aside a few hours each month to check through your investments in great detail, aided by the *Financial Times*, the *Investors Chronicle* or the daily, evening or Sunday newspaper of your choice. The important point is to make sure that you have current information to hand and to give sufficient time to your investments to help make them work better for you.

The books I recommend to beginners for developing a further understanding of unit trusts, investment trusts, gilts, deposits and family finance are Bernard Gray's *Beginners' Guide to Investment*, Michael Brett's *How to Read the Financial Pages*, Alison Mitchell's *New Penguin Guide to Personal Finance* and *Which? Way to Save and Invest*, published by the Consumers' Association. These primers are excellent and, if you want to become really expert on the very worthwhile subject of your own finance, there is nothing to stop you reading them all. You would happily read a few books on gardening or cookery, so why not investment, which is so germane to your financial health. You would certainly obtain a great deal of very worthwhile advice and pick up a large number of further hints to help you improve your family's finances.

11

FINANCIAL ADVISERS

Find out how your adviser is authorised and remunerated, and note the many questions you should ask. Remember that many financial commitments are long-term, so always insist on written proposals and think them over carefully.

I hope that as a result of reading the last ten chapters you feel more able to make the best possible arrangements for your family's finances. I have not tried to give a comprehensive survey of all the financial packages currently on offer. Even if I had managed to do so, it would have made this book a difficult and boring read and, anyway, it would not have been too long before some of the contents were out-of-date. Instead, I have tried to concentrate upon the principles and approach to investment, which should never become dated.

Of course, you will still need a financial adviser to help you with some of the more complex packages. I hasten to add that I would need one too.

WHO CAN GIVE ADVICE?

The Financial Services Act states very clearly that any investment adviser (including life insurance and pensions) must be authorised. The chief regulator is SIB – the Securities and Investments Board. Some firms, including banks and building societies, may be regulated directly by SIB. Others will obtain their authorisation from one of three self-regulatory bodies.

1. PIA – Personal Investment Authority

2. IMRO – Investment Management Regulatory Organisation

3. SFA – Securities and Futures Authority

In addition, solicitors, accountants, actuaries and insurance brokers may be regulated by their own professional bodies. If you are unsure about whether your adviser is authorised, check with the appropriate body, or with the SIB Central Register (Telephone: 0171-929 3652). With a few exceptions, it is a criminal offence to give investment advice without authorisation.

FINDING AN ADVISER

Finding a good financial adviser may not be easy. The best approach is to ask your friends for a recommendation. Personal endorsement is often the best way to obtain any professional service, whether it be a solicitor, architect or financial adviser. This method of selection is not foolproof. However you find an adviser, it is always difficult to evaluate the quality of financial advice. For instance, it could take many years to discover that you have been put into an inappropriate pension plan. But getting to grips with the principles laid down in this book should at least prepare you to ask the right questions and understand the essential features of what an adviser is recommending.

Feeling comfortable with your adviser is important. If there is no rapport between you, your needs may be misunderstood, or you may not get that extra personal attention. But again, caution is required; advisers want your business and may go out of their way to be personable. Try not to confuse the flattery of salesmen with keen and competent attention.

Since it is difficult to judge the quality of financial advice in advance, it is probably worth having at least initial consultations with several advisers, to compare what they have to say. You should ask them how long they have been in the business and obtain details of their training and qualifications. Test their knowledge on different kinds of investments. They may be completely clued up on pensions (no bad thing if that is what you are looking for), but much less knowledgeable about PEPs and unit trusts.

Find out whether the adviser is independent, or tied to, or employed by, a particular company. In that event, the adviser will be limited to advising on the products of the company in question. Be wary if you have never heard of the company; you should be looking for a company with a household name and a fine reputation that it will be anxious to protect at all costs.

Another important question is the exact nature of the advisers' authority under the body with whom they are registered. Can they handle clients' money and are they authorised to act for clients on a discretionary basis? Generally speaking, the more authority they have the more confident you can be that they will know their onions.

There is no shortage of sources of financial advice, from the small one-man band on the high street, through the medium-sized firm of independent advisers, to the multi-branch operations of banks and building societies. Firms of accountants, solicitors, actuaries, pension consultants and stockbrokers often have specialist teams providing financial advice. You can find them listed in *Yellow Pages*.

Insurance companies may sell their wares through any of these types of adviser. They also usually have their own sales forces and outside firms they have appointed as representatives. The latter will be able to sell only the products of the company they represent.

In practice, most large banks and building societies sell only the products of the insurance company to which they are tied. They often also have subsidiary companies which can offer independent as opposed to tied advice. However, you will not normally be offered independent advice unless you ask for it. In April 1995, Bradford & Bingley is an exception among larger banks and building societies in offering independent advice to everyone.

In the absence of a personal recommendation or introduction, you can always write to *Money Management*, Greystoke Place, Fetter Lane, London EC4A 1ND (Telephone: 0117 976 9444). They will send you a free list of three independent, fee-based advisers in your area.

Independent Financial Advisers Promotion (Telephone: 0117 971 1177), which is sponsored by life insurance companies, will also send a list of six advisers near to you. They may be remunerated by fees or commission.

The Society of Pension Consultants, Ludgate House, Ludgate Circus, London EC4A 2AB (Telephone: 0171 353 1688) will send out a list of its members, as will the Association of Consulting Actuaries, 1 Wardrobe Place, London EC4V 5AH (Telephone: 0171 236 5514). Members of both trade bodies specialise in pensions, though some advise on life insurance investments as well. Also APCIMS, 112 Middlesex Street, London E1 7HY (Telephone: 0171 247 7080), representing stockbrokers, publishes a list of its members and their services.

The key question is – how is the agent, representative or independent adviser remunerated? Do not be shy about asking. It is *your* money you are both playing with and, under the Financial Services Act, you are entitled to a straight answer.

TIED ADVICE

If the adviser is not independent, but a representative or tied agent of a particular company, then any remuneration will come from that company in the form of commissions (and salary in the case of some representatives). In this event, the financial packages you will be offered will be confined to the products of the company in question.

Tied agents have to tell you what, if any, commission they receive – or the effective equivalent cost of selling a policy taking account of salary, bonuses, company car and so on. In addition, as I explained in Chapter 8, you should be given illustrations of how the overall performance of a policy can be affected by all the charges deducted by the company managing a plan.

Whoever drafted the Financial Services Act presumed that you would realise that tied agents and representatives would receive a substantial commission on the products of the single company that they are representing. A company representative or tied agent does have to recommend to you the financial product of their company that is best suited to your particular needs. If there is no such product, he has to tell you.

INDEPENDENT ADVICE

Independent advisers must give you exact and full details of how much they will make by selling you any specific product. You should also ask the individual who is dealing with you if he or she receives different commissions on any of the range of products on offer.

Some independent advisers always charge fees, some choose to be paid only by way of commission from insurance companies, unit trusts and the like, and others give you a choice.

Stockbrokers charge a commission, which is added to the cost of any contracts, so you know exactly where you stand on Stock Exchange transactions. However, if they introduce a unit trust or pension plan or life insurance product they will also receive a commission from the company providing the investment. Usually this will not cost you any more, as the commission comes out of the initial charge, which you would have to pay anyway. However, many advisers of all kinds will often agree to refund some of their commission, particularly if you are investing large amounts. Likewise, if you buy a unit trust direct from the management company, it may have an unofficial policy of returning some of the commission which would otherwise have been paid to an intermediary. *There is certainly no harm in asking.*

Obviously, it pays you to know the general commission rates on various financial products. Then, if you receive recommendations to buy a number of high-commission financial packages, and some excellent low-commission and no-commission products are missing, you will be on red alert.

It is very tempting for advisers to recommend endowment policies. Commissions range from about two-thirds of your first year's premium to the whole of it. Bear in mind that for a mortgage a repayment loan will usually do the same job and there are more tax-efficient alternatives.

Personal pensions also attract high commissions. For example, on a twenty-five-year scheme, over 60% of your first year's premium could go in commission and, on a ten-year scheme, about 30%. Single premium bonds pay commissions of about 5%.

Unit trust commissions average about 3% of your investment. However, most tracker funds have very low initial and annual charges and some pay no commission, so recommending them would be a great test of character for any adviser.

Investment trusts pay regular commissions to agents, but this is a moving scene so ask for precise details.

With gilts and National Savings, there are no commissions; TESSAs usually have no commission, as they are most often bought directly from building societies. Some banks and building societies do pay commission on money introduced into savings accounts. This should not affect your return, but you should make sure that there is not a better-paying TESSA available from another large bank or building society.

If you have negotiated a fees-only deal with an independent adviser, all commissions should be credited to your account. This way, you will know exactly where you stand and can be more certain of receiving absolutely independent advice. Make absolutely sure that all commission is rebated. Also, bear in mind that advisers are often paid renewal commission – a small annual percentage of the value of the investments you are retaining. Ask what will happen to any renewal commission.

Fee-paying advisers can charge anything from £75 to £150 an hour. But before you hold up your hands in horror, calculate how much they would receive from percentage commissions on your investments. An adviser could take just as long to find the right unit trust whether you are investing £2,000 or £20,000. For large sums of money, fees can work out much cheaper; for small sums, a commission basis can make more sense.

Under the Financial Services Act, an independent adviser has to give you the best advice. Of course, this means that the adviser has to know all about your personal financial circumstances, how much risk you are prepared to take, and your expectations from any particular investment. Be very wary, therefore, if your adviser does not ask you some very detailed questions about your financial affairs.

SOME GOOD QUESTIONS

When your financial adviser gives you final recommendations, now that you have read this book, you will naturally want to ask a number of pertinent questions. Here are a few suggestions that may be appropriate:

1. Why an endowment-policy? Don't they pay agents very large commissions? Aren't they more expensive, less flexible and less tax-efficient than investment with PEPs?

2. Wouldn't a straightforward capital repayment mortgage be a better proposition?

3. What about a pension-linked mortgage?

4. Why all unit trusts and no investment trusts?

5. Why no tracker funds? Aren't they much cheaper?

6. Why switch to another product? How much does it cost to switch?

7. Why no National Savings certificates? Aren't they very tax-efficient?

8. Why no TESSAs? Aren't they tax-efficient too?

Your final question should be to ask for alternative proposals, taking points like these and any others you raise into consideration. You should then compare the commission that the agent will receive on the first set of proposals against the second. If the difference is substantial, you should need a lot of convincing that your interests are the adviser's paramount consideration.

Most advisers are thoroughly reputable, but they are also human, so hefty commissions can be very tempting. Once your adviser realises that he or she is dealing with someone who knows a thing or two about personal finance, your relationship will be all the sounder.

BE ON YOUR GUARD

Another point to be on guard about is unnecessary switching of products, which will almost certainly cost you money and, unless you are on a fees-only basis, will generate more commission for your adviser. It rarely pays to switch products; usually a better plan is to make the most of the financial products to which you are already committed.

A final and very important point. Always ask your financial adviser to put any proposals in writing. There is no hurry; so think them over carefully and ask for clarification about any of the points that trouble you, even a little. Remember that many of the commitments you are likely to enter into are long-term and, in some cases, it can be very expensive to change your mind later.

I hope these first eleven chapters will have given you a better understanding of the many options available and of some of the pitfalls. If you want to refresh your memory from time to time, you might find it helpful to reread the summaries at the beginning and end of most of the chapters.

The second part of this book is only for those readers who want to try their hand at investing directly in shares. If you have understood a good proportion of the preceding chapters, you should not find shares too difficult. Compared with some of the complexities of personal finance, I find them very easy indeed. Investing directly in shares can also be very rewarding and much more fun.

MORE ACTIVE INVESTMENT

PREFACE

The second part of this book is for beginners in equity investment. A number of chapters, such as 'Bull and Bear Markets', and 'Portfolio Management', are based on similar ones in my previous book on investment, *The Zulu Principle*. However, they have been substantially adapted to simplify and further explain the principles involved.

In *The Zulu Principle*, I assumed that readers were connected with the business of investment in some way or had read the glossary at the end of the book. Either way, they would know the difference between an ordinary share, a preference share and a convertible debenture; the meaning of terms like price-earnings ratio, dividend yield and asset value; and the effect and significance of scrip and rights issues. In this book, I have made the opposite assumption – that readers are not connected with the business of investment and may not even have read a primer.

Like any other subject, investment only becomes really interesting when you understand the basic principles, so I aim to teach them to you as quickly as possible. The first two chapters will explain the language of finance and how to read accounts. They are based on the glossary of *The Zulu Principle*, but the chapter on reading accounts is a much more extensive and simpler version.

I must caution complete beginners that they will not find these first two chapters an easy read. It takes five years of theoretical study and practical experience to qualify as a chartered accountant, so it is not surprising that my two chapters on 'The Language of Finance' and 'Reading Accounts' are absolutely crammed with essential facts.

I could have written another complete book on the subject, but, instead, decided to give you the necessary medicine in two short, sharp doses. If you find the first two chapters difficult, I recommend you read them again when you have completed the rest of the book. If, after doing this, you still have doubts about the language and principles of investment, I suggest you read a primer such as Bernard Gray's *Beginners' Guide to Investment* or Michael Brett's *How to Read the Financial Pages*, concentrating on the chapters dealing with shares and share valuation.

Once you have read and understood the first two chapters of this part of my book, you should be in the home straight and well on your way to grasping what share investment is all about. The only other chapters that you might find a little complicated are Chapter 17 on 'Price-Earnings Ratios and Growth Rates' and Chapter 18 on 'Creative Accounting'. In that event, I suggest you also re-read these after you have finished the rest of the book.

Common sense will tell you that a complete beginner would need to do plenty of homework to become reasonably effective at selecting shares. To make your task easier, I have focused on a relatively narrow and very rewarding area of investment – leading growth shares. One of their many attractions is that, if you select them well in the first instance (which this book will help you to do), most of the time you will be able to sit back and leave the management of the companies to continue with their good work.

Chapters 15-19 focus on selecting growth shares. All the shares mentioned are simply for illustrative purposes and should not be thought of as recommendations. You should concentrate upon the *method* of finding them.

My hope is that, as a result of reading the following chapters, you will have a better knowledge of the basics of stock market investment and a better understanding of the approach to the problem of share selection. With any subject, you must first learn the basics, then how to use them. As soon as you feel ready, there is then no substitute for practical experience. Once you begin to invest, you will find that your commitment will sharpen your awareness of the financial world and your understanding of it. As Goethe once said:

> Whatever you can do, or dream you can . . . begin it.
> Boldness has genius, power and magic in it.

12

—

THE LANGUAGE OF FINANCE

Get a firm grasp of the basics and jargon of finance. Only then will you be able to understand fully the business pages and converse intelligently with your stockbroker.

If you wish to be an active investor, you must be prepared to invest a proportion of your patient money directly in shares, the prices of which, I hasten to warn you, can go down as well as up. The rewards of share investment can be far greater than from making a deposit or investing in dated gilts, but so are the risks.

FOUR IMPORTANT STEPS

To be a successful stock market investor, you need to take the following steps:

1. Learn about shares so that you fully understand financial jargon and buzz words – the language of finance.

2. Learn how to read company accounts.

3. Find a good stockbroker who will help and advise you.

4. Study the various approaches to investment and choose one that suits your temperament and financial requirements.

Let us start with the language of finance. Rather than give you a long list of definitions, I prefer to take a hypothetical company and plot its development. This way, you will encounter most of the financial terms and expressions that you need to know.

FEELGOOD PLC

We will name the company Feelgood plc and assume that it is in the health food business with 10 million shares in issue. Those shares can be bought and sold on the *stock market* (they have a public quotation) and are priced at 100p each. The *market capitalisation* of Feelgood is £10m (10 million shares multiplied by 100p).

The underlying *net assets* of the company include shops, fixtures and fittings, stocks and *debtors* (people and businesses which owe money to Feelgood) minus the amount due to *creditors* (people, banks and businesses to which Feelgood owes money). In the case of Feelgood, the total net assets are worth £7m, giving a net asset value per share (NAV) of 70p (£7m divided by 10 million shares). The profits of Feelgood for the previous financial year were £1m before tax, which, at the full rate of 33%, left *profits after tax* of £670,000 (£1m of pre-tax profits less £330,000 corporation tax).

These profits of £670,000 are also called the earnings of the company. The *earnings per share* (EPS) of Feelgood are 6.7p (£670,000 divided by the 10 million shares in issue).

PRICE-EARNINGS RATIOS

Feelgood's share price is determined by the balance of buyers and sellers in the market and reflects how much investors are prepared to pay for the future earnings of the company. A common measure of their willingness is the ratio of the price of the shares (100p) to the earnings per share (6.7p). It is called the *price-earnings ratio*. Feelgood, therefore, has an historic price-earnings ratio of 15 (the ratio of 100p to 6.7p = 15), which in May 1995 was slightly more than the ratio of the average company's share price to its earnings. An abbreviation for price-earnings ratio is *P/E ratio* or, as it is sometimes called, *the multiple*.

The P/E ratio of a company fluctuates with its share price and earnings per share. If Feelgood's share price were to rise to 200p, the P/E ratio would rise to 30 (30 times 6.7p equals 200p – or, put the other way around, 200p divided by 6.7p equals 30). Similarly, if the following year earnings fell to, say, 4p per share and the share price remained at 100p, the P/E ratio would rise to 25. In fact, it would be far more likely that the share price would fall on the announcement of reduced earnings to, say, 50p, which, with earnings of 4p, would give a reduced P/E ratio of 12.5 (12.5 times 4p equals 50p). The market would give a lower rating to Feelgood's earnings because they were falling.

DIVIDENDS

If Feelgood decides to pay a dividend of 2.1p per share, the *dividend yield* of Feelgood shares is calculated by first adding back the basic rate of income tax (now 20%), which is assumed to have been paid, and then expressing the answer as a percentage of the share price. The calculation is made in two stages as follows:

$$\frac{2.1p \times 100}{80} = 2.63p \text{ which is the } gross\ dividend$$

The dividend yield is therefore:

$$\frac{2.63p \text{ (the gross dividend)}}{100p \text{ (the share price)}} \times 100 = 2.63\%$$

If the shares rose from 100p to 200p the dividend yield would fall to:

$$\frac{(2.63p \times 100)}{200p} = 1.31\%$$

With earnings per share of 6.7p, Feelgood could have paid a higher dividend. The board, however, decided to be prudent and, as a result, the *dividend cover* is 3.2 times (6.7p earnings per share divided by the dividend of 2.1p).

Feelgood would be shown in the prices section of the *Financial Times* like this:

1995

	Price	+or-	High	Low	Market Cap £m	Yield Gross	P/E
Feelgood	100	+2	140	75	10.0	2.63	15

RAISING FURTHER FUNDS

If the directors of Feelgood need to raise further funds, they might arrange for a *rights issue*, offering all existing shareholders the right to buy one more share, at a price of, say, 80p, for every four shares they already own. This particular rights issue would raise £2m (10 million divided by four, multiplied by 80p).

If the directors are doubtful about all the shareholders taking up their rights, they might decide to *underwrite* the issue through their stockbrokers or *merchant bankers* (specialist banks which advise on takeovers, flotations and other financial deals), who arrange for a number of *institutions* (insurance companies, pension funds, etc.) and perhaps some private clients to agree to buy any of the shares not subscribed for by existing Feelgood shareholders. In exchange, the broker or merchant banker is paid an *underwriting fee*, a substantial proportion of which is passed on to the institutions and private clients who have agreed to take the risk of buying the shares.

SCRIP ISSUES

At a later stage of Feelgood's development, the shares might rise to as much as 1,000p each. The directors might then decide that the shares were too *heavy* (highly priced) and that there would be a more liquid market in them if they were priced substantially lower and there were a larger number in issue. To achieve this happier state of affairs, they might arrange for a one-for-one *scrip issue* – existing shareholders are given one free share for each share they own. The shareholders then own two shares instead of one and, as a result, there are double the number of shares in issue.

The value of Feelgood has not changed so, strictly on the arithmetic, the share price should be expected to fall to 500p after the issue. However, scrip issues are often accompanied by dividend increases, and are usually made by expanding companies. After a split, shares appear to be cheaper, so they frequently perform better than the market as a whole.

DEBENTURES, LOANS AND CONVERTIBLES

In an expansionary phase, the directors may decide not to *dilute* Feelgood's share capital by having a rights issue and issuing more shares, especially if the share price is depressed. The fewer shares in issue, the more any future increase in profits and dividends benefits each existing shareholder.

If interest rates are relatively low, instead of a rights issue, the directors might decide to borrow from the company's bankers or raise a *debenture*. A debenture is a loan which is usually secured on particular assets of a company, such as factories and machinery. It carries a fixed rate of interest and is repayable on a specified future date. For example, Feelgood might raise a £2m 10% debenture, secured on its freehold shop properties, repayable in ten years' time, in the year 2005.

The interest payable on the debenture is paid out of profits or, if the company is losing money, is added to losses. If the debenture interest falls into arrears, the debenture holders have the right to appoint a *receiver*, who moves into the company and takes charge of the secured assets with a view to selling them off to repay the debenture holders. In that event, or if the company goes into *liquidation* (when a liquidator, usually an accountant, is appointed to wind up a company), the debenture is repaid first (well before other creditors), out of the proceeds of the sale of the secured assets.

CONVERTIBLE LOAN STOCK

From the company's point of view a softer, less restrictive alternative to a debenture is a *convertible loan stock*, which also has a fixed rate of interest and is repayable at a specified future date. Feelgood might decide to raise the £2m with, for example, a Feelgood 8% Convertible 2010. Notice that the interest rate is 2% lower than for the debenture.

Convertibles are not secured on any particular assets of a company, so in a liquidation they rank behind debenture holders but before ordinary shareholders. In exchange for less security and lower interest than a debenture, convertible loan stockholders have the right to convert their loan stock into ordinary shares.

The terms of conversion vary from one stock to another. Typically, loan stockholders have the right to convert every year on a set date until the time that the loan stock is *redeemed* (repaid). The Annual Report gives the details of conversion terms which, in the case of Feelgood, might be that every £100 worth of loan stock can be converted into 80 ordinary shares at a price of £1.25 per share. If the shares have a market price of 100p, the extra 25p is called the *conversion premium*. Convertible loan stockholders are usually prepared to pay more than the equivalent share price for the extra security of a loan stock and for the extra yield (in this instance, the 8% loan stock interest is far more than the 2.63% dividend yield on Feelgood's shares).

The interest payable on a convertible loan stock is a charge against profits before any dividends are paid to ordinary shareholders, but after payment of debenture interest. Note the order in which payments are made – sometimes there are insufficient profits to go around.

CONVERTIBLE PREFERENCE SHARES

Another, even softer, alternative way of raising further funds is a *convertible preference share*. Preference shares occupy a grey area somewhere between debt and equity, although current accounting practice puts them under the heading of shareholders' funds in the balance sheet. However, if preference shares have a *redemption date* (a date set for repayment), and will one day have to be repaid, I regard them as debt.

In the event of a liquidation, the capital of convertible preference shareholders is repaid before ordinary shareholders, but after all the debentures, convertibles, loan stocks and other creditors. The dividends payable to convertible preference shareholders are only paid after all other interest payments.

An important point to understand about a convertible preference share is that the effective yield is higher than might appear because 20% tax has already been deducted. The calculation is the same as for working out the dividend yield of an ordinary share. Simply multiply the stated yield by $\frac{100}{80}$.

If Feelgood issues an 8% convertible preference share, the effective dividend yield is 10% – $\frac{(8\% \times 100)}{80}$

The conversion terms of convertible preference shares vary in the same way as with convertible loan stocks.

UNSECURED LOAN STOCK

If Feelgood were a larger company, it would have a further option for raising funds – the issue of an *unsecured loan stock*. Feelgood might, for example, issue a 12% unsecured loan stock 2005. In a liquidation this would rank behind debentures, but before convertible loan stocks and other creditors. An unsecured loan stock holder has no right to convert into ordinary shares, and, as the stock is also less secure than a debenture, usually enjoys a higher rate of interest. Only very strong companies can issue unsecured loan stocks, which are unappealing to the general run of investors.

PREFERENCE SHARES

Preference shares without any conversion rights would also be unpopular with institutions because Feelgood is a small company and the institutions are not particularly keen on preference shares which do not confer the right to participate in future profits. For capital repayment, preference shares rank before ordinary shareholders in a liquidation, and their fixed dividend is payable before a dividend can be paid on the ordinary shares. Sometimes a preference share is designated a *cumulative preference share*, which means that the dividend is accrued, if passed in any year. When a company is brought back from the dead by radical reorganisation or a stroke of good fortune, a cumulative preference share can sometimes be very valuable because of the accumulated dividend arrears, which have to be paid as the company begins to make profits again.

LISTING OF SHARES

All the stocks in the FT Actuaries All-Share Index are *listed*, which means they have satisfied the Stock Exchange's criteria for a quotation on the main market. In mid-1995, a new market for small, young and growing companies was introduced. The Alternative Investment Market (AIM) is regulated by the Stock Exchange but has much less stringent listing criteria than the main market, making it a much riskier proposition. Companies do not need to have a trading record and there are no restrictions on market capitalisation or the number of shares in public hands. AIM is a successor to the Unlisted Securities Market, which in April 1995 still had about 200 companies quoted but was due to be phased out completely by the end of 1996. It will also largely supersede the Stock Exchange's Rule 4.2 which provides a facility for dealing in infrequently traded shares. For the majority of investors who want to invest in leading growth shares, there is no need to give these markets any further thought. Any transaction in quoted shares appears in the Daily Official List (the register, published every day, of all listed securities and the prices of transactions in them).

THE STOCK MARKET

If you wanted to buy some shares in Feelgood, your first step would be to open an account with a *broker* (who would act as your agent in buying and selling stocks). Once your broker knew you, he or she would take your order by telephone. If you decided to buy 1,000 shares in Feelgood for, say, 100p each, you would ask your broker the price for 1,000 shares, which might be 98–102p per share. This means that the *marketmaker* (a firm offering to act as a principal and buy or sell shares for its own account) is prepared to sell 1,000 shares in Feelgood at 102p (*the offer price*) and buy at 98p (*the bid price*). In fact, your broker would also check with other marketmakers to give you the keenest overall price for buying or selling. The difference between the bid price and the offer price is called the *spread*, which in this case is 4p.

As soon as the *bargain* (transaction) is completed, your broker sends you a *contract note* which, in addition to the price of the shares purchased, includes stamp duty of 0.5% and the broker's commission. This is negotiable, ranging from 1.65% to 0.5%, or even less, according to the amount of business you transact and the size of the deal. You then receive the broker's statement and, in due course, *a share certificate* for your 1,000 shares in Feelgood.

Until July 1994, the buying of shares took place within an account, which normally lasted two weeks, occasionally three. The account period ran from Monday to Friday, either eleven or eighteen days later, and settlement of deals transacted in the account took place on the second Monday after the final Friday. In 1994 that regime was replaced by a system of rolling settlement in which deals were settled ten working days after the day of the transaction. This change was the first step in a process which is planned to lead eventually to the introduction of an automated settlements system called Crest. In mid-1995, the Stock Exchange reduced the delay before settlement from ten to five working days.

KEY DEFINITIONS

I will now set out the most important definitions. If you have any residual doubts after studying them, I recommend that you read Bernard Gray's book, *Beginners' Guide to Investment*, and pay particular attention to Chapter 15, on valuing shares.

DEFINITIONS RELATING TO THE VALUATION OF QUOTED SHARES

1. MARKET CAPITALISATION – The total number of shares the company has in issue multiplied by the share price, which is constantly changing.

2. DIVIDEND YIELD – The dividend yield of a company can be determined by expressing the gross annual dividend as a percentage of the share price. If a company pays 10p a share gross dividend and the shares are 100p, the dividend yield is 10%. If the price rises to 200p, the dividend yield falls to 5%.

   Dividend yields can be both historic and prospective. The historic dividend is based upon last year's dividend payment, whereas the prospective dividend yield is based upon the dividend forecast for the year ahead. Dividends are usually paid twice yearly, with an interim payment after the end of the half-year and a final payment after the full year's accounts are issued. The dividend yield of a company is based upon the total dividends paid or payable to ordinary shareholders by the company in a given year.

3. EARNINGS PER SHARE – The after-tax profits of a company attributable to ordinary shareholders, calculated on a per share basis (by dividing the number of shares in issue into the after-tax profits).

4. PRICE-EARNINGS RATIO – The number of times earnings per share need to be multiplied to equal the current market price of a share. Based on last year's earnings per share, this is called the historic P/E ratio, and on forecast earnings, the prospective P/E ratio.

5. NET ASSET VALUE – The total assets of a company, minus all of its short- and long-term liabilities, provisions and charges. Sometimes simply abbreviated to NAV.

6. NET ASSET VALUE PER SHARE – The net asset value of a company divided by the number of ordinary shares in issue. The NAV per share is a particularly pertinent measure of value with property companies and investment trusts, which are asset-based.

13

READING ACCOUNTS

Learn how to read the annual accounts of the companies in which you invest. This is the only way to find out what the management has been doing with your money.

After buying your shares in Feelgood, you will want to keep a close eye on them. You will see the share price quoted in your daily newspapers and your broker can always supply you with up-to-the-minute prices. Make sure he also advises you of any directors' share dealings and other important announcements.

Within four months of the end of the first six months of its financial year, Feelgood will prepare an *interim report* covering its activities and the profit or loss for the period. This report will be unaudited and must either be sent to shareholders or be advertised in two national newspapers. The interim reports are also notified to the Stock Exchange, so your broker will be fully aware of them.

PRELIMINARY ANNOUNCEMENT

Two to three months after the end of Feelgood's financial year, the company will make a *preliminary announcement* of its profits and taxation for the previous year and the dividend it proposes to pay. Again, this is notified to the Stock Exchange and will usually be covered in the following day's papers.

A few weeks later, you will receive by post notice of the Annual General Meeting, a proxy card and the *Annual Report and Accounts*, which includes detailed accounts and usually contains a comment on current trading conditions. You should read the Report and Accounts from cover to cover, so let me show you how to make sense of it.

AUDITOR'S REPORT

Always check the Auditor's Report *first* to make sure that it has not been qualified in any way and confirms that the accounts give a true and fair view of the financial position of the company. Many companies that had clean Auditor's Reports for years have since emerged as being very suspect indeed, so the slightest qualification should be enough to encourage you to dispose of your shares immediately.

CHAIRMAN'S STATEMENT

Next, you should read the Chairman's Statement to obtain a general impression of what has happened to the business during the year and, perhaps more importantly, the outlook for the future. The chairman does not have to make a statement; if he does not do so, you should study the Directors' Report in detail.

The Companies Act states that the Directors' Report must give you a fair review of progress during the year, an indication of likely future developments and of research and development activities. You will also be advised about any shares in the company purchased by the company itself, important events since the year-end, political and charitable donations, significant changes in fixed assets and the names of the directors and details of their shareholdings. Other mandatory information in the Annual Report and Accounts includes a geographical analysis of turnover outside the UK, other shareholdings in the company over 3% and whether Feelgood is a *close* (controlled) company for tax purposes.

You are obviously looking for both the tone and content of the chairman's or directors' comments to be optimistic: you need to be reassured that the company is likely to continue to produce increased earnings per share at a satisfactory rate. An interesting guideline on how to interpret the usual broad and platitudinous statements made by many company chairmen is to be found in the excellent book, *Interpreting Company Reports and Accounts*, by Geoffrey Holmes and Alan Sugden. The authors take an imaginary company, 'Polygon Holdings', in a range of industries and industrial climates, and give their suggestions for estimating this year's profits based upon the chairman's comments on current trading:

Activity	Industrial climate	Chairman's remarks	Previous year £m	Reported year £m	Estimate of current year £m
Building	Continued recession	'Further decline inevitable'	1.0	0.8	0.5–0.6
Paper	Cyclical upturn	'Marked improvement'	2.2	1.8	2.4–2.8
Bookmaking	One of the UK's few growth industries	'Continued progress'	1.0	1.2	1.4–1.5
Plastic extrusions	Demand flat	'Market share increasing but lower margins'	0.6	0.75	0.6–0.8
Interest charges	Rates down 2%	'Improvement in liquidity likely'	–0.8	–1.0	–0.8
		Pre-tax total	4.0	3.55	4.1–4.9

The authors also draw attention to the necessity of keeping an eye open for any details of discontinued loss-makers (usually an excellent sign), of judging the chairman's previous record of forecasting (a helpful guide to this year's accuracy) and of being wary of vague statements like, 'Unforeseen difficulties have occurred.'

CONSOLIDATED BALANCE SHEET

The first set of figures to concentrate upon is the *Consolidated Balance Sheet* (accounts which include the share capital, assets and liabilities of all companies within the group to give a complete picture on the specified date on which the financial snapshot is taken). The Balance Sheet of Feelgood at the end of May 1995 looks something like this:

CONSOLIDATED BALANCE SHEET

	1995 £000
FIXED ASSETS	
Intangible assets	500
Tangible assets	5000
Investments	–
	5500
CURRENT ASSETS	
Stocks	8500
Debtors	1000
Cash in hand	2000
	11500
CREDITORS	
Amounts falling due within one year	7000
NET CURRENT ASSETS	4500
TOTAL ASSETS LESS CURRENT LIABILITIES	10000
CREDITORS	
Amounts falling due after more than one year	2750
PROVISIONS	
Deferred taxation	250
MINORITY INTERESTS	–
	3000
NET ASSETS EMPLOYED	7000
	£000
CAPITAL AND RESERVES	
Called-up share capital	2500
Profit and loss account	4500
SHAREHOLDERS' FUNDS	7000

To keep the accounts as simple as possible, I have not shown comparative figures. In practice, there would be another column showing the same details for the previous year. Watch out for any major fluctuations. For example, if a hefty cash balance disappears one year and is replaced by an overdraft in the next, you should be on the lookout for a full explanation.

FIXED ASSETS

Under the Companies Act, *Fixed Assets* have to be shown in three categories:

1. INTANGIBLE ASSETS, which are usually brand names, copyrights, trademarks and goodwill. These kinds of assets are difficult to value with any precision, although in many cases they are very valuable.

2. TANGIBLE ASSETS, which are those held by a business for the purpose of earning its profits – they are, therefore, usually not for sale. These fixed assets include land and buildings, plant and machinery, and motor vehicles. In the case of Feelgood, they include shop freeholds and leases, and fixtures and fittings. Precise details are given in the *Notes to the Accounts*, which also show the amount of *depreciation* (the loss of value of an asset due to use, passage of time and obsolescence) which has been written off to arrive at the *net book value*. It is important to understand that the real value may be substantially more or less than the net book value, which makes no pretence of being an open-market valuation. Fixed assets, particularly land and buildings, are frequently revalued and, on occasions, shown at the revised valuation in the company's balance sheet.

3. INVESTMENTS, which are essentially long-term investments not being held with a view to resale. Listed investments are shown at cost and the market value will also be noted.

CURRENT ASSETS

We then come to the *Current Assets*, which include cash and any other assets, like stocks and debtors, that will eventually be turned into cash in the normal course of business. In the case of a manufacturing company, the first item, *Stocks*, is broken down into three categories in the notes: raw materials, work in progress and finished goods. The method used to value stocks has to be consistent. Raw materials, for example, are usually valued at the lower of cost or net realisable value.

In the Notes to the Accounts, *Debtors* are analysed in some detail between trade and other debtors and pre-payments and accrued income. Trade debtors arise in the normal course of business from selling goods on credit. Other debtors might include money owing to the company from the sale of a subsidiary or a fixed asset. Pre-payments and accrued income include a proportion of rent, rates, telephone rental and other similar bills paid in advance. Any bad and doubtful debts will have been written off or provided for in the accounts, so the figure you see in the balance sheet should represent the recoverable balance. Any debtors falling due after more than one year should also be shown separately.

Cash is one of those delightfully simple assets which needs no further description or qualification.

CURRENT LIABILITIES

Creditors have to be shown under two headings: amounts falling due within one year and amounts falling due after one year. The detailed Notes to the Accounts usually show the first category in great detail. With Feelgood, they include bank overdraft (if any), trade creditors, current corporation tax, accruals and deferred income, other loans and the dividend payable.

NET ASSETS EMPLOYED

The difference between Current Assets and Current Liabilities represents *Net Current Assets*. Below that is the figure for Total Assets minus Current Liabilities, which in Feelgood's case is £10m. The only amounts that need to be deducted to arrive at the Net Assets Employed in the business are the following:

1. CREDITORS – Amounts falling due after more than one year. The Notes to the Accounts set these out in detail. With Feelgood, the total of £2.75m includes long-term bank loans (if any), mortgages, obligations under finance leases and hire purchase contracts and other long-term loans.

2. PROVISIONS – Amounts retained to cover any liability or loss which is likely to be incurred. With Feelgood there is only deferred taxation of £250,000 but, with other companies, provisions might also include pension commitments.

3. MINORITY INTERESTS – Represent the share of the assets of subsidiaries that are not wholly owned. There is none in Feelgood, but the problem does often arise. For example, a company might own 70% of one of its subsidiaries. In that event, 100% of the

assets and liabilities would be *consolidated* in (brought into) the accounts of the parent company. So as not to overstate the position, 30% of the net assets of the subsidiary would then be deducted as one figure under the heading of minority interests in the parent company's balance sheet.

CONTINGENT LIABILITIES

Contingent Liabilities are liabilities that have not crystallised by the date of the balance sheet. They are not sufficiently well-defined to permit substantial provisions being made for them in the accounts. They must, however, be shown as a note. Dangerous ones to beware of are significant sums concerning the disposal of subsidiaries and guarantees of major liabilities over which the company has no control.

CAPITAL AND RESERVES

Returning to the Feelgood balance sheet, the Net Assets Employed amount to £7m in total (£10m less £3m). The shareholders own these assets through their shareholdings. There are 10 million ordinary shares in issue with a par value of 25p, resulting in *Called-up Share Capital* of £2.5m – the amount invested by the original shareholders. In this instance, as in many others, it has been supplemented by profits (£4.5m) ploughed back over the years under the heading of *Profit and Loss Account*. Adding this figure to the Called-up Share Capital of £2.5m gives a total for shareholders' funds of £7m which does, of course, reconcile with the £7m of Net Assets Employed.

In a company's accounts you will often see Share Premium Accounts, Revaluation Reserves and Capital Reserves under the general heading of Capital and Reserves. All that you need to remember is that they are all part of Shareholders' Funds and will be represented by assets on the other side of the company's balance sheet.

THE CONSOLIDATED PROFIT AND LOSS ACCOUNT

The Consolidated Profit and Loss Account for the year ended 31 May 1995 is also very straightforward. Against each major figure there is usually a number relating to a more detailed explanation in the Notes to the Accounts. The *Turnover*, for example, is usually analysed both geographically and divided into different types of business. Cost of Sales, Selling and Distribution costs and Administrative Expenses are all shown separately. Other items that have to be highlighted (usually in the Notes to the Accounts) are chairman's emoluments, directors' emoluments, including pensions and other benefits, and the auditor's remuneration.

Interest payments and interest received may be shown net in the Profit and Loss Account, but in that event would be shown separately in the Notes to the Accounts. In the case of Feelgood, there is only £50,000 of interest payable. The profits for the financial year after deduction of £330,000 of taxation are £670,000. Although there is none in the case of Feelgood, there is then quite often a further deduction for minority interests. If one of the subsidiaries were only 70% owned, 100% of the profits would have been added to the group's profits in the consolidated figures, but a deduction of 30% (less tax) would be made from the minority interests figure to reduce the net addition back to 70%.

CONSOLIDATED PROFIT AND LOSS ACCOUNT

	1995 £000
Turnover	6000
Cost of sales	3000
Gross profit	3000
Selling and distribution costs	1200
Administrative expenses	750
	1950
Trading profit	1050
Interest receivable	–
	1050
Interest payable	50
	1000
Taxation	330
Profit for the financial year	670
Minority interests	–
Profits attributable to shareholders	670
Dividends paid and proposed	210
Amounts transferred to reserves	460
Earnings per ordinary share	6.7p

CASH FLOW STATEMENT

Every set of annual accounts is now also required to show a *Cash Flow Statement*. The statement splits cash flow into different categories and attempts to classify how the profits are spent and where the money goes. There are always lots of figures so concentrate upon the most important one – *the net cash inflow from operating activities should not be materially different from the profit arising from trading operations.* This is such a vital point that I will illustrate it with an example from a typical set of accounts of Sainsbury. The group's Cash Flow Statement immediately refers you to Note 24 which is set out below.

Note 24
RECONCILIATION OF OPERATING PROFIT TO NET CASH INFLOW FROM OPERATING ACTIVITIES

	Group	
	1992 *£m*	*1991* *£m*
Operating profit	667.7	585.0
Profit sharing	(49.4)	(44.0)
Depreciation charges	135.6	120.2
Increase in stocks	(1.5)	(52.3)
Decrease (Increase) in debtors	4.7	(9.7)
Increase in creditors	31.7	109.2
Net cash inflow from operating activities	788.8	708.4

The Operating Profit is £667.7m, from which £49.4m is deducted for the retail employees' Profit Sharing Scheme. There is then a very substantial £135.6m added back for Depreciation which, although charged against profits, does not absorb cash. The rest of the adjustments are related to working capital requirements – increases or decreases in stocks, debtors and creditors.

The final result is a healthy £788.8m *net cash inflow from operating activities*, which compares very favourably with the £667.7m of *operating profit*. Many Reports and Accounts are not as well set out as Sainsbury. The less clear they are, the more vigilant you should be. Concentrate upon the key figures. *When net cash inflow from operating activities is less than operating profit*, creative accounting might have been at work.

Why is cash flow so important? First, as a check that trading profits and therefore earnings are 'real' (backed up by hard cash), and second, because free cash flow funds the expansion of a company. By the term 'free cash flow' I mean cash flow after dividends and after capital expenditure.

Food retailers, such as Sainsbury or Tesco, have excellent cash flow. From the opening day of a new supermarket the tills ring up disposable cash. Bread, for example, is supplied on credit by the bakers, sold for cash and eaten within a day or so. A few weeks, and in some cases months, later, the baker's account is settled by the supermarket, which has enjoyed the use of the cash in the meantime. At the end of its financial year the cash profits of a supermarket are spent on taxes, dividends, the repayment of debt and, of course, on new supermarkets to generate further growth. The only worry is when over-expansion and over-building causes conditions to become so competitive that there is a price war. They rarely last for long, though – why spoil a good thing?

CAPITAL EXPENDITURE

I mentioned *capital expenditure* (money invested in fixed assets such as land, buildings, plant and machinery) which is often necessary for a company's expansion. Capital expenditure for which no provision has been made, or capital expenditure which has been authorised but not yet contracted for, has to be shown in the accounts as a note. On occasions, the amount of the potential future liability can be considerable and could in some cases wipe out a company's cash balances. At the very least, it will diminish them or further increase the company's indebtedness.

There are some companies which need to keep investing capital just to maintain the status quo and stay alive. Steel companies, for example, are very capital intensive. They frequently need to invest in new plant and equipment to replace machinery that is in a bad state of repair or has become obsolete. I much prefer the more upbeat type of capital expenditure on brand new, additional factories together with state-of-the-art equipment – the stuff that makes for real expansion.

SUMMARY

When reading a company's Annual Report, most people focus on the Profit and Loss Account. In fact, this is not the most important page. I suggest you read an Annual Report in this order:

1. **The Auditor's Report** – Any qualification should encourage you to sell your shares.

2. **The Chairman's Statement** – This should give you a good idea of what the company's business is all about and of major developments during the year. The chairman will also usually give you an indication of the future outlook for the company.

3. **The Balance Sheet** – This is a snapshot of what you as a shareholder actually own.

4. **The Profit and Loss Account** – Now you can turn your attention to profits and losses.

5. **The Cash Flow Statement** – Profits are only 'real' if they are backed up by hard cash. Profits can be massaged, but cash is hard to fake.

6. **Notes to the Accounts** – Read these carefully too. Sometimes significant points are tucked away in the small print.

I hope that you now feel that you have a better understanding of the key points in company Reports and Accounts. If you want to go into further detail, you should read the book I mentioned earlier, *Interpreting Company Reports and Accounts.* I frequently refer to this excellent work, which is already in its fifth edition.

14

YOUR STOCKBROKER
AND YOU

**Before choosing a stockbroker, decide on the extent to which you want
to have your hand held and how much you are prepared to pay in
commissions for that luxury.**

PROSHARE

Before appointing a stockbroker, the small investor should consider
joining ProShare which was formed in April 1992. ProShare is an independent, not-for-profit organisation, funded by the London Stock
Exchange and industry, which exists to promote the benefits of owning
shares. Membership is open to the public and aims to provide members
with comprehensive, jargon-free information on all matters relating
to share ownership and financial planning.

ProShare is not a trade association or professional body representing the interests of financial products providers or a provider of

such products itself. It is a public interest body which seeks to represent the views and concerns of private investors and to increase public understanding and appreciation of the advantages of stock market investment.

ProShare's activities encompass political lobbying, dissemination of information written in layman's language, guidance on the establishment of employee share schemes and representation, based on research, of the needs and concerns of individual (as distinct from institutional) investors.

Membership currently costs £29.95 per annum, for which members receive an attractive and interesting monthly magazine and access to a number of special discounts on investment-related products and services.

ProShare Investment Clubs is a 'one-stop shop' for potential and existing investment clubs and their members. It provides a comprehensive manual on how to set up and run a club. It answers all the questions a club or its members are likely to ask and allows them to enjoy the fun and excitement and learning experience of investing in the stock market through a pooled fund. Clubs taking full membership are registered with ProShare Investment Clubs which is a member of the World Federation of Investors and they receive a monthly newsletter together with special offers and invitations to regional and national conferences. The ProShare Investment Clubs Manual can be purchased separately for £25 or as a component of full membership at £50.

Further information can be obtained by writing to ProShare (UK) Limited, Library Chambers, 13 & 14 Basinghall Street, London EC2V 5BQ or telephoning 0171 600 0984.

FINDING A STOCKBROKER

Now that you have some understanding of the language of finance, your next step is to appoint a good stockbroker to help you with your investments.

Finding the right stockbroker is not an easy task for investors with small portfolios. Many brokers prefer to concentrate their efforts on the institutions and do not want the administrative hassle of dealing with small accounts.

The Association of Private Client Investment Managers and Stockbrokers, 20 Dysart Street, London EC2A 2BX, will supply a free brochure giving details of those brokers who are interested in private clients with funds of £10,000 (in some cases less), and describing the kinds of services they can offer.

For active investors there are two main options: execution-only (simply dealing), which is the cheaper of the two, or a more comprehensive, and therefore more expensive, service which might be called 'hand-holding'. I hasten to say that I like my hand held, by which I mean receiving investment recommendations, immediate advice about directors' dealings and major new developments, copies of press cuttings and brokers' circulars, the occasional share placing, market updates and a friendly word. The more active your account the more help you can look for from your broker.

A further problem for private clients is the level of commission charged by traditional stockbrokers. This can range from about 1.65% down to 0.5% and even lower for really major clients. There are also often hefty minimum charges, usually of about £25 a transaction, which can be particularly onerous for very small bargains.

SHARELINK

In the past, I always thought that execution-only stockbroking was a false economy, but that was before I visited Sharelink in Birmingham.

In March 1995, Sharelink's minimum charge was £10 per bargain in each company up to £1,000, 1% for orders of £1,001 to £2,500, 0.75% on the next £2,500, and only 0.1% on the excess over £5,000. On a £10,000 order their charge added up to £48.75 (0.49%), but on a £20,000 order this dropped to only 0.29%. This is cheap, even by the standards of execution-only brokers, and very cheap indeed when compared with more traditional brokers offering a fuller service.

However, the main revelation from my visit was the discovery of Sharelink's new service called Sharefinder, which covers the leading 650 companies and has three essential features: a weekly performance summary, a weekly buy/sell guide and individual company reports.

The weekly performance summary costs £2.95 a copy and gives details of P/E ratios, NAVs, yields, gearing and relative performance. The buy/sell guides cost £4.95 each and give details of brokers' consensus recommendations for the same 650 shares. These statistics are useful now and then, but the best value for money is Sharelink's company report for £4.95. Each report is produced to order, so you can always be sure of the latest information. It has details of how many brokers have recommended the share as a buy, a sell or a hold. There is also a computerised consensus commentary, which I tested against three shares I know well and found to be remarkably good in picking up the salient points. In addition, the report includes five-year statistics of earnings, dividends, P/E ratios and key financials together with shareholdings, charts and all the latest announcements. At £4.95, this is excellent value for someone contemplating a sizeable investment in a leading company.

Sharelink has also introduced weekly computer searches for shares that comply with differing selection criteria such as high yield, asset value over book value and above average earnings growth in relation to P/E ratios. Sharelink is not in the business of offering investment advice. However, the information it now provides adds a new dimension to its services and makes it a very attractive halfway house for small investors who do not need their hands held too firmly. For further information, telephone 0121 200 7777.

FIDELITY

Fidelity Brokerage, the UK stockbroking arm of Boston-based Fidelity Investments, the worldwide stockbroking and investment management group, is another well-known company that offers a stockbroking service for investors who make their own investment decisions.

Again, you will not be left completely on your own. Fidelity provides a broad range of market and company information free over the phone (telephone calls are free, too) from their sophisticated market monitoring systems.

The service will have particular appeal for active investors – people looking for ease of dealing and cost savings on larger and regular deals.

First, Fidelity Brokerage operates a flat-rate commission scale which works in bands, so you know exactly where you are on charges. In mid-1995, any trade up to the value of £2,500 costs a flat £25; for one between £5,000 and £7,500 the cost is a flat £60 – on a par with Sharelink and about 50% less than the average traditional stockbroker.

Discounts are also given for closing bargains, frequent dealers and for bed and breakfast deals. More importantly, however, Fidelity's dealers will actively negotiate the best price for shares in the market place, and savings on share price can often negate the commission costs.

To simplify the cash settlement process, Fidelity has followed the US practice and offers a money market banking facility linked directly to the stockbroking account. Also designed to make life easier for the investor, all client portfolios are held in a designated nominee account (stocks are held by Fidelity Brokerage but registered to the individual customer). So Fidelity does all the paperwork, but the investor can still attend AGMs, receive any perks, company reports, and so on.

Finally, for investors who want to venture into foreign shares, Fidelity Brokerage also offers dealing in US, European and other major world markets, as well as in unit trusts, offshore funds and currency funds – all within the same stockbroking account.

So, for independent investors who do not need advice, Fidelity provides a convenient, low-cost solution. For further information, telephone 0800 222 190; lines are staffed from 9a.m. to 6p.m. seven days a week.

TRADITIONAL BROKERS

As I have explained, a traditional broker's commission on purchases and sales of stock can range from 1.65% to less than 0.5%, according to the size of the transaction and the importance of the client. If you want your hand held, you should not begrudge your broker a reasonable commission on each transaction, provided he gives you good service. You want a broker who is switched on and really anxious to help you.

You have to bear in mind that your broker would be unnatural if he were not to some extent commission-orientated. The more you turn over your portfolio, the more commission your broker will earn in the short run. Do not be alarmed though, most brokers have the long-term interests of their clients at heart and will not try to persuade them to deal simply to earn more commission.

MINIMUM LEVEL OF SERVICE

The problem for many small investors is that they feel they cannot be too demanding because their account is so tiny and unimportant to the broker. However, there is an absolute minimum of information that the private investor, however small, can and should be able to request. As the account grows there is another, higher level of service that can be progressively demanded. Let me outline the minimum standard you can reasonably expect as a small private investor:

1. Any verbal or written recommendation from your broker should

be accompanied by details of the current P/E ratio of the share in question, the dividend yield, the NAV per share, the market capitalisation, the past record of earnings growth, the consensus of estimated future growth, the prospective P/E ratio, borrowings and your broker's reasons for buying.

2. Any execution should be carried out efficiently, at the price limit mutually agreed with the broker.

3. Subsequently, you should be kept informed of any major new developments, such as directors' share dealings, any announcements made by the company and details of any sharp price movements.

DATASTREAM CHARTS

As your relationship develops and you become a major client, you should expect your broker to provide a copy of the Datastream relative strength chart for any share in which you are interested, and if necessary obtain a copy of the annual and interim accounts for you.

The Datastream chart will show you graphically how the price of your share has been performing against the market as a whole. More of this later.

PRESS CUTTINGS

Your broker should also be able to supply the last six months' press cuttings and a copy of the Extel card, which gives summarised financial statistics of the company. You cannot expect this kind of service until you are paying your broker sufficient commissions to justify special treatment. You should restrict your requests for the fullest information to those companies in which you are very likely to invest. Obviously, you do not want to wear your broker's patience too thin with hundreds of spurious enquiries.

CONCENTRATE ON THE FACTS

I have, in the past, dealt with brokers who ring me up to say, 'English China Clay looks very good. There is a rumour that Hanson is going to bid.' Or, 'Tesco's results are coming out on Wednesday. They will be better than expected. The shares look very cheap.' I hate this kind of share tip. It is worse than useless – a definite drawback to good money management.

When a broker tells me a share looks attractive, I immediately ask for details of the price-earnings ratio, the asset value, the record over the last five years, the growth rate and the consensus of brokers' forecasts. I want facts and try to limit fancy. If you do the same, your broker will quickly get the message that you, too, are one of those strange people who actually wants to concentrate upon the known facts first, second and last.

Once you have established a *modus vivendi* with your broker, he or she can and should become an invaluable ally and aid to the successful management of your investments. It is important to start off as you mean to continue. While you will always be interested to hear your broker's views on investments, you should be far more interested in the feedback on the enquiries you have initiated. That is the information you need to beat the market.

15

A DISCIPLINE

Develop an edge over other investors by concentrating on leading growth shares. Temper and refine your method with reading and constant practice.

To invest successfully, you must try to develop an edge over other people who have the same objective. The best way of achieving this is to have a method, a system, an approach of your own, that you can improve by experience and practice. A narrow area of speciality in which you can become a relative expert. A discipline that will have strict ground rules drawn from my demanding criteria for selecting leading growth shares. A discipline to protect you from persuasive tips and a casual and sloppy approach.

It is impossible for most people to devote sufficient time to investment and become expert in every aspect of such a complex and wide-ranging subject. If, however, you focus your efforts on one area of investment, you will have a much better chance of succeeding. You need to use a laser beam rather than a scattergun.

There is no need for you to learn about the Japanese or German markets, turnarounds, cyclicals, asset situations or shells. You can, if you wish, concentrate simply upon *leading UK growth shares*. As you can see from the graph, the FT-A All-Share Index has performed very well over the last twenty years and on an income-reinvested basis has handsomely beaten inflation as measured by the RPI. Leading UK growth shares also have the advantage of no currency complications and comprehensive coverage by the press, brokers and newsletters. I recommend beginners to focus on them.

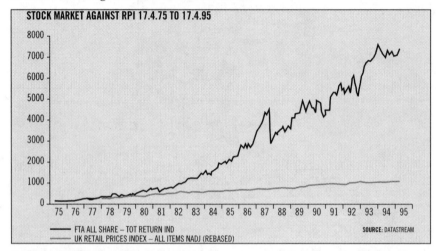

STOCK MARKET AGAINST RPI 17.4.75 TO 17.4.95

—— FTA ALL SHARE – TOT RETURN IND
········ UK RETAIL PRICES INDEX – ALL ITEMS NADJ (REBASED)

SOURCE: DATASTREAM

Before examining growth shares in more detail, I want to make three important suggestions:

1. AIM TO BEAT THE INSTITUTIONS

    It is important for you to gain confidence and realise that you can beat the institutions. They sound formidable but, with a few exceptions, as we have seen in Chapter 4 on unit trusts, they do not perform outstandingly well.

    You have a major advantage – you have much less money to invest. An institution managing a few billion pounds might have a portfolio of 500 shares or even 1,000. You will only have about ten shares in your portfolio and there is no doubt that your first selection will be better than your tenth, which in turn would obviously be far better than your hundredth, if you had to find that number. You will be surprised how difficult it is to select even ten excellent growth shares – I very much doubt if there are as many as 100 in the UK.

    Your second advantage is that, with a small portfolio, your own input is more important and meaningful. You might notice

that a food retailer is opening several new supermarkets, that a local engineering company is taking on another 200 people or that a friend is delighted with his new computer. Professional managers notice these things too, but they have much less impact on a portfolio containing 500 shares.

2. DO NOT WORRY ABOUT THE MARKET AS A WHOLE

You might be worried about the general level of the market and be wondering whether or not it is the right time to invest. The short answer is that *nobody* knows if the market is about to go up or down. In April 1995, the stock market was relatively buoyant. Having started the year at historically high valuations (a dividend yield of 4% and a historic P/E ratio of 18), profits and dividends in the March reporting season grew sufficiently, as companies emerged from recession, to make shares seem good value again. Increasing optimism about interest rates on both sides of the Atlantic then pushed ratings higher again giving shares another boost. With analysts expecting further strong earnings growth, bullish forecasts of a higher level at the end of the year do not seem unreasonable.

Remember though, for every hope, there is a matching worry. Even as the market was rising, evidence emerged of a possible slowdown in the economy in the shape of manufacturing output figures no higher than in the previous three months. There were similar straws in the wind from the US, where the plunging value of the dollar also threatened higher interest rates. However, in late April 1995, the Coppock technical indicator (which has an excellent track record on buying signals in the UK) turned positive.

In Chapter 21, I outline the characteristics of both bull and bear markets and the signs at the top of a bull market and the bottom of a bear market. Provided you are investing patient money that will not need to be withdrawn suddenly, I recommend remaining fully invested if you feel bullish, but tuning this down to 50% if you feel bearish or are losing sleep at night worrying about your investments. Overall, your portfolio will perform far better if you concentrate on selection rather than trying to deal in and out of the market.

3. REMEMBER THAT SELECTION IS MORE IMPORTANT THAN TIMING

You should not be unduly concerned about the general level of the market provided you can find shares that are *relatively* very attractive and offer excellent long-term growth prospects. Remember that, since 1919, investment in the stock market has beaten deposits by more than 6% per annum. I have recently read an interesting study, which supports this argument. *Market Timing vs Industry Selection*, by the American firm CDA/Wiesenberger, tracks two gifted men – Mr A, who has the ability to time the market to a tee, and Mr B, who has always been fully invested in the best sectors. Both investors began with $1,000 on 31 March 1980 and by 30 September 1992 Mr A had been in and out of the market on nine occasions, timing each move to perfection. His $1,000 had grown to $14,650.

However, Mr B, who had always been fully invested in the best sector, turned his $1,000 into $62,640. During the same period, a $1,000 investment in the S & P 500 would have grown to a mere $6,030. The results achieved by Mr A and Mr B would have been hard to emulate, but they do show clearly that selection is far more important than timing.

The final illustration of this vital principle is the Coca-Cola story. The company was floated in 1919 at $40 per share, but the price quickly slumped to $20 because of wild gyrations in the sugar price. Since then we have had the financial crashes of 1929, 1974 and 1987, a few major wars and a depression or two.

In spite of all these vicissitudes each $40 share in Coca-Cola is now worth well over $2m.

GROWTH SHARES

Now, let us return to our focus on growth shares, which are such an attractive investment medium for people prepared to tie up their patient money for the long haul. Once the right selection has been made, the upside potential is unlimited and can, as in the case of Coca-Cola, produce massive capital gains.

There are many more examples closer to home. If you had bought just the minimum allocation of 100 shares in Sainsbury when it was floated in July 1973, your original investment of £145 would now be worth over £6,000, after a peak of £8,000 a couple of years ago. Over forty times your money in twenty-two years. Rentokil and Racal have also been sparkling investments. During the same period, £10,000 in Racal would have grown to over £1.2m and £10,000 in Rentokil to over £500,000. As you can see from the charts, both companies have beaten the market by very substantial margins.

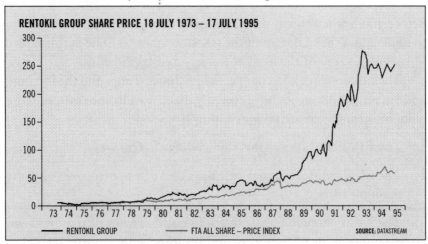

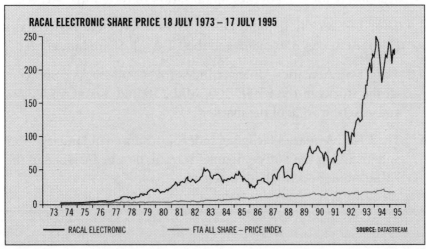

To obtain profits like these you have to begin with relatively small companies, but remember that for every one that succeeds, many fall by the wayside. Greater skill is required to select a small company that has the potential to become a giant. These kinds of companies have a much greater operational risk. In this book, I intend to concentrate upon FT-SE 100 stocks and shares in the Mid 250 Index only. These leading companies range from market capitalisations of about £200m to £20bn and offer the comfort of relative security. There will be an occasional failure, but many fewer than with a portfolio of shares in smaller companies. If you want to buy smaller companies and take the extra risk for the extra reward, you should read my earlier book, *The Zulu Principle*. In it I outline the necessary selective criteria in great detail which should help you to make the right decisions, if you are prepared to put in the time and effort.

THE FT-SE ACTUARIES SHARE INDICES

Before you begin to focus on individual shares, it is important for you to understand the make-up of the UK stock market. The performance of various sectors of the market is measured by indices.

The London Stock Exchange, the *Financial Times* and the Institute and Faculty of Actuaries have recently made a welcome revision to its main indices, which are now as follows:

1. The FT-SE 100 Index (the 100 leading shares).

2. The FT-SE Mid 250 Index (the next 250 companies, size being the main measure).

3. The FT-SE Actuaries 350 Index (a combination of the first two, accounting for 91% of the capitalisation of the entire market).

4. The FT-SE SmallCap Index (about 570 stocks that lie between the FT-SE Actuaries 350 Index and the FT-A All-Share Index).

5. The FT-SE Actuaries All-Share Index (over 900 stocks embracing all the stocks in the FT-SE 100, Mid 250 and SmallCap indices and covering 98% of the market).

6. The FT-SE Actuaries Fledgling Index, introduced in January 1995 and including the 800 companies too small to be included in the FT-SE Actuaries All-Share Index.

MARKET STATISTICS OF THE INDICES

Index	Approx Market cap	Number of Companies	Approx %age of market by size
FT-SE 100	Above £1.4bn	100	70
FT-SE Mid 250	£200m-£1.4bn	250	21
FT-SE 350			
Actuaries Index	Above £200m	350	91
FT-SE SmallCap	£40m-£200m	570 approx	7
Fledgling	About £0.5m to £40m	800 approx	2

As I explained in Chapter 12, there are a large number of companies which are currently traded on a matched-bargain basis under the Stock Exchange's Rule 4.2. Many of these companies will transfer to the new Alternative Investment Market in June 1995 – others have said they will not go to the expense of doing so.

The term 'matched-bargain' means that you can only sell shares once a willing buyer has been found. Few if any marketmakers are prepared to take the risk in the meantime. Because of this, the market in these companies, which are mostly very small and account for an insignificant percentage of the total market, tends to be very illiquid. We will, therefore, give them no further thought.

Put very simply, the FT-SE 100 Index is for leading stocks, the FT-SE Mid 250 for medium-sized companies, the FT-SE SmallCap for small companies and the Fledgling Index for minnows. To give you a better idea of the constituents of the indices, you will find in Appendices I and II the complete FT-SE 100 Index and the Mid 250 Index in mid-1995. In addition, I have set out for you below a random selection of thirty companies from the SmallCap Index, just to give you a general idea of its constituents:

Allders
Ashtead Group
Boosey & Hawkes
Budgens
CentreGold
Chemring Group
City Centre Restaurants
Cordiant
The Davis Service Group
Dorling Kindersley
Europcamp
Filofax Group
First Choice Holidays
Goal Petroleum
Gold Greenlees Trott

The Go-Ahead Group
Healthcall Group
HTV Group
Johnson Group Cleaners
Kelt Energy
London Clubs International
Macro 4
Manchester United
Menvier-Swain Group
Misys
National Express Group
Peel Holdings
Phonelink
The Sage Group
Singer & Friedlander Group

The new Fledgling Index contains all the remaining quoted companies below the FT-SE SmallCap Index, provided that they have traded on at least fifty business days before their annual review. It is an interesting mix. There are firms that have just left the nest plus older companies that have done a lot of flying but now have broken wings.

When investing in a fledgling company, most investors hope that it will eventually become one of the greats. A fine example is Hanson, which began life as the Wiles Group worth only £2 million and now has a market capitalisation of over £12 billion.

However, Hanson is the exception. Most companies fail to climb the ladder to the FT-SE 100 or just make it and, after a year or so, fall back into obscurity.

Sometimes there can be a reincarnation. A company that has lost its original purpose, but still has a little cash or another interesting asset, often becomes a shell for an entrepreneur seeking a quote as a personal vehicle. Then the whole process starts again.

Here are ten typical fledgling companies to give you the flavour and feel of them:

ABI Leisure Group	Frank Usher Holdings
Banner Homes Group	Graystone
Cakebread Robey and Co.	Martin Shelton Group
Dee Valley Water	Treatt
Enviromed	Utility Cable

In some of these shares, institutions could have problems if they tried to deal in real volume. In moments of crisis, marketmakers in smaller companies only offer to buy or sell as few as 1,000 shares and mark the price up or down immediately after they deal. Finding yourself trapped in shares of this kind can be a very unpleasant experience.

Institutions tend to invest mainly in the FT-SE 100 Index stocks because market *liquidity* is so much better. They can buy and sell the shares in volume without unduly affecting prices. The Mid 250 Index also includes some very sizeable companies: for example, in April 1995, Lucas is capitalised at over £1.6bn and is an obvious candidate for promotion to the FT-SE 100 Index. Even near the bottom of the Mid 250 Index you will find a company like Babcock International Group capitalised at over £200m.

MEASURE YOUR PERFORMANCE

If you follow my recommendations, you will initially only select your investments from the leading 350 UK shares. The FT-SE Actuaries 350 Index is therefore the standard against which you should measure the performance of your shares.

Once your portfolio is largely invested, make a note of the level of the 350 Index from your Saturday *Financial Times* or by simply asking your broker. Whenever you review the performance of your portfolio as a whole, you can take the opportunity to see how it has fared against the index. You might enjoy doing this once a month, but if not, every six months should suffice. It does not have to be a big hassle, but it is important to measure how well or badly you are doing against the appropriate standard. Otherwise you risk preening yourself because your portfolio has risen by, say, 20% while the index might have doubled during the same period.

You should not expect to achieve great results in the first year or so. You can also be more tolerant if there is strong evidence that you are improving. However, after three years of investing, you should be at least matching the market or beginning to beat it by a small margin. If not, face the facts – not everyone can be good at managing shares. You can always switch to a tracker fund and use your own time far more productively.

THE REVIEW PANEL

A Review Panel meets quarterly to decide on the index constituents. The main criterion for a company being in one index or another is its size measured by market capitalisation. I say 'main' because if one shareholder owns say 70% of the shares, the free float would be only 30% and the Review Panel would take this into consideration. It also makes allowances for companies that appear to be experiencing temporary blips.

As a result of the Panel's March 1995 review, there were no changes in the FT-SE 100 Index, but RJB Mining, Unitech, TLG, Matthew Clark, Premier Consolidated Oilfields and Brake Bros were promoted to the Mid 250 Index to replace John Laing, Saatchi and Saatchi (now Cordiant), Aegis Group, Dawson International, Persimmon and Bilton which were demoted to the FT-SE SmallCap Index.

When companies are promoted their shares frequently rise within a few days. This is primarily because tracker funds, which only invest in index stocks, sell the shares of demoted companies and buy those of promoted companies to keep in step with the index.

There is a second reason for a share price rising following a promotion. A company makes it to the Mid 250 Index and then to the FT-SE 100 Index usually as a reward for growth and vigour; the accompanying publicity often draws attention to the achievements of the company and attracts further buying. It therefore pays to keep a close eye on contenders for promotion and demotion. For example, if you are thinking of selling a share that is likely to be demoted, it would be better to act well before the Review Panel's next quarterly meeting. Conversely, the purchase of a share likely to be promoted should be made quickly before its promotion is announced.

THE TOP 350 COMPANIES

Let us look at the advantages of concentrating your investments in the leading 350 UK shares:

1. Very few of them will fade away entirely. They are relatively safe investments.

2. The liquidity of the market in these stocks is far better than with smaller companies. There are usually many more marketmakers and you are unlikely to find yourself trapped in a leading stock, unable to deal because the market is too restricted.

3. Many of the FT-SE 100 shares have proved themselves to be great growth stocks and the Mid 250 Index includes many shares that are future candidates for the FT-SE 100 Index. There is, therefore, greater evidence of past growth, which in turn leads to there being more confidence in future hopes and estimates.

We are searching for companies among the top 350 that have grown at an above-average rate, are likely to continue to do so *and are not already too pricey*. I will be setting out for you a set of criteria to help you make the right selections. You will be able to pass them on to your broker, who should be able to search for them with *Company REFS* and *Datastream* (a computerised analytical system with a very large data base used for sophisticated searches for stock market and other company data).

SUMMARY

1. To beat the market you must try to develop an edge over other people who have the same objective. The best way of achieving this is to have a method, a system, an approach of your own, that you can temper and refine by experience and constant practice.

2. I suggest that you begin with growth shares in the FT-SE 350 Actuaries Index, which represents 91% of the market capitalisation of all UK quoted companies. They are much safer and the market liquidity is also better than for companies in the SmallCap Index and below.

3. Do not worry unduly about macro-economics and the level of the market as a whole. Selection is far more important than timing.

4. At least every six months, measure your performance against the appropriate index. If, after three years, you are failing to beat the market, you would be better advised to switch to a tracker fund or find another way of delegating the management of your equity funds.

16

──

CRITERIA FOR SELECTING GROWTH SHARES

Apply strict criteria when selecting long-term growth shares. This way you will avoid disastrous losses and find more stock market winners.

The word 'growth', when related to growth shares, describes companies that have the ability to increase earnings per share (EPS) at an above-average rate year after year. Although growing companies frequently make acquisitions, it is the capacity to produce *organic growth from within* that is the distinguishing characteristic of a great growth share.

PAST GROWTH IN EARNINGS PER SHARE

In normal times you would look for EPS growth of a minimum of 15% per annum, totalling at least 100% over the last five years. A steady 15% growth rate would, in fact, double earnings during a five-year period. However, there might have been a small setback one year and, if so, this should not worry you unduly. You should expect earnings to have increased in at least four out of the last five years. In particular, make sure that in the last recessionary year, earnings were up by at least 10%.

Before your eyes glaze over at the enormity of the task, let me reassure you that your broker will help you with the necessary research. You only need to understand the basic thinking behind each of the criteria I will be outlining. Taken together, they will build into a checklist for you to pass on to your broker.

There can be exceptions to the rule of insisting upon a five-year record of earnings growth. For example, a significant change of management can make some of the prior years invalid for comparison purposes. A major change in the direction of a company might also justify accepting a shorter period of growth. In the next chapter, I outline in more detail *Company REFS'* minimum earnings requirement for classifying a company as a growth share.

OPTIMISTIC OUTLOOK

Past earnings are one thing, but share prices constantly look forward to the future, which is much more difficult to predict. You have to make your own assessment by using these valuable pointers:

1. The Chairman's Statement at the time of the Annual Report and at the interim stage must be optimistic in both content and tone.

2. The dividend policy must be positive. If a company has been steadily increasing its dividend and the rate of increase drops or the dividend is only maintained, this is often a warning signal.

3. The consensus of brokers' forecasts, which is just one element in a wealth of statistical information provided by my new investment service, *Company REFS*, should project strong earnings growth. *REFS* is available on a monthly or quarterly basis. You can either become a subscriber or ask your broker to give you the details from his own copy.

    I will explain *Company REFS* to you in much more detail in Chapter 23 on Recommended Reading. I am sure you will find it an invaluable companion in your search for growth shares.

    The Estimate Directory and the *Earnings Guide* are monthly publications which give details of the individual brokers' forecasts that build up to the consensus.

4.   Common sense is vital for an overview. For example, when the Clintons took charge of American healthcare, the outlook for drug stocks, which included some of the best performing shares during the 1980s, suffered a blow from which they have never really recovered. Although the companies' worst fears were not realised, increasing pressure from governments and large private health-care providers means that the industry's extraordinarily attractive margins are unlikely to return.

Similarly, the very optimistic forecasts which made super-market groups such strong performers a few years ago have been proved unfounded by intensifying competition in the industry. With companies like Tesco and Sainsbury unable to continue their ambitious expansion plans in a naturally limited market they have had to move overseas (which always adds risk to the operations of a business) to seek further growth.

COMPETITIVE ADVANTAGE

The third important criterion is to make sure that your selected company has a competitive advantage, which makes it hard to beat and difficult to emulate. This kind of edge over competitors is usually the result of *at least one* of the following attributes:

a)   *Excellent brand names*, such as Coca-Cola, Nestlé, Sony and Marks and Spencer. Reputations of this stature and quality take years to build and are immensely valuable. In their particular fields, companies like Photo-Me International for passport photographs and, on a much lesser scale, Glass's Guide for the pricing of sec-ond-hand cars, also have valuable names that would be difficult to compete with.

b)   *Patents*, like Wellcome's Retrovir for the treatment of AIDS, which was one of the attractions of the company to Glaxo when it launched a £9bn bid at the beginning of 1995. Glaxo also had a strong patent in Zantac, for the treatment of ulcers, but the impending expiry of that drug's protection from competition has started to worry analysts. While companies have a sixteen-year free run with a well-patented product, they can often make a for-tune for shareholders.

c)   *Copyrights*, which last fifty years, are usually for popular records, film libraries or important publications.

d) *A franchise created and granted by the Government*, such as television broadcasting, or the supply of water, electricity or gas. However, the beneficiaries suffer from some kind of regulation, so the utilities, for example, are unlikely to be allowed to make extraordinary profits for any length of time. The utilities' operating environment will almost certainly become considerably less benign should the Labour Party form the next government.

e) *An established position in a niche industry*, such as Druck's leadership in the UK in pressure-measuring devices. Photo-Me International occurs to me again as a classic example of a company with an established niche in passport photographs.

f) *Dominance in an industry*, such as Rentokil's in pest control. The company would no doubt prefer me to use its term 'environmental services', but this is my book.

The first attribute, an excellent brand name, is the most desirable and would take years of inefficient management to spoil. Patents, copyrights and franchises are also great while they last, but very much a case of making hay while the sun shines.

An established niche business can be more problematical. There is always the danger of the profit opportunity in the sector of the industry attracting a major new competitor. A watching brief is therefore essential.

Size in itself and apparent dominance in an industry can also be very dangerous to rely upon completely, as IBM and General Motors would be among the first to testify. The problem in both cases was that the businesses became subject to vigorous international competition. It is one thing to be dominant in your home market but quite another on an international basis. Dominance in an industry is a great advantage for a company, provided it remains constantly alert to the threat of overseas competition, dramatic new trends in the industry and technological developments.

When considering whether or not a company has a competitive advantage, these are the essential questions to ask yourself:

1. Is the industry difficult to enter?

2. Would the company be very difficult to compete with?

You want both answers to be a very positive 'yes'. You are looking for a business that is protected by strong barriers to entry.

ATTRACTIVE INDUSTRY SECTOR

Being in an attractive sector of industry is a vital part of a company's competitive advantage. It will not surprise you to learn that in some industries the managers have a tailwind behind them while in others they are heading into a Force 10 gale. The chart shows the widely differing percentage performance of selected sectors from the FT indices during the last fourteen years.

PERCENTAGE PERFORMANCE OF SELECTED FTA SECTOR INDICES 1980-MID 1995

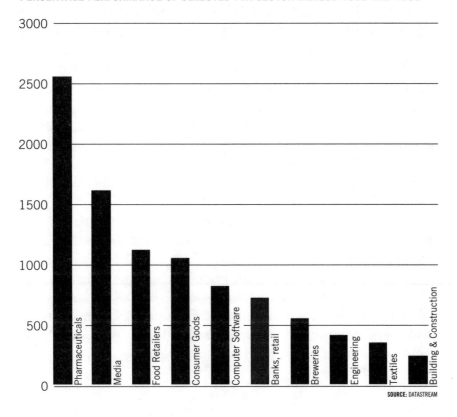

SOURCE: DATASTREAM

As you can see, pharmaceuticals, which includes companies owning patented drugs with international appeal, *has been* far and away the best performer. High on the list, too, are media companies and food manufacturers, which are also protected by strong brand names.

Near the bottom, as you might expect, you find contracting businesses, which are highly cyclical and have no particular advantages. General engineering companies also tend to have few branded products of their own. All of these industries are easy to enter, and it is relatively easy to set up in business from scratch.

You may wonder why anyone ever invests in companies of this nature. There is, of course, a price for everything. Sometimes, when industry is right at the bottom of the cycle and capital goods shares have fallen well below asset value, they are picked up by a few institutions and adventurous spirits. There might be a quick one-off gain as they recover, but I would recommend that you steer clear of them and invest in companies that have a competitive advantage in industries that are well placed to prosper. For the long term, the sectors I favour include pharmaceuticals (in spite of the Clintons), food retailing and manufacture, brewers, business services, leisure, media and stores. This is a very sweeping generalisation, which needs to be qualified. Within the engineering and electrical section of the market, you will find some excellent growth companies with branded products. Nine times out of ten though, you will find that great growth stocks tend to be found in the 'easy' industries I have mentioned. I cannot remember in recent years a British motor manufacturer, machine tool manufacturer or building contractor that has had earnings growing at a substantial and *sustainable* rate. So give these industries a wide berth if you are looking for growth.

During 1993, after some painful investment experiences with shares like Sage and Micro Focus, I decided to avoid investing in any further computer software companies. They can make you some amazing gains, if you invest right at the beginning and they have a successful run, but equally you can suffer some horrible losses. Because the industry's technology is moving so fast, a company's key products can suddenly become out of date. I therefore decided to cast software companies out of my selection process for growth shares.

RETURN ON CAPITAL EMPLOYED

You may find it difficult to judge from these subjective measures whether or not a company has a true competitive advantage. Fortunately, there is a very convenient financial cross-check. If a company has a worthwhile edge over its competitors, this should be reflected in the return it enjoys on *capital employed*. (All the money in the business – the total of ordinary share capital and reserves, preference shares, debentures, loan stocks and other debt). The better the quality of the business, the higher the percentage return the management should be able to make on the assets under its control. Your broker should be able to obtain five-year figures from *Company REFS* or *Datastream*. In the interests of consistency, *Company REFS* calculate the percentage return after deducting intangible assets from capital employed. Here are the figures for four leading companies:

	Last Annual Report %	5-year Average %
Rentokil	78.1	53.7
Sainsbury	18.8	17.4
BTR	23.6	19.6
Glaxo Wellcome	30.7	25.2

The five-year average irons out short-term fluctuations and accounting quirks and helps you to judge the capacity of a business to employ capital well. You should also keep an eye on the trend in case it is changing.

STRONG FINANCIAL POSITION

Next, you must ensure that a company does not have *excessive* debt. My limit is 50% of net assets and preferably much less. The calculations are made for you in the *Investors Chronicle* annual reviews of company results. Your broker can also let you know the percentage of debt, sometimes called gearing, which he can obtain from *The Hambro Company Guide* or *Company REFS*.

Often really great growth companies generate so much cash that they have no debt at all. Companies like Rentokil quickly build cash mountains. They spit out cash, which they use to expand and pay dividends. In contrast, car and truck manufacturers have to devote a large proportion of their profits to buying new machinery just to stay in business. Not much of their cash is left over afterwards for expansion and dividends.

STRONG CASH FLOW

It is vital to make sure that a company has strong cash flow and, at the same time, to double check that there has not been excessive use of creative accounting. This is easy to do by simply reconciling the *net operating cash flow* of a company with its *net operating profits*. The former should be at least the same as, and preferably more than, the latter. Nowadays, in the Notes to the Accounts, the two figures are usually highlighted. I have shown you how to reconcile the two figures in Chapter 13, but if you have any difficulty, simply ask your broker to give you the details.

GROWING DIVIDENDS

I may be old-fashioned but I always prefer companies that pay steadily increasing dividends. I make this one of my criteria because some institutions do not invest in dividend-less companies and I do not want to prejudice their future involvement. In addition, the dividend policy of a company can often give a valuable guide to the future outlook.

HIGH RELATIVE STRENGTH

A dynamic growth share with strong fundamentals should perform better than the stock market as a whole. Let us assume that the FT-SE 100 Index stood at 3,000, and that you invested in a FT-SE 100 stock at 100p. If, during a three month period, the Index fell 10% to 2,700, the relative strength of your shares would be good if they were significantly over 90p (100p less 10%). You should, however, be especially disappointed if your shares fell to, say, 80p, as you would lose 20% instead of the market average of only 10%. In these circumstances, the relative strength could only be described as poor.

In a more bullish environment, if the FT-SE 100 Index rose by 5% to 3,150, you would expect and hope that your shares would also rise by 5% to at least 105p. If they rose to say 120p, the relative strength would be excellent.

Relative performance is a very good indicator of how your shares are doing against the market. When you invest, it is good practice to make a note of the level of the relevant index, so that you will always have a basis for comparison purposes.

Charts are an essential tool in the investor's kit, if only because they present you with an easily understood picture of the price action of a share relative to the market. A Datastream chart of relative strength should be easily obtainable from your broker.

Here are the charts of BTR and ICI, showing their share prices as compared with the performance of the FT-A All-Share Index during the same twenty-year period:

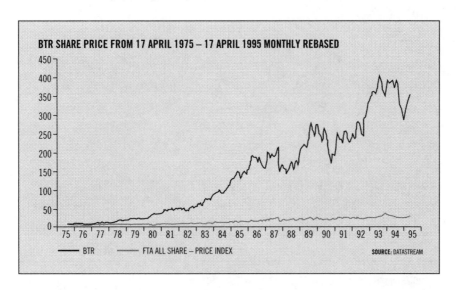

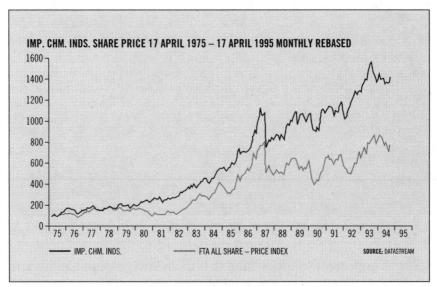

As you can see, BTR has massively outpaced the market, whereas ICI's performance has been lamentable. BTR's enormous relative strength has resulted in the BTR graph having to be drawn on a very different scale than ICI, as otherwise it would have gone off the page.

Now look at the charts below, which show only the relative strength of BTR and ICI against the market.

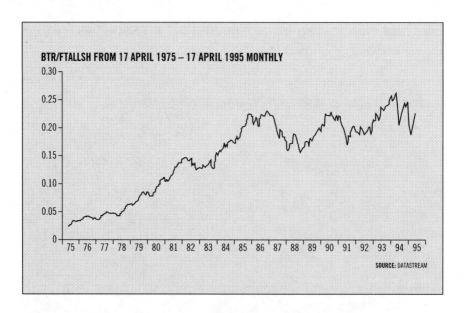

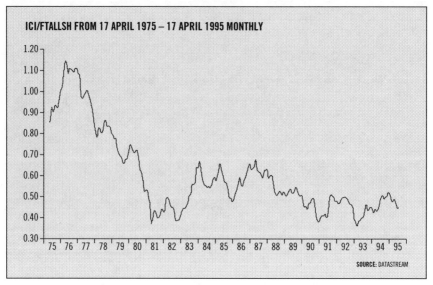

It is important to understand that the relative strength of a share that simply matches the performance of the market would appear as a straight horizontal line. The key point of interest is the trend and whether or not it is likely to continue. Clearly, ICI's relative strength has been poor, whereas BTR's has been excellent, showing a steady and strong upward trend.

I am a little old-fashioned and still prefer a two-line chart that shows the share price against the market, but one-line relative strength charts do give you a very quick idea of whether or not you are on to a winner.

If you buy the *Financial Times* each day, you should also keep an eye on the daily new highs and lows. These will give you an excellent feel for the shares that are making real headway and those that are losing momentum.

As a rule of thumb, I recommend investing in a growth share only when the price is within 15% of its high during the previous two years. This may sound paradoxical, as obviously you would prefer to buy a share at a lower price, but poor relative strength may be giving you a warning that there is something wrong with your judgement of the fundamentals.

SOMETHING NEW

As an important and added bonus, I like to find that growth shares are benefiting from 'something new' – new management, new products or technology, new events in the industry as a whole or a new major acquisition. New management is by far the most important of these as the impact of a new chief executive or new team of key executives can be both far-reaching and on-going. Archie Norman joining ASDA and Stuart Wallis joining Fisons are recent examples.

The importance of new products needs no elaboration. Suppliers of new products and new services in comparatively immature industries with unlimited markets can be described as 'new economy companies'. Old economy companies are tired and shrinking and include businesses making products for mature and limited markets in which there is already substantial established, often international, competition. The difference between a new drug for a previously incurable disease and bicarbonate of soda is obvious and the same is true for filing cabinets compared with the storage of records by microprocessing and computers. A new technical breakthrough can sometimes sweep all before it and produce massive earnings gains.

New events in the industry as a whole include the failure of major competitors. After the failure of Harry Goodman's International Leisure Group in March 1991, life was made much easier for Airtours and Owners Abroad, both of which increased their profits substantially.

Another kind of new development can stem from Government legislation. For example, the granting of new television franchises has had a major effect on companies like Carlton Communications.

A new major acquisition can radically change the market's perception of a company and its direction. Hanson has been held in much higher esteem since the company took over Imperial Tobacco, as has BTR following its purchases of Thomas Tilling and Hawker Siddeley. The market will certainly have a new appreciation of Tomkins after its controversial takeover of RHM. If the acquisition works out well, as it appears to be doing, Tomkins will grow in stature; if not, it will be consigned to the doghouse.

SMALL MARKET CAPITALISATION

All things being equal, I prefer companies with a small market capitalisation. A company at the bottom of the Mid 250 Index might be capitalised at only £200m, compared with Glaxo Wellcome, for example, with a muscle-bound market capitalisation in April 1995 of £25bn. The task of doubling Glaxo Wellcome is a mammoth one, whereas a £200m company might easily double over a few years. The operating risk is higher with a smaller company, but so is the potential reward. Smaller companies are also far less well researched by brokers and institutions, increasing the possibility of finding a bargain among them.

REASONABLE ASSET POSITION

With smaller companies and those with some debt, it is more important to have the comfort of some assets to fall back on, in case the business encounters troubled times. I like a reasonable asset position as secondary support for a share price, but I recognise that the assets per share of established major companies like Rentokil are almost irrelevant. Does it really matter if Rentokil has assets representing only a small fraction of its share price? No one is bothered about the assets per share, nor are they ever likely to be, provided the company has sufficient working capital, is not over-geared and has a relatively strong balance sheet. You only need to know that a company like Rentokil can keep on doing its thing – growing at an above average rate and paying increasing dividends.

MANAGEMENT SHAREHOLDING

It is reassuring to see the directors sharing both the risks and the rewards of share ownership. There is no better way of ensuring that management has the 'owner's eye'. I am not worried about the size of their shareholdings, provided that they are not merely nominal. Purchases and sales of shares by management can also provide valuable clues to the trading outlook.

SUMMARY

For ready reference, I will restate the criteria mentioned so far:

1. Ideally earnings per share should be growing at 15% per annum or more totalling at least 100% over the last five years and be up by at least 10% in the previous year. A shorter period is allowable for companies which have had a major management change for the better or have changed direction. In the next chapter I outline *Company REFS' minimum* requirement for classifying a company as a growth share.

2. Chairman's Statement, interim reports and brokers' consensus forecast to be optimistic.

3. The company to have a competitive advantage arising (in order of invulnerability) from an excellent brand name, patents, copyrights, government franchise, established position in a niche indus-

try or dominance in an industry. You want to invest in companies that are *difficult to compete with* and are operating in industries that are *difficult to enter*.

4.   Further evidence of competitive advantage is provided by a company's return on capital employed. The five-year details are available in *Company REFS* and through your broker from Datastream. You are seeking companies with a return of 20% or more in a constant or upward trend.

5.   Choose companies that are in attractive sectors of industry, like health and household, brewers, food retailers and manufacturers, business services, media, leisure and stores. Avoid shipbuilders, machine tool manufacturers, building contractors and those textile, electrical and engineering companies which do not have branded products. Also avoid computer software companies, because fast-changing technology can make them very vulnerable to major setbacks.

6.   Debt to be not more than 50% of net assets and preferably very much less.

7.   *Net operating cash flow* to be at least the same as and preferably more than *net operating profits*.

8.   Share price to be within 15% of its two-year high and to be relatively strong compared with market averages.

9.   'Something new' is not mandatory, but can be a very attractive bonus. Look for 'new economy' companies with new products or technology, and for companies with new management, new events in their industry or a new major acquisition.

10. Prefer smaller market capitalisations, but do not hesitate to reach upwards for exceptional opportunities.

11. A reasonable asset position is desirable, especially for smaller companies with debt.

12. Management to have the 'owner's eye' through a significant shareholding.

You now have all the criteria except the most important one – how to buy a share at a very attractive price relative to its growth rate.

17

___

PRICE EARNINGS RATIOS
AND GROWTH RATES

**Measure how much you are being asked to pay for the future
growth of a company. This is the way to find shares that
have been overlooked by the market.**

There is a limited number of significant growth companies in the UK,
possibly only a hundred or so. If you buy shares in any one of them,
you will probably do very well over a period of years. You will, however, fare very much better if, in addition to choosing the right company, you buy its shares at the right price.

I have explained to you the criteria for selecting a growth share,
so let us now get down to the very important question of the price you
should pay.

EARNINGS PER SHARE GROWTH

We have established that the earnings of a company are the profits
after tax attributable to the ordinary shareholders. If a company has

227

earnings of 10p per share and a P/E ratio of 10, the shares would be priced at 100p and, with a P/E ratio of 20, the shares would be 200p. The annual rate of growth in earnings and the projected future rate of growth are the main factors which determine the multiple. The P/E ratio is the measure of how much you are paying for future growth and how much others have paid before you.

Earnings are the engine that drives the share price. If the engine fails or falters, the shares will fall. The two charts show, at a glance, the close relationship between the earnings and the share prices of Rentokil and BTR over the last fifteen years. There can be no doubt that earnings per share growth and the performance of share prices are umbilically linked, although there may be long periods during which they get out of kilter.

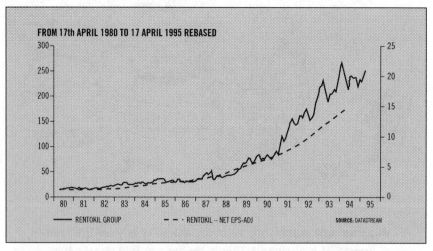

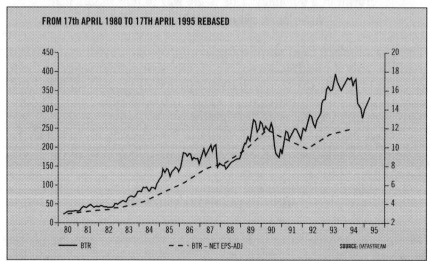

FT-SE Actuaries Share Indices

	May 5	Day's chge%	May 4	May 3	May 2	Year ago	Div. yld%	Net cover	P/E ratio	Xd adj. yld	Total Return
FT-SE 100	3251.7	−0.4	3264.3	3262.6	3248.2	3106.0	4.20	1.97	15.10	54.06	1263.33
FT-SE Mid 250	3555.1	−0.1	3560.0	3548.7	3542.8	3771.0	3.63	1.80	19.09	47.14	1357.93
FT-SE Mid 250 ex Inv Trusts	3560.4	−0.1	3565.5	3554.7	3550.7	3788.2	3.78	1.86	17.78	49.42	1358.85
FT-SE-A 350	1614.4	−0.3	1619.8	1618.0	1611.8	1579.8	4.07	1.94	15.84	25.63	1282.46
FT-SE-A 350 Higher Yield	1628.2	−0.3	1632.8	1631.7	1625.6	1574.0	5.00	1.72	14.57	33.19	1067.84
FT-SE-A 350 Lower Yield	1600.5	−0.4	1606.7	1604.2	1597.9	1545.2	2.99	2.37	17.64	17.58	1067.27
FT-SE SmallCap	1804.07	+0.2	1800.25	1790.53	1782.71	1940.53	3.37	1.59	23.32	22.50	1428.72
FT-SE SmallCap ex Inv Trusts	1782.28	+0.3	1777.76	1768.24	1760.96	1919.42	3.58	1.66	21.10	23.26	1417.09
FT-SE-A ALL-SHARE	1595.73	−0.3	1600.38	1598.05	1591.88	1572.45	4.02	1.92	16.25	24.91	1288.75

■ FT-SE Actuaries All-Share

	May 5	Day's chge%	May 4	May 3	May 2	Year ago	Div. yld%	Net cover	P/E ratio	Xd adj. yld	Total Return
10 MINERAL EXTRACTION(24)	2858.35	−0.2	2863.75	2854.81	2851.17	2707.93	3.60	1.96	17.67	52.95	1177.01
12 Extractive Industries(7)	3711.78	−0.5	3731.48	3710.66	3724.11	3885.04	3.79	1.96	16.79	91.94	1051.07
15 Oil, Integrated(3)	2865.63	−0.1	2868.05	2859.43	2852.00	2655.15	3.69	2.05	16.54	50.43	1205.84
16 Oil Exploration & Prod(14)	2089.03	−0.5	2099.87	2101.11	2104.68	2000.22	2.37	0.72	73.21	31.57	1229.05
20 GEN INDUSTRIALS(279)	1909.62	−0.2	1913.61	1903.77	1893.49	2097.39	4.11	1.65	18.40	31.18	999.10
21 Building & Construction(38)	970.00	+0.1	969.10	967.37	969.85	1321.17	4.10	1.89	16.14	17.71	780.26
22 Building Matls & Merchs(31)	1757.48	+0.2	1754.41	1747.10	1742.24	2045.38	4.21	1.91	15.57	34.53	853.11
23 Chemicals(22)	2321.67	......	2320.95	2314.57	2316.85	2525.48	4.07	1.38	22.18	33.48	1053.68
24 Diversified Industrials(18)	1851.12	−0.2	1855.19	1845.23	1837.59	2098.34	5.15	1.46	16.60	40.72	980.61
25 Electronic & Elect Equip(37)	1991.92	−0.8	2008.81	1984.11	1965.17	2065.89	3.66	1.92	17.73	14.64	991.72
26 Engineering(72)	1900.16	−0.4	1908.27	1902.32	1881.67	1963.42	3.27	1.87	20.47	23.87	1110.12
27 Engineering, Vehicles(13)	2249.89	−0.4	2259.60	2235.31	2231.22	2466.25	4.07	0.49	62.76	47.72	1125.93
28 Paper, Pckg & Printing(27)	2915.00	+0.1	2912.97	2883.45	2872.88	2921.15	3.28	2.31	16.52	38.72	1170.44
29 Textiles & Apparel(21)	1617.43	+0.3	1612.87	1603.39	1600.71	1803.69	4.36	1.63	17.61	26.92	942.49
30 CONSUMER GOODS(93)	3066.75	−0.3	3074.57	3074.11	3055.29	2737.27	4.23	1.71	17.24	57.81	1087.24
31 Breweries(18)	2329.65	−0.5	2340.74	2332.02	2296.89	2284.83	4.16	2.03	14.81	12.45	1067.55
32 Spirits, Wines & Ciders(10)	2756.62	−0.5	2771.82	2780.43	2759.66	2969.65	4.21	1.83	16.23	54.52	951.07
33 Food Producers(24)	2450.82	−0.4	2460.35	2455.04	2446.11	2373.22	4.15	1.95	15.43	53.07	1066.19
34 Household Goods(10)	2569.76	+0.4	2558.95	2563.06	2512.04	2727.35	3.58	0.86	40.36	50.32	950.03
36 Health Care(17)	1748.35	+0.1	1746.06	1737.10	1719.97	1730.82	2.80	0.88	50.55	23.68	1035.52
37 Pharmaceuticals(12)	3817.48	−0.3	3828.62	3825.46	3800.83	2769.34	4.07	1.57	19.59	61.12	1245.66
38 Tobacco(2)	4023.61	+0.5	4004.02	4023.61	4043.46	3749.92	5.63	1.63	13.59	131.29	952.30
40 SERVICES(93)	1980.87	−0.4	1989.66	1985.85	1979.66	2045.17	3.30	2.09	18.08	23.35	993.92
41 Distributors(32)	2456.69	......	2457.66	2440.45	2434.71	3068.36	3.89	1.95	16.49	44.19	874.51
42 Leisure & Hotels(29)	2257.77	+0.2	2252.96	2245.05	2254.13	2234.75	3.41	1.58	23.19	35.81	1138.78
43 Media(43)	2929.53	−0.6	2948.16	2951.35	2896.91	3063.00	2.67	2.28	20.55	48.91	1037.97
44 Retailers, Food(16)	1889.56	−0.7	1902.48	1913.79	1912.69	1639.27	3.57	2.47	14.16	17.14	1150.89
45 Retailers, General(44)	1661.82	−0.8	1675.68	1670.87	1670.35	1760.91	3.31	2.12	17.79	11.49	911.07
48 Support Services(37)	1558.66	......	1558.76	1548.97	1553.66	1666.24	2.75	2.42	18.80	13.59	963.42
49 Transport(21)	2238.39	−0.2	2242.47	2224.51	2222.64	2486.72	3.84	1.89	17.20	29.32	895.96
51 Other Services & Business(7)	1247.98	+0.4	1243.33	1243.32	1240.47	1222.38	3.62	1.21	28.45	10.90	1092.74
60 UTILITIES(37)	2329.92	−0.3	2335.87	2339.55	2345.47	2202.98	4.67	1.93	13.89	6.85	918.01
62 Electricity(17)	2211.05	−0.2	2217.72	2214.63	2230.01	2074.60	4.63	2.67	10.14	19.89	946.23
64 Gas Distribution(2)	2006.36	−1.0	2025.80	2045.00	2048.44	1897.93	5.97	0.65	32.09	0.00	942.37
66 Telecommunications(5)	2029.24	......	2029.32	2031.17	2033.15	1967.61	4.03	1.68	18.46	0.13	880.75
68 Water(13)	1831.34	−0.2	1835.30	1837.86	1836.64	1653.41	5.47	2.73	8.38	4.62	933.82
69 NON-FINANCIALS(662)	1722.88	−0.3	1727.74	1724.52	1718.86	1706.13	3.97	1.84	17.09	24.09	1248.69
70 FINANCIALS(117)	2292.61	−0.4	2301.44	2304.29	2289.66	2173.99	4.62	2.34	11.58	58.71	940.41
71 Banks, Retail(9)	3061.98	−0.4	3073.64	3087.35	3067.72	2720.74	4.49	2.95	9.42	86.03	950.38
72 Banks, Merchant(8)	3300.99	+0.4	3286.68	3277.93	3298.31	2925.42	3.51	2.54	14.01	31.67	1012.97
73 Insurance(26)	1272.25	−1.0	1285.23	1289.63	1270.90	1320.43	5.58	1.67	13.40	42.72	911.45
74 Life Assurance(6)	2541.41	−0.7	2559.10	2537.03	2520.96	2388.51	5.35	1.33	17.60	91.02	1019.74
77 Other Financial(22)	1986.76	......	1986.47	1988.27	1985.89	1894.03	3.86	2.32	13.94	25.59	1088.02
79 Property(46)	1367.65	......	1367.32	1357.42	1351.27	1622.19	4.40	1.19	23.90	12.85	801.06
80 INVESTMENT TRUSTS(133)	2727.37	−0.1	2729.39	2717.72	2702.35	2830.26	2.33	1.03	51.88	20.96	928.96
89 FT-SE-A ALL-SHARE(912)	1595.73	−0.3	1600.38	1598.05	1591.88	1572.45	4.02	1.92	16.25	24.91	1288.75
FT-SE-A Fledgling	984.25	+0.2	982.28	976.77	974.25	−	3.07	1.13	36.15	10.65	995.14
FT-SE-A Fledgling ex Inv Trusts	978.41	+0.2	976.07	971.23	968.97	−	3.24	1.16	33.24	11.16	989.77

THE TOP 350 COMPANIES

Let us look at the leading 350 companies in May 1995 to ascertain the average *historic* price-earnings ratio then. As you will see from the FT table on the previous page, investors were buying the shares of the leading 350 companies on an average of 15.84 times *historic* earnings. If average earnings were 20p a share, that would result in an average share price of 317p (15.84 times 20p).

RANGE OF P/E RATIOS

The top 350 companies in mid-1995 were a disparate bunch, with *historic* price-earnings ratios ranging from as little as 4 to well over 100. The index included stocks like Pilkington on a multiple of 35, discounting an anticipated recovery; utilities like Manweb on a multiple of only 8, fearing that the regulator might restrict prices; dull dogs like Lloyds Chemists on a multiple of only 7.5, and growth stocks like Eurotherm on a multiple of 23.

Here are a few more well-known companies taken from the *Financial Times* as examples of the wide range of historic P/E ratios in mid-1995:

Glaxo	16.4	Blue Circle	18.8
Argyll	12.9	Burton	21.9
Sainsbury	14.6	Dixons	25.3
GEC	15.7	Prudential	15.4
Rentokil	22.3	Amersham	19.3
Christies	28.4	Reuters	23.0
Kwik-Fit	15.6	Bowater	14.7
Powergen	10.7	Welsh Water	6.8
Hanson	12.2	British Petroleum	14.1

Sometimes, the multiples reflect the anticipated growth rate and at other times the extent of the likely recovery in profits. Astronomic P/E ratios of 30 and over usually anticipate a substantial degree of recovery.

THE PEG FACTOR

The P/E ratio is, however, a one-dimensional measure. More meaningful is the relationship between the P/E ratio of a company and the expected rate of growth of its earnings per share. I call this the Price-Earnings Growth factor – PEG for short. A PEG is a kind of thumb-rule way of measuring whether or not a growth company's prospective price-earnings ratio is high or low *in relation to the company's prospective growth rate*.

The concept is easily illustrated by an example. Say a company is growing at 12% per annum and has a prospective P/E ratio of 12, the PEG would be $\frac{12}{12}$ = 1.0. If the growth rate was a much more attractive 24%, the PEG would be $\frac{12}{24}$ = 0.5.

In principle, any company with a PEG noticeably under 1.0 is worth serious attention and further investigation.

PEGs only apply to growth companies. Recovery and cyclical stocks rarely become great growth companies. In *Company REFS*, we define a growth company as one with at least four years of increasing earnings per share, past or future. The minimum qualification would therefore usually be two years of past growth and two years of projected growth. The REFS definition is deliberately a slender one, so as to catch as many nascent growth companies as possible and also those experiencing a management change. You do not want to wait for five years of past growth before investing – by then most of the action may be over.

When using a PEG there is no need to be frightened of relatively high price-earnings ratios, provided the growth rate is there to justify it *and seems to be sustainable*. Obviously, any company growing at more than say 30% per annum will have great difficulty keeping up the pace and will eventually falter. The PEG approach works best in the middle ranges; I particularly like companies growing at about 20%-25% per annum on P/E ratios of 12-15.

The attraction of buying shares with a low PEG is that it provides a safety factor. Even if next year's profits are slightly disappointing, the share price is unlikely to fall much as the shares were already very cheap in relation to the original forecast and are probably still quite cheap in relation to the actual results.

GROWTH STOCKS

In April 1995, I had a close look at the monthly table of growth companies with the lowest PEGs in the FT-SE 100 and Mid 250 indices.

FT-SE 100 – LOWEST PEGs FOR GROWTH COMPANIES

Growth companies with lowest price-earnings growth factors based on consensus forecast eps for the 12 months ahead.

page	MKT Cap £m	1 Mo Rel Str %	Share price (p) 12 Months High	Low	Recent	Company	Prosp PEG	Prosp PER	Prosp Eps Growth Rate %	5-Year Eps Growth Rate %	3-Year Eps Growth Rate %	Prosp DY %	Last AR ROCE %
	10,710	+1.2			526	Index weighted average	1.37	12.6	12.2	3.7	12.8	4.9	21.7
	3,042	+1.2			451	Index median	1.15	13.0	10.3	2.1	6.3	4.8	17.9
761	6,103	+2.4	221	158	201	Vodafone	0.48	18.4	38.0	23.6	12.3	2.4	53.9
621	3,228	–5.4	459	378	403	Royal Bank of Scotland	0.56	8.5	15.1	12.6	74.5	5.5	na
624	8,591	+3.8	904	721	805	RTZ....................................	0.57	11.4	20.0	–11.2	–12.5	4.1	13.7
129	23,762	+4.7	436	377	431	BP	0.71	12.9	18.1	–16.9	–26.7	3.7	10.5
798	1,975	+0.4	438	332	359	Wolseley	0.74	10.9	14.7	5.2	31.4	3.7	19.7
100	2,165	+7.2	322	256	297	Blue Circle........................	0.76	11.8	15.5	–18.2	–21.7	5.2	12.7
167	1,505	+3.2	345	226	254	Caradon............................	0.77	10.8	13.9	na	2.6	5.1	18.7
169	2,128	+1.0	951	797	925	Carlton Comms.................	0.78	14.1	18.0	–0.4	20.1	3.4	34.0
735	3,621	–2.1	252	198	237	TSB	0.81	8.8	10.9	30.0	122	5.8	na
661	2,347	+0.2	630	499	548	Siebe	0.81	13.2	16.2	2.4	9.2	3.1	17.2
517	9,349	+7.0	540	424	538	National Westminster Bank	0.83	7.8	9.4	–10.8	77.6	5.9	na
608	2,375	+4.4	245	200	241	Rentokil	0.87	16.5	18.9	24.3	25.3	2.2	74.2
450	7,967	+5.5	616	522	614	Lloyds Bank	0.91	9.3	10.2	52.0	27.9	6.1	na
110	2,258	+8.9	500	388	451	Bowater............................	0.92	12.8	13.8	3.9	6.8	4.3	19.7
4	6,194	+4.1	474	381	472	Abbey National.................	0.93	9.2	9.9	9.0	15.1	5.8	na

FT-SE MID 250 – LOWEST PEGs FOR GROWTH COMPANIES

Growth companies with lowest price-earnings growth factors based on consensus forecast eps for the 12 months ahead.

page	MKT Cap £m	1 Mo Rel Str %	Share price (p) 12 Months High	Low	Recent	Company	Prosp PEG	Prosp PER	Prosp Eps Growth Rate %	5-Year Eps Growth Rate %	3-Year Eps Growth Rate %	Prosp DY %	Last AR ROCE %
	953	–0.7			354	Index weighted average	1.45	13.5	15.0	–1.7	10.2	4.5	19.5
	492	+0.3			275	Index median	0.90	12.7	12.7	0.3	8.7	4.3	17.0
434	246	–3.6	176	143	143	Kwik-Fit	0.34	10.7	31.9	2.3	–14.1	4.2	16.2
807	1,069	–1.3	609	461	528	Yorkshire Water	0.35	6.1	17.3	na	12.1	6.5	10.0
684	314	–13.5	238	180	212	Stagecoach Holdings	0.38	11.4	30.0	na	48.5	2.9	20.4
464	1,603	+6.2	211	158	198	Lucas	0.40	14.8	36.6	–26.7	0.6	4.5	10.4
790	396	+0.9	110	85	105	Wickes	0.41	12.1	29.6	–9.2	105	3.2	19.0
669	879	+2.3	570	473	564	Smith (David S)................	0.44	10.7	24.2	–5.4	3.0	3.2	10.6
480	202	–1.5	614	517	554	Matthew Clark..................	0.45	11.4	25.4	–3.2	13.4	4.7	27.1
112	1,409	–4.0	348	273	282	BPB..................................	0.47	10.5	22.3	–18.6	16.9	4.5	15.0
730	299	+1.2	333	274	291	Travis Perkins	0.50	10.7	21.5	–21.3	–9.5	4.4	12.3
401	1,017	–2.2	364	286	312	IMI	0.52	13.9	26.8	–11.2	–16.0	4.5	14.3
89	1,186	+1.0	460	303	335	BICC	0.53	13.8	26.1	–21.2	16.8	5.6	15.4
493	383	–1.7	482	290	305	Meyer...............................	0.54	9.1	16.8	–25.1	–4.5	5.1	11.2
334	657	–0.7	390	293	315	Glynwed	0.58	11.7	20.2	–18.5	–13.5	5.2	18.4
774	246	–1.0	458	350	364	Watmoughs.......................	0.61	13.8	22.6	3.6	2.5	3.2	12.9
626	757	+9.0	152	103	119	Rugby Group	0.61	11.7	19.1	–5.2	0.4	4.1	15.1
691	952	+3.4	235	189	229	Storehouse	0.63	13.4	21.4	60.5	112	3.8	15.0
271	826	+2.1	423	356	418	EMAP..............................	0.64	16.0	25.2	2.0	17.2	3.2	137
16	483	–0.6	510	410	425	Airtours	0.66	8.6	13.2	45.3	20.6	4.3	41.6
703	262	+5.7	260	186	209	Takare	0.66	11.7	17.8	32.9	23.7	1.7	8.1
451	227	–36.1	334	187	187	Lloyds Chemists	0.66	5.6	8.5	15.0	11.3	7.8	29.8
115	267	+9.4	523	413	523	Brake Bros........................	0.67	14.1	20.9	13.0	7.1	2.4	26.8
233	755	+8.5	434	269	397	Danka Business Systems....	0.68	19.9	29.0	27.4	27.4	0.7	32.3
715	278	+1.9	895	575	628	Tibbett & Britten	0.69	13.5	19.5	19.0	19.9	3.6	25.3
223	392	+15.6	194	139	166	Cray Electronics	0.69	14.1	20.5	211	58.4	2.6	37.3
637	1,185	–6.6	427	304	309	Scottish Hydro-Electric	0.69	8.1	11.8	na	na	6.2	20.0
165	259	–7.6	410	326	355	Capital Radio	0.69	15.9	22.9	–3.1	23.2	3.1	122
444	313	+9.0	542	279	329	Lex Service	0.70	9.6	13.7	5.3	80.6	6.0	13.8
462	428	–0.9	439	381	435	Low & Bonar	0.71	11.7	16.4	2.5	4.2	3.8	19.2
485	598	+13.3	225	122	209	Medeva	0.72	12.4	17.3	54.4	18.6	2.5	82.1
470	849	+9.8	290	218	258	MAI..................................	0.72	11.5	15.9	11.7	13.8	4.7	17.2

REFS figures are based on brokers' consensus forecasts and *always refer to the twelve months immediately ahead*. For example, examining a company on 1 April with a financial year ending on 31 December, REFS adds nine months (three quarters) of the current year to three months (a quarter) of the consensus estimate for the following year. In this way, the statistics are always up-to-date and dynamic and the figures in the REFS tables are always directly comparable.

You will see from the tables that the index median for the FT-SE 100 prospective PEG is 1.15 and that it is 0.9 for the Mid 250 Index. The 'median' means the midway company in the list. For example, if there were seven companies, the median statistic would be the fourth one.

There are a few surprising omissions from the table. Some well-known growth companies like Hanson and Guinness have not made the grade because they had temporary setbacks in earnings, so their next year's growth will include an element of recovery.

THE BATON PASSES

A further very important factor in buying a rapidly growing stock, and in judging whether or not the P/E ratio is expensive, is the exact timing of your purchase. Take the example of MTL Instruments, a small electronics company manufacturing measuring instruments and safety devices. In February 1991, the price of the shares was 124p, and earnings per share in the last reported year to December 1989 were 11.3p. Therefore, if you had bought the shares then, you would have paid eleven times 1989 earnings and, with 20% growth forecast, nine times earnings for the year ended December 1990.

One month later, in March 1991, the results for 1990 were announced. You would have known from the half-year results that the profits were going to be excellent, but when you bought in February 1991 many investors were still valuing the shares on the historic 1990 multiple. The forecast for the year to December 1991 was optimistic, enabling analysts to estimate confidently that there would be a further 20% uplift in earnings. Within a few weeks the market began to think of the company on a prospective P/E ratio for 1991, which made the shares seem to be far cheaper than they were at the time of your purchase. When a baton is passed in a relay race, attention focuses on the next runner and the next lap – moving from the historic to the prospective P/E ratio.

This phenomenon is particularly pronounced with *fast-growing* companies near the end of one financial year (or half-year). You frequently enjoy a one-off gain by investing in them as the market adjusts to absorb the results of the previous year and digests the news that the following year may be even better. The process is aided by the press and brokers, as some of the companies are not household names and receive very little attention throughout the year. They have their moment in the sun when their results are announced.

FUTURE ESTIMATES

Your first step in finding a growth share that seems to fulfil my other criteria is to check the prospective PEG. *Company REFS* gives a synopsis of the earnings and dividend history and estimates for each company (pretax profits will also be shown soon) in one of the many panels of statistics in the company entry. Very similar details can also be found in the *Hambro Company Guide* or requested from your broker.

EARNINGS, DIVIDEND ESTIMATES				
		94AR	95E	96E
norm eps	p	42.9	46.8	50.4
change	p		−0.60	−0.30
brokers	n		14	14
std dev	p		1.21	6.14
growth	%	7.52	9.09	7.69
per	x	16.6	15.2	14.1
dps	p	27.0	30.2	32.6
div yield	%	4.75	5.31	5.72

The panel shows Glaxo Wellcome on 3 April 1995 and indicates that the brokers' consensus forecast for the year ending 30 June 1995 is for growth of 9.09%. For 1996 further growth of 7.69% is forecast. REFS takes three months (a quarter) of the 1995 estimate and nine months (three quarters) of the 1996 estimate to give a forecast for the twelve months immediately ahead of 8.02% growth.

The prospective P/E ratio for the same period is calculated in a similar way and comes to 14.4. The PEG is then calculated like this:

$$\frac{\text{Prospective price-earnings ratio (14.4)}}{\text{Estimated future growth rate (8.02\%)}} = \text{Prospective PEG (1.79)}$$

You can readily see that 14.4 divided by 8.02 results in a very high and therefore unattractive PEG of 1.79.

In *Company REFS* all of these calculations are made for you every month and set out in the company entry and in the tables.

ATTRACTIONS OF LOW PEGs

The attraction of buying shares on low PEGs is that not only do you obtain the benefit of future growth, but you also reap rewards from the eventual status change in the multiple. For example, a gem of a company, with earnings of 10p a share on a multiple of 13 and a share price of 130p, might be growing at 20% per annum. When earnings are reported up the usual 20%, its EPS rise to 12p. Analysts begin to realise that the company should be on a multiple of *at least* 20 and the shares move up to 240p. Out of the rise of 110p, only 26p is due to the rise in earnings. The far larger balance of 84p comes from the status change in the P/E ratio, with more to follow from that source as the shares continue to be better appreciated by investors.

The added advantage of buying shares on cheap PEGs is that you have a very comfortable cushion against unexpected setbacks. For example, if our gem of a company, growing at 20% per annum, reports earnings up only 15%, the shares are still inexpensive. Even with average growth of 13%, they are not dear.

You can sometimes find bargains like these down the scale in the SmallCap Index. There are, however, much greater risks with smaller companies, so I suggest that, if you want to try this, you read *The Zulu Principle* first.

Meanwhile, you will be concentrating on the leading 350 companies and your aim will be to find shares which satisfy the criteria I have given you in Chapter 16. You also want any company you select to have an attractive PEG – a low P/E ratio in relation to its growth rate. There is a great advantage in having a formula that is easy to remember and does not require any calculation. I suggest, therefore, that you aim to find leading shares with PEGs of 1.0 or less – prospective P/E ratios of no more than estimated future growth rates. The shares of a company growing at 20% would be attractive on a P/E ratio of 20 or under, but a company growing at 7% would need to be on a multiple of under 7 to be of any interest to you. It is reassuring to note that, over a long period, it has been very rewarding to buy the market when the prospective price-earnings ratio is equal to the forecast future growth rate.

SUMMARY

1. The annual prospective rate of growth in earnings per share is the main single factor that determines the P/E ratio of a growth share.

2. To relate the growth rate to the P/E ratio, simply divide the prospective price-earnings ratio by the estimated future growth rate. This establishes a price-earnings growth factor (PEG).

3. The PEG factor is not infallible; it is simply an indicator that a company *appears* to be cheap in relation to its future growth rate. Before making an investment in a company with an attractive PEG, it should be checked out thoroughly to make sure that it satisfies most of the other investment criteria outlined in the previous chapter.

4. As a start, you should aim to buy leading shares in the FT-SE 100 Index and the Mid 250 Index that satisfy the investment criteria I have outlined and have PEGs of 1.0 or under. The prospective P/E ratio of any share you select should be no more than the estimated future growth rate. In this way, you will benefit from both the growth in earnings and the eventual upward status change in the P/E ratio.

5. Use *Company REFS*, the *Hambro Company Guide* or your broker to obtain the brokers' consensus forecast.

If you prefer to make your own calculations of PEGs, work on a twelve months immediately ahead basis and be sure to exclude cyclical and recovery stocks. The REFS definition of four years consecutive earnings growth (past and future) is a convenient *minimum* standard to define a growth company.

6. Fast-growing stocks can often be purchased advantageously just before they announce their yearly or half-yearly results, when attention will shift from the historic to the prospective P/E ratio.

7. The PEG factor works best when growth rates are clearly sustainable. Shares with P/E ratios of 12-15 and growth rates of 20%-25% are ideal candidates.

18

—

CREATIVE ACCOUNTING

Accounting standards are improving rapidly but there is still scope for management to inflate earnings figures. Read the Annual Accounts from cover to cover, especially the small print.

In the previous chapter, I resisted the temptation of telling you that the earnings of a company might not be all that they appear to be. I wanted you to concentrate without distraction on the basic thinking behind establishing a P/E ratio, a growth rate and a PEG factor.

In recent years there has been an accounting revolution, stimulated by many high-profile company scandals like Asil Nadir's Polly Peck and Maxwell Communications Corporation during the reign of Robert Maxwell.

It is very easy to see why there were so many abuses. Most company managements are under pressure to produce increased profits and earnings per share year after year. Sometimes the treatment of an item of expenditure or income is optional, and management, needing to produce growth in earnings per share and, perhaps, to secure bonuses, can be tempted to choose the least conservative method of accounting.

METHODS OF TRANSFERRING PROFITS FROM ONE YEAR TO ANOTHER

Management can do this in many ways. For example, an invoice for services rendered can be issued just after or just before the end of a company's financial year. If the amount in question is brought into the year just ending, the profits of that year will be boosted. If not, they will be depressed by the omission and the following year will get the benefit. The final results are therefore determined by the whim of the person making this kind of decision.

Take a company in the building business which has an unsold house on its books at the end of its last financial year. The house could have been built during the first six months of the year at a cost of £100,000 and the estimated selling price might be £200,000. Accounting prudence demands that at the end of the year the house should be valued for accounting purposes at cost or market value, whichever is the lower. On the first day of the current financial year, the house could be sold for the full asking price of £200,000 and, hey presto, the profit of £100,000 comes into the current financial year, not the previous one. There is nothing sinister in this. The profit will not be made until the house is sold, but one day can make all the difference to the annual profits.

You can readily see that many an entrepreneur anxious to preserve his company's unbroken record of earnings per share growth would make every effort to sell the house in a year in which profits were poor. Conversely, if business had been excellent and the future outlook appeared murky, our entrepreneur might deliberately delay a sale by a few days to swing the profit into the more difficult period ahead.

I have illustrated my point with only one house, but there could be many. In some businesses, several million pounds could easily be shunted from one financial year to another with this kind of approach.

Provisions are another area which offers scope for transferring profits to another year. Let us assume that our entrepreneur has had a good year and wants to keep something in reserve for the future. When reviewing outstanding debtors, he simply decides to adopt an exceptionally cautious view over the amount to be provided for bad debts. Unless he is obviously wrong, the auditors are unlikely to challenge his prudence. Similarly, he might argue that a more substantial provision should be made against the value of old stock and work in progress. These simple examples show how easy it is to transfer profits from one year to another.

WELL-KNOWN METHODS OF CREATIVE ACCOUNTING

There are many other areas of accounting with plenty of scope for skulduggery, including research and development costs, advertising expenditure, currency fluctuations, reorganisation expenses, methods of stock valuation, changes in methods of depreciation, the sale of fixed assets, capitalisation of interest, earn-outs and changes of financial year end. I explain all of these in *The Zulu Principle*.

An excellent and more detailed book on the subject, *Accounting for Growth*, was written by Terry Smith in 1992. He outlined the various accounting devices and awarded a selection of leading companies 'blobs' for each time they adopted arguable methods for boosting their earnings per share. Some companies with household names ended up with as many as eight or nine blobs out of a possible total of twelve.

Let me give you just one example of the methods I have listed, so you can see the kind of scope there has been for creative accounting. Polly Peck was the most notorious perpetrator of boosting profits with currency transactions. A large amount of money was borrowed in hard currency, like Swiss francs, at a cost of, say, 7% per annum, and invested at a much higher rate of about 20% in a weak currency. The difference of 13% per annum was brought into the accounts as a profit. On the other side of the coin, the weak currency depreciated in value during the year by, say, 15%, but this was shown as a reduction of capital in the Balance Sheet. There was a small note in the Annual Report under the heading of Accounting Policies stating that, 'The effect of variances in the exchange rates between the beginning and end of the financial year on the net investment in subsidiary companies is dealt with through reserves.' Easy to see with hindsight.

THE ACCOUNTING REVOLUTION AND FRS3

Sir David Tweedie, the head of the Accounting Standards Board, is a tough guy who takes a very hard-line approach on closing the gaps in accounting practice. In particular, a recent regulation, FRS3, now governs the presentation of profit and loss accounts and has become mandatory for all UK companies.

In the minds of many observers, the new rules have gone a step too far. In the past, there was a distinction between exceptional and extraordinary items – the former had to be deducted from trading profits, but the latter could be shown below the line, so they would not affect earnings. Exceptional items were those that were thought to be unusual but germane to the business and therefore likely to recur in some form in future years: for example, unusually large bad debts and major strikes, both of which are part of the cost of being in business. In contrast, extraordinary items, like discontinuing a business, were excluded because they are unlikely to recur.

Sir David Tweedie has lumped all exceptional and extraordinary items together and makes no distinction – all of them now have to be deducted from profits and, as a result, from earnings per share. This has the desirable effect of removing the decision-making process (whether or not an item is extraordinary or exceptional) from management, but the undesirable effect of distorting the results of all companies, including many with items of expenditure or revenue which could *genuinely* be classified as extraordinary.

The Accounting Standards Board does not object to company management showing their own version of earnings per share in parallel with the mandatory FRS3 presentation. The Board does, however, insist that the management's interpretation is not only fully justified and explained, but also consistently applied. Needless to say, some managements will only bother to show another version when the results are very poor on the basis of FRS3, so the management's version should be treated as suspect, unless it is confirmed by the financial press and brokers.

THE INSTITUTE OF INVESTMENT MANAGEMENT AND RESEARCH (IIMR).

Every analyst aims to arrive at a benchmark figure of earnings per share by which to measure the price-earnings ratios and to establish the growth rates of the companies they are reviewing. Through their professional body, the IIMR, analysts recommend the following adjustments to establish underlying (also called 'headline') earnings per share:

1. All trading profits and losses (including interest), even those of an exceptional nature, should be included in the earnings.

2. Profits and losses on the sale of fixed assets or of a business should be excluded. (This does not apply to assets purchased for resale).

3. Profits and losses arising in activities discontinued during the year, or in activities acquired during the year, should remain in the earnings figure.

4. The costs of eliminating a discontinued operation, or making an acquisition, and the profits and losses on any disposals, should be excluded.

5. Items related to prior periods and the effect of any changes in accounting policy and the correction of previous accounting errors, should be excluded from current earnings.

6. Goodwill should not be brought into the calculations in any way.

7. Changes in pension fund arrangements should be included in the earnings figure and prominently displayed.

8. Capital and trading items in currencies other than the reporting currency should be handled in the same way as the equivalent items arising in the domestic currency.

9. The calculation of the headline earnings number should include tax adjustments to reflect the fact that certain items are excluded from headline earnings.

10. Apart from these adjustments, the calculation of headline earnings should normally reflect the tax charge as shown in the company accounts.

11. Companies should be encouraged to ensure that adequate
    disclosures are made to enable the effect of minority interests to
    be calculated on any adjustments that may be made to arrive at
    the headline figure if these are not already required.

The main thrust of these recommendations is to distinguish between
capital and trading items. Non-trading expenses, like the disposal of
fixed assets or an entire operation, extraordinary litigation costs,
diminution in the value of fixed assets and bid defence costs, would
be taken out to establish the correct headline earnings figure.

The difference between headline earnings and reported FRS3 earnings can be massive. The example given by the IIMR to illustrate their
argument changes pre-tax profits of the company in question from
£45m to £23m and the FRS3 EPS figure of 39p to a headline EPS of
only 20p.

THE INVESTOR'S DILEMMA

Where does all this leave the investor? Sir David Tweedie has tightened
the rules of the game, but as a result he has also made it very difficult
for investors to make judgements of true earnings per share and growth
rates. He argues that he is concerned with making sure that accounting
standards are complied with; he does not want investors to judge
companies from a single (and previously unreliable) figure, such as one
year's earnings per share.

Earnings per share are now shown after extraordinary and exceptional items, which have to be clearly explained. In particular, the
results of acquisitions, other continuing operations and discontinued
operations have to be distinguished between. Your task will be to decide
if any of these items should be added back or deducted, to give you a
truer picture of earnings per share.

Financial journalists and brokers have now become used to the
new reporting standard so their analysis is no longer littered with a
confusing range of profits and earnings figures. The best articles (like
the two examples from the *Investors Chronicle*) will refer to whichever
figure is most meaningful and if there is a marked difference between
underlying and reported profits they will explain what has caused the
disparity.

INVESTORS CHRONICLE

COURTAULDS
Fibres, Coatings, Chemical

Buy

Ord price: 534p			Market value £2.14bn	
Touch: 532-535p			1992-3 High: 618p Low: 370p	
Dividend yield: 3.3%			PE ratio: 14	
Net asset value: 135p			Net debt:40%	

Year to 31 Mar	Turn-over £bn	Pre-tax Profit £000	Stated Earnings per share (p)	Gross Dividend per share (p)
1989	2.61	197	35.7	17.3
1990	2.63	202	39.0	14.8
1991	1.91	186	36.5	16.0
1992†	1.94	186	35.0	17.3
1993†	2.07	193	37.6	17.8
% Change +7	+4		+7	+3

Market makers: 15   Normal market size: 25,000
Last IC comment: 2 April 1993, page 8

Stripping out the effects of FRS3, pre-tax profits and earnings eased very slightly even though the former was boosted by £6m by the lower pound. However that does not detract from a robust performance in difficult conditions.

Continuing business increased sales by 89 per cent but margin pressure meant that operating profits rose by only 1 per cent. Particularly badly hit were the marine coatings and US rayon operations. European markets were generally tough. However Courtaulds has been quick to rationalise problem areas. For instance, last year it closed its Canadian rayon plant in order to streamline North American production. Courtaulds' overall workforce shrank by 8 per cent.

There were bright spots. A £50m order for Light Armoured Vehicles offset continued aerospace weakness to increase profits from performance materials. Courtaulds' relatively immature, Far East arm continued to grow with the booming tiger economies. Most impressively, the new super fibre, Tencel, made a positive contribution and should make profits of £20m a year by the second half of this decade. A £49m payment from its pension fund surplus helped Courtaulds maintain aggressive capital investment and pay down debt to £222m, which allayed fears of a rights issue. Profits this year could rise to £215m, which puts the shares on a future PE of only 13. **That doesn't reflect Courtaulds' underlying quality.**

DIPLOMA
Electronics, building supplies

Fairly priced

Ord price: 489p			Market value £272m	
Touch: 487-490p			1992-3 High: 483p Low: 260p	
Dividend yield: 2.8%			PE ratio: na	
Net asset value: 134p			Net cash: £26m	

Half-year to 31 Mar	Turn-over £m	Pre-tax Profit £m	Stated Earnings per share (p)	Gross Dividend per share (p)
1992†	61.9	2.5	0.5	3.67
1992†	74.0	8.1	9.3	4.38
% Change +20	+224		+1,450	+19

Market makers: 7   Normal market size: 3,000
Last IC comment: 22 May 1992, page 44

These figures were distorted by FRS3, by the acquisition of medical supplies distributor Anachem and by a further £1.1m of rationalisation costs. However, the underlying picture is attractive but appears to be discounted in the share price.

Operating profits from building supplies grew only slowly from £2.3m to £2.7m and it was this arm that took the £1.1m reorganisation hit. The whole division experienced an improving order book as the half progressed and Diploma's chairman, Christopher Thomas, is confident that business will continue to increase. The second half has, so far, been busy.

While Anachem made a first time contribution of £1m, profits in the rest of the electronics arm increased from £2.7m to £4.5m. Diploma distributes semi conductors and other hi-tec electronic equipment, both in the UK and in the USA but it was only in the former market that profits increased. Although Mr Thomas is careful not to talk up the recovery too much, sales are clearly picking up and this business is operationally geared.

Further recovery in both divisions suggests that full year profits could reach £22m according to broker Hoare Govett. **Since underlying earnings will grow by around a third, a future PE ratio of 19 seems reasonable.**

Some shares are difficult to buy and sell. Profits marked (†) are affectd by new accounting rules.

GRAPHS OMITTED.

245

NORMALISED EARNINGS

Brokers' circulars usually present the figures using both FRS3 and 'normalised' earnings. Normalised earnings are based largely on IIMR headline earnings, but there are a few essential differences such as very large redundancy costs, fundamental reorganisation costs and exceptional tax charges.

There is a subjective element in deciding exactly what to exclude from normalised earnings. *Company REFS* uses the following criteria:

1. The amount must be sufficiently large to have a material and distorting effect on the earnings per share trend.

2. It must be clearly identifiable and separate from normal trading.

3. It must be unusual in nature and not expected to recur in the normal course of events.

4. It will have been or is likely to be ignored by most analysts in establishing an actual earnings performance base, upon which to build future estimates.

All of these four criteria must be satisfied for any adjustment to be made to IIMR headline earnings. If any adjustments are made, the tax effect is also calculated and brought into the resultant 'normalised' earnings figure.

Normalised earnings possess three important characteristics:

1. They reflect the underlying *trading* performance of the company.

2. They can be used as a *measure* of performance against expectations.

3. They clarify the *historic record of the operating performance* of a company.

The main limitation of normalised earnings is that they reflect the results achieved by the business during an accounting period when a company had a certain structure which may have changed. For example, normalised earnings include the results of trading businesses which have been discontinued or sold and only part of the results of companies acquired during the year.

You can see that, in a way, the whole exercise of calculating earnings per share has gone full circle. FRS3 became necessary because there was so much abuse, but it was so draconian that analysts have found it necessary to calculate their way back to a kind of pre-FRS3 position. The main difference today is that the basis of the calculations does not now depend on the judgement of a company's directors, and every exceptional item is analysed in a harsher light.

Company REFS uses normalised earnings for its key statistics but also gives details of historic, IIMR and FRS3 earnings and cash flow. The consensus forecasts in *The Estimate Directory* and *Earnings Guide* are based on brokers' individual forecasts which obviously cannot anticipate exceptional events so they are comparable with historic normalised earnings. For their historic data *Datastream* has decided to stick to FRS3 earnings

RECONCILE CASH FLOW

One of the most reliable cross-checks on earnings is a company's cash flow during the same period. I explain how to reconcile operating profits and operating cash flow in Chapter 13. In 1991, for instance, ICI had profits before tax of £1bn and excellent operating cash flow of £1.5bn. In contrast, British Aerospace had profits before tax and exceptional items of £154m, and operating cash inflow of minus £95m. A prize also goes to Polly Peck, which in its farewell set of accounts showed pre-tax profits up 44% at £161m – but in the new style of cash flow statements, NatWest Securities calculated that the operating cash *outflow* would have been £129m. The main reason was a staggering increase in working capital of £288m. When there is a large divergence the wrong way, you know that creative accounting has been at work.

Whatever else you do, keep an eye open for profit boosting by the methods I have mentioned and cross-check operating profits with operating cash flow. Growing cash in hand is always comforting to see in the balance sheet – unlike earnings per share, cash is hard to fake. Always read the Annual Report and Accounts from beginning to end and remember that footnote 25(d) or even 17(e) might contain a very important message for you.

CONVERTIBLES

Before ending this chapter of caveats, I must mention two more areas where you need to remain alert: the issue of convertible shares, options and warrants, and fluctuations in the rate of tax being paid by a company.

Any calculation of earnings per share should allow for convertible loan stocks, bonds and preference shares being converted and options and warrants being exercised. Where these total less than 10% of the shares in issue, they are not worth complicating your thinking, so I suggest that you ignore them. The conversion of a loan will save some interest, and the exercise of warrants or options will bring fresh cash into the company. There will be a little dilution of earnings, but not enough to worry about.

Fortunately, the calculations are usually made for you. All the options and convertibles are shown in the Notes to the Accounts under the heading of Called-up Share Capital or something similar, and the potential effect of reinvesting the proceeds is reflected in earnings per share.

TAXATION

Frequently, companies have tax losses brought forward that are available to set off against current profits. This can result in an abnormally low tax charge flattering earnings per share in the year during which the tax loss is used. Earnings per share growth is based upon earnings after tax. The tax charge should therefore be adjusted back to a normal level to obtain a true picture. Companies operating in enterprise zones and companies in Ireland often enjoy tax breaks and receive capital grants. Heavy capital expenditure in some engineering and leasing companies also lowers the tax charge.

I am not suggesting that you should worry unduly about the complications of company taxation. Normally, a company pays out about a third of its profits in taxation. If profits before tax were £12m you would usually expect profits after tax to be about £8m. If profits after tax were £10m, tax would have been levied at only 16.7%, about half the normal rate. In that event, you should ask your broker why the tax charge is so low or try to find out from press comment or the company's accounts. The main worry about a low tax charge is that it might suddenly revert to a normal rate and stunt earnings per share growth as a result.

The key point is to try to determine if a company paying a low tax charge will in future continue to pay low taxes or whether the benefit will suddenly come to an end. If it is the latter, try to recalculate earnings per share (with your broker's help if necessary) and base your earnings figures on a normal tax charge of about a third.

SUMMARY

1. Sir David Tweedie, through the Accounting Standards Board, is rapidly lifting accounting standards and putting the profession's house in order.

2. There will always be some scope for creative accounting, so be on the alert and read press and broker comment carefully. You should also make a point of reading the detailed notes to the Report and Accounts (sometimes called the Financial Statement) as well as the Chairman's Statement. Read all documents you receive from your selected companies from cover to cover. Be on the alert for warning signals like qualification of the Auditor's Report or a proposed change of auditor.

3. If you want to understand creative accounting better, I suggest you read Chapter 4 of *The Zulu Principle*.

4. Meanwhile, keep your eyes open for press and broker comment drawing attention to profit boosting. The best possible cross-check is to compare operating profits with operating cash flow as explained in Chapter 13. Your broker should be able to tell you if there is a large divergence between the two figures, in which case creative accounting has probably been at work.

5. Earnings per share are now presented in accordance with FRS3 so that both extraordinary and exceptional items are included in the results. However, brokers and the press have now accepted a common standard for normalised earnings based upon IIMR headline earnings with the further adjustments explained in detail in this chapter. In particular, this has helped to distinguish capital profits and losses from trading revenue.

6. *Company REFS* uses normalised earnings for its key statistics but also gives details of historic, IIMR and FRS3 earnings and cash flow. The consensus forecasts in *The Estimate Directory* and *Earnings Guide* are based on brokers' individual forecasts, which obviously cannot anticipate exceptional events and are therefore comparable with historic normalised earnings. *Datastream* has decided to stick to FRS3 earnings for its historic data.

7. Whenever convertibles, options and warrants total more than 10% of the share capital, adjust earnings figures by assuming dilution and potential interest savings.

8. Adjust earnings to allow for a normal tax charge if the tax for the year has been reduced as a result of a non-recurring event.

The introduction of FRS3 is nothing to be alarmed about. Before FRS3, there were so many abuses of accounting standards that all EPS and growth rate figures were suspect. Some companies made little or no use of creative accounting, others went to town, using every possible device to boost earnings. Many investors did not realise that this was happening on such a large scale. At least, now, the relevant facts about exceptional and extraordinary items are clearly stated and the press, brokers and analysts are aware of the devices, which are more likely to be highlighted and explained.

19

THE SELECTION PROCESS

Learn how to use a series of sieves to select the officers from the army of growth stocks.

Let us take stock of the progress you have made so far:

1. You should have a better understanding of the language and jargon of finance.

2. You are aware of the key points in company accounts. In particular, you know that you cannot rely upon earnings per share figures without reading the accounts and checking press and broker comment.

3. You know how to find and appoint a helpful stockbroker who will cater for your needs.

4. You know the criteria for selecting a leading growth share.

5. You know how to buy a leading growth share at the right price – on a P/E ratio that is low in relation to the growth rate.

All that remains now is to put theory into practice. To begin with, you could try running a ghost portfolio, but that is never quite the same as real money and no stockbroker is going to help you without the incentive of earning some commission.

An execution-only broker will take your account, however small. A more traditional broker will probably need you to start with £5,000 to £10,000. Let us assume that you have set aside £9,000 as patient money which would be just right for taking advantage of the maximum annual PEP allowance. A married couple could have £9,000 in each of their names.

Your aim is to find future growth shares which meet the twelve criteria listed in Chapter 16. Some of the requirements, like excellent brand names and attractive sectors of industry, you will know yourself or can easily ascertain. You will, of course, be reading the financial section of your daily newspapers and some extra reading that I will recommend in Chapter 23. Once you begin to direct your mind that way, you will be surprised how quickly you get a feel for the financial pulse of the stock market and for the individual companies in which you are actively interested.

THROUGH THE SIEVE

If you were intent upon forming a private army of 100 men aged between twenty-one and thirty, and you advertised in the national press, you might receive as many as 5,000 replies. At an early stage, your task would be to sieve the applicants you decided to interview. Your aim would be to end up with an aggressive elite force of 100 strong and intelligent men. Your first sieve would be their IQ, determined, perhaps, by their ability to gain a certain standard in a written examination. Your second sieve might be to reject the men who could not pass a tough physical fitness test. Your third would be to select only those with an aggressive temperament. For officer material, you would then look further at the men with past experience and the right kind of personality and character.

Picking shares is just the same. You start off with 350 applications from all the leading shares. You are looking for officer material among this already elite group; you only need to select a maximum of ten.

Your broker can help you with Company REFS or Datastream to apply a few of the necessary sieves and then you (aided by your daily reading and this book) and your broker (aided by his or her experience and knowledge of the market) will apply the rest. Each sieve will rule out large numbers of applicants and, in the end, you will be left with an elite force of officers – shares that have passed all the tests.

Once you have selected a really good growth share you can usually sit back to enjoy compound earnings growth. Of course, there will be the occasional upset but, if you have chosen well, there will be many more long-term winners than losers.

SOME SUGGESTED CRITERIA

If you intend to concentrate on quality growth stocks from the top 350 companies, you need to establish some selection criteria to reduce the list to a manageable number of potential investments. Here are a few suggested sieves:

1. Earnings per share growth of at least 100% over the last five years.*

2. Earnings per share growth of at least 10% over the last year.

3. Only one earnings setback during the last five years.

4. A return on capital employed of at least 20% a year.

5. Borrowings to be less than 50% of net assets.

6. Dividends to have been at least maintained during the last five years.

If you want to be even stricter, you could add a few more sieves of your own. For example, you might decide to buy shares only when the directors have been net buyers during the preceding six months, or you might decide to exclude shares with shrinking profit margins and/or reducing returns on capital employed.

It may surprise you to know that in May 1995 fewer than 20 companies out of the 350 would have passed through the six main sieves listed above and less than half of those would have been *really reliable in terms of future earnings*. Quality companies like Reuters

---

*This is a harsh criterion. A less demanding alternative is *Company REFS'* measure of a growth share, which requires four years of earnings per share growth whether it be past or a combination of past and future.

and Rentokil were not surprisingly included, but at a price. The trouble is that other investors are well aware of their attractions. As a result, the shares of Reuters, in particular, appear to be *relatively* expensive, both in relation to the market and to its sector.

There is still an argument for buying shares of such high calibre, even if you have to pay a premium for the privilege. In May 1995, Reuters, for example, had a relatively high forward price-earnings ratio of 17.7 and a quite expensive PEG of 1.13. The growth has, however, been very reliable in the past and even if it slows down a little it looks like being so in the future. The *Company REFS* graph shows the share price with the solid black line and the relative strength against the market with the dotted line. The two plots should be read separately. The circular dots joined by a solid black line show past earnings per share and those joined by a dotted line show the brokers' consensus forecast of future earnings per share for the current and following years.

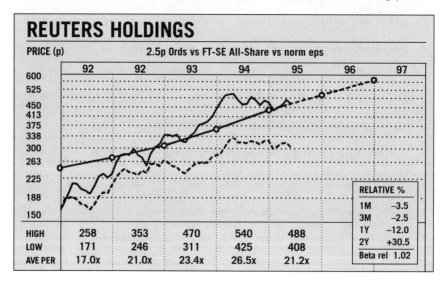

Even if your timing is a little out, within a year with projected growth of 10–15%, your purchase price would become much more reasonable in relation to earnings. However, if there was an earnings setback, the shares would come tumbling down from their relatively high multiple, as investors rushed for the exit. To minimise the risk of a downwards status change, you should always consider the twelve criteria I have outlined in Chapter 16.

The most important of these criteria is competitive advantage or, as Warren Buffett puts it, 'a strong business franchise'. You can check the super-profits resulting from a company's edge over its competitors by examining its returns on capital employed. To make sure that the competitive advantage is at least being maintained, you can also check the recent trends of sales, profit margin and return on capital employed. In 1994-5, both Reuters and Rentokil passed all of these tests with flying colours.

It is also important to check that net cash flow from operating activities is at least the same as, and preferably more than, operating profits, as explained in Chapter 13. Fortunately, super growth stocks of great stature rarely use creative accounting in a big way and are often very strong cash generators. There is therefore usually very little to worry about on this score. It is interesting to note that Terry Smith in his book, *Accounting for Growth*, awarded no black blobs for creative accounting to Rentokil and only two to Reuters; the possible total was twelve with companies like Grand Metropolitan having nine,

Guinness five and an average for industrial companies of about four.

Another sieve that I sometimes use is the relative strength of selected shares against the market as a whole. Each month REFS gives details of the relative strength of all shares over the previous month, two months, year and two years. In a bull market, it often pays to buy shares which are within 15% of their two year high and seem to be performing relatively well. However, in a bear market this idea does not work so well.

You will remember that one of my twelve criteria for selecting a growth share is to make sure that the company is in an attractive sector.

Shipbuilders and housebuilders are far too cyclical to become great growth stocks. Airlines have their difficulties too. When Richard Branson was asked how to become a millionaire, he replied that first you become a billionaire and then you buy an airline.

Reverting to our two earlier examples, Reuters is in the Media sector, and Rentokil is in Support Services. In the past, both sectors have enjoyed considerable growth and this seems very likely to continue in the future. I want to make it absolutely clear that I am not recommending the purchase of Reuters, Rentokil or any other share. By the time you read this book the investment statistics I have referred to will already be out of date. I am simply trying to show you the way to select the 'officers' from the 'army' of 350 leading shares. It is the *approach* that you should concentrate upon – not the individual shares.

INTER-LINKING CRITERIA

I hope you can see how my selection criteria tend to inter-link. A company with a strong competitive advantage and a resultant high return on capital employed has little need for creative accounting; the management is probably more concerned to report the lowest possible profit in order to save tax. This kind of company will also naturally generate a great deal of cash and tend to have substantial cash balances or negligible debt. In stark contrast, companies with little or no competitive advantage are always struggling to put on the bravest possible face and present the most favourable picture to the investment community, so that they can raise more money when necessary. They tend to have growing debt and plenty of problems. They are to be avoided – you are looking for cash-generators not cash-eaters.

SMALLER GROWTH COMPANIES

The famous American investor, T. Rowe Price, was widely known as the father of growth stocks. For many years, American investors had regarded all stocks as rising or falling with the economic cycle. Rowe Price had different ideas; in 1939, he wrote 'Earnings of most corporations pass through a life cycle which, like the human life cycle, has three important phases – growth, maturity and decadence.' Rowe Price invested in young stocks which he thought would be likely to grow faster than the economy. He was particularly keen on three key financial measures, the trends of sales per share, margins and return on capital.

There is a great deal to be said for investing in small-to-medium-sized growth stocks to catch their early heady growth phase. In their infancy, companies like Reuters and Rentokil were superb investment opportunities. In contrast, companies like Coloroll and Ratners may have seemed at one stage to have excellent future prospects, but they could not keep up the pace and soon ran into difficulties. You can see from these few examples that, if you choose the right stocks, there is an extra reward and equally, if your initial choice is wrong, you can lose your entire investment.

There is no doubt that on average over the last forty years small companies have performed better than the market as a whole. A Hoare Govett study showed that between 1955 and 1993 small companies appreciated in value 4.3% per annum better than the FT-SE All-Share Index.

Small company dividends also grow faster. A most startling statistic demonstrates this well and also proves the power of reinvesting gross dividends. £1,000 invested in 1955 in the companies making up the bottom tenth of the market would have become worth £89,000 by the end of 1994. However, with dividends reinvested gross (as you can in a PEP), the £89,000 would have been transformed into an astonishing £800,000. This performance would have been about four times better than the index over the same period.

In my book, *The Zulu Principle*, I refer to larger companies as 'elephants' and make the comment that 'elephants don't gallop'. I also refer to smaller companies as 'fleas' and observe that they 'can jump over 200 times their own body height'. The interesting question is why smaller companies should perform so much better than larger ones. To my mind, there are a number of reasons:

1. It is far easier to grow from a small base. To double profits of £500,000 to £1m is a much easier task than doubling profits from £50m to £100m. Every large company began life as a small company.

2. Small companies frequently operate in highly profitable niche markets that are not sufficiently large to attract competition from major companies. For small companies it frequently takes many years of above-average growth before they reach saturation point in their particular niche market.

3. A discovery or technical breakthrough by a small hi-tech or

bio-tech company can have a dramatic effect on the company's share price and its market capitalisation. Similar discoveries by GEC or ICI might have a barely noticeable impact on their shares.

4. Small companies are frequently highly geared operationally, so a small increase in sales can have a disproportionate impact on profits. If things go well this can be a considerable advantage.

5. Small companies invariably have younger management which is usually highly motivated by much larger percentage share-holdings.

6. Small company management is less hampered by corporate infra-structure and tradition. This makes management more venture-some and less prone to inertia.

7. In general, small companies are far more likely to be taken over.

However, do not become too excited. Every one of these advantages has within it the seeds of a potential disadvantage which is worth examining in more detail:

1. Operational risks are greater. Small companies tend to borrow more heavily, lack reserves and are less likely to be backed by banks at critical moments.

2. Small companies are usually less diversified. This can be an advan-tage in good times, but diversification can be a comfort if the out-look turns bleak.

3. Small companies are usually more dependent on their home market, as they are unlikely to have had sufficient corporate life to have developed a substantial export business.

4. The stock market is often inclined to overestimate the prospects of small hi-tech and bio-tech companies.

5. Young management is obviously less experienced and less able to deal with a turndown in business or a major setback.

Over and above all of these disadvantages, the market in small company shares is usually thin, with fewer marketmakers (sometimes only one) and much larger percentage spreads. If your selection is wrong you can often be stuck with the shares until a substantial buyer comes to your rescue.

If you want to succeed in the small company jungle, it is absolutely essential to do your homework. Small companies tend to be much less well-researched than companies in the FT-SE All-Share Index. Reliable statistics and forecasts are often hard to find, although I believe that Company REFS has come to the rescue of the small investor with a wealth of monthly (or quarterly) key investment statistics and information. The principles for selecting shares remain exactly the same as for larger companies, but the difference between being right or wrong is much more extreme. To put it in a word, investing in small companies is *dangerous* unless you have a method and know exactly what you are doing. Of course, you will make mistakes, but the importance of having a method is that you can gradually refine and improve it as you learn from past errors of judgement.

If you are keen to invest in small companies, I suggest that you first read my book, *The Zulu Principle*, and Peter Lynch's two books, *Beating the Street*, and *One Up On Wall Street*. Then I recommend *Company REFS*, initially on a quarterly basis. Study the guide book, in particular, as it sets out how each and every statistic is calculated and how it should be used for stock selection.

Do not be in a hurry to invest in small companies. Proceed gingerly and with the utmost caution. Over a period the luck element is likely to average out and the financial rewards of investing in small companies should bear a very direct relationship to the effort you put into it.

20

HIGH YIELDERS

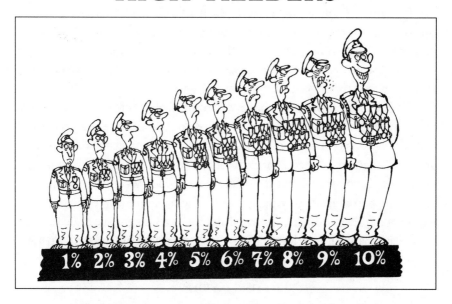

If you need income, carefully selected stocks can give you both an above-average yield and long-term capital growth.

ALTERNATIVE METHODS OF INVESTMENT

There are several different methods of approaching the basic principle of investing in growth stocks. You could, for example, build a well-spread portfolio of growth stocks in emerging and fast-developing regions like China, India and Latin America. Alternatively, some investors prefer to base all their decisions on technical factors, studying supply and demand, volume and chart patterns. They are not concerned by fundamentals like earnings per share growth and balance sheet strength, as they argue that all of these are reflected in the share price.

Other, very different, approaches to investment have little do with growth. Instead, they weed out high-yielding shares, or those with assets substantially in excess of share prices, or cyclical stocks due for a bounce. The main snag of following any of these methods is that your final selections tend to have a shorter time fuse and need to be watched more closely. You buy them with a comparatively limited objective in mind. With a high yielder, you sell when the yield drops to a more normal level. With a cyclical, you wait for the cycle to turn, and with an asset situation (using value analysis) you sell when the share price rises nearer to underlying asset value or there is a bid for the company.

In contrast, once you have chosen the right growth shares, you can reasonably hope for a long and happy ride. Obviously, you have to keep an eye subsequently on the companies in question, but, on most occasions, you can look forward to at least a few years of above-average growth and substantial capital gains.

In *The Zulu Principle*, I have written full chapters on turnarounds and cyclicals, asset situations and value analysis. Some investors find it difficult to pay a high multiple for an excellent growth stock and prefer instead to hunt for bargains that are well backed by assets or a high yield. If you think that this kind of approach would suit your temperament better than buying growth stocks, I suggest you read *The Zulu Principle* post-haste. Meanwhile, I will try to give you the flavour of investing in high-yielding stocks, just to give you the general idea of an alternative method of investing.

CUTTING DIVIDENDS

It is argued with some justification that well-chosen high-yielding stocks tend to out-perform the market. I say 'well-chosen' because many stocks that appear to have a high yield can be on the brink of cutting their dividends.

No company reduces its dividend lightly, as stock market confidence in management is immediately affected by a reduction. Companies only cut their dividends when there is little choice – when profits are down drastically or cash is in short supply. Even then, many companies prefer to have a rights issue (raise money from their shareholders) and use a proportion of the proceeds to pay a dividend (back to the same shareholders). This is an absurd and very tax-inefficient idea when you think about it, because many shareholders have to find the money out of taxed income to subscribe for the rights issue, only to receive back income which has been taxed again. Nevertheless, you can see why many leading companies are tempted to do this – arguably, confidence would have been severely eroded if P & O had raised less money in its 1992 rights issue and cut its dividend instead. Raising cash from shareholders to pay them dividends has now become accepted as normal practice in the UK, although the press and some investors are beginning to query the logic.

One way for a company to pay shareholders a dividend while at the same time avoiding a cash outflow is to give them shares instead. This is called a scrip dividend. The practice, which had been falling into disuse, was revived in 1992 by a number of large companies including BAT, the tobacco and insurance group.

According to current tax law in the UK, when a company pays a dividend it is obliged to send a proportion (now 20%) to the Inland Revenue. Because this can be offset against future taxes on profits, it is known as Advance Corporation Tax or ACT.

However, ACT can only be offset against UK profits, which for many international groups have been a dwindling proportion of the whole through the recession. Many companies have had to write off substantial amounts of ACT.

Offering shareholders new shares works for the company because ACT is only paid on cash dividends. The practice only makes sense for shareholders themselves if the shares are likely to remain a good investment.

THE OFFICERS OF HIGH YIELD

So, bearing in mind the caveat that high yields can presage dividend cuts, we are now intent upon selecting, say, ten officers of high yield from the army of stocks in the 350 Index. The first task is to reduce the size of the army; this is achieved by simply eliminating all those shares with prospective yields of less than the level you set – say, half as much again as the market average. In May 1995, the right kind of minimum requirement would have been about 6.7% per annum, so only the shares forecast to yield more would survive this sieve. You will notice the key word 'forecast' – it is used deliberately because a prospective dividend yield is not always a reliable guide to the future, although sometimes brokers' forecasts are all you have to go on.

As you can see from the page of high-yielding shares from the Tables Volume of *Company REFS*, there were only seven companies in the FT-SE 100 Index that, in March 1995, had prospective dividend yields for the twelve months immediately ahead of over 6.7% per annum, and there were only nineteen in the 250 Index. Our

FT-SE 100 – HIGHEST DIVIDEND YIELDS
Highest dividend yields based on consensus forecast for the 12 months ahead.

page	Mkt Cap £m	1 Mo Rel Str %	Share price (p) 12 Months High	Low	Recent	Company	Prosp DY %	Prosp Div Cov x	Prosp PER	5-Year Eps Growth Rate %	Prosp Eps Growth Rate %	Last AR Net gear %	PCF
	10,142	−0.6			514	Index weighted average	4.91	2.2	12.4	2.5	12.6	36.0	11.4
	3,013	−1.0			429	Index median	4.82	2.1	12.5	0.9	11.2	31.7	9.1
598	2,218	−0.0	570	416	428	Redland	7.33	1.4	11.9	−18.3	16.5	26.3	5.8
711	1,896	+1.8	555	435	475	Thames Water	7.03	2.7	6.6	na	3.3	42.3	6.5
71	12,805	−8.2	473	372	416	B.A.T	7.00	2.0	9.0	1.6	17.6	46.4	9.0
325	2,456	+3.3	653	491	542	General Accident	6.94	2.2	8.2	−12.2	−4.1	na	na
552	3,375	−1.8	741	558	560	P & O	6.90	1.3	14.0	−15.1	8.1	52.5	9.3
525	1,946	+1.7	602	457	507	North West Water	6.78	2.7	6.7	na	6.5	38.5	5.9
650	1,826	+0.3	606	462	499	Severn Trent	6.74	3.1	6.0	na	15.4	27.1	4.8
204	3,199	+1.6	593	474	511	Commercial Union	6.68	1.7	10.9	−6.7	−2.9	na	na
359	12,204	+0.4	275	220	235	Hanson	6.66	1.6	11.8	−5.4	20.8	50.9	21.9
692	2,518	+3.9	352	284	312	Sun Alliance	6.59	2.4	7.8	−20.6	10.5	na	na
127	12,711	−4.8	315	253	293	British Gas	6.54	1.6	12.2	−1.7	18.6	69.6	5.8
400	1,553	−7.5	565	294	295	Inchcape	6.53	1.7	11.0	5.3	3.9	18.9	7.9
439	2,186	+2.5	485	408	446	Legal & General	6.46	1.3	14.4	1.6	22.6	na	na
448	7,420	+3.0	597	522	572	Lloyds Bank	6.35	2.2	9.0	21.2	6.0	na	na
330	19,366	+1.7	692	532	634	Glaxo	6.32	1.5	12.8	13.2	8.1	12.2	11.0

FT-SE MID 250 – HIGHEST DIVIDEND YIELDS
Highest dividend yields based on consensus forecast for the 12 months ahead.

page	Mkt Cap £m	1 Mo Rel Str %	Share price (p) 12 Months High	Low	Recent	Company	Prosp DY %	Prosp Div Cov x	Prosp PER	5-Year Eps Growth Rate %	Prosp Eps Growth Rate %	Last AR Net gear %	PCF
	958	−1.0			361	Index weighted average	4.56	2.5	13.6	−2.1	17.5	24.6	12.2
	477	−2.0			257	Index median	4.53	2.3	12.3	−1.2	13.6	16.0	9.1
17	304	−5.2	63.2	41.5	43	Albert Fisher Group	10.9	1.1	10.0	−14.8	10.1	48.1	5.9
356	398	−7.7	393	214	225	Hambros	8.57	1.3	11.1	−6.3	39.6	na	na
470	398	−7.9	177	155	155	Man (E D & F) Group	8.05	2.1	7.3	na	4.1	241	−21.2
362	995	−0.7	201	136	142	Harrisons & Crossfield	7.98	1.2	13.3	−16.4	25.9	48.2	11.0
367	248	+0.7	152	104	107	Hazlewood Foods	7.97	1.7	9.3	−1.5	5.4	90.4	5.6
88	1,108	+2.5	460	303	313	BICC	7.72	1.2	13.3	−20.9	18.7	71.8	7.0
105	848	−4.0	460	378	378	Booker	7.65	1.4	12.0	−6.8	12.9	73.8	6.7
673	627	+3.6	578	462	498	South West Water	7.37	2.5	6.9	na	1.4	74.4	6.8
556	198	−1.9	293	170	171	Persimmon	7.32	2.0	8.7	−17.8	19.4	20.7	13.3
377	237	+0.9	413	247	253	Heywood Williams	7.30	1.7	10.1	−18.8	16.3	−16.4	14.7
699	842	+4.9	260	144	159	T & N	7.26	1.6	10.5	−13.8	na	55.6	6.0
570	389	−11.3	660	454	454	Powell Duffryn	7.21	1.6	10.5	−3.7	11.0	17.5	7.7
453	391	+5.1	391	282	324	London & Manchester	7.16	1.2	14.5	7.9	4.2	na	na
31	1,408	−0.7	602	446	475	Anglian Water	7.08	2.6	6.7	na	4.0	35.6	5.0
378	223	+4.2	223	114	127	Hickson	7.02	1.4	13.0	−14.0	−4.9	51.3	6.5
442	266	−6.3	545	279	279	Lex Service	7.01	2.3	7.9	−20.8	18.8	4.7	−29.5
739	811	−2.4	409	319	347	Unigate	6.77	1.8	10.5	4.0	0.0	46.0	7.2
702	986	−6.8	186	107	107	Tarmac	6.75	1.8	10.4	−44.3	35.5	18.3	7.5
374	688	−2.5	409	282	283	Hepworth	6.70	1.6	11.6	−10.5	15.7	16.7	8.8
381	1,220	+0.4	187	152	177	Hillsdown	6.66	1.7	11.3	−16.0	7.6	47.4	5.7
231	977	+4.4	489	394	425	Dalgety	6.65	1.7	11.1	2.6	1.6	33.2	6.6
806	1,030	+4.2	609	461	510	Yorkshire Water	6.63	3.1	6.0	na	15.5	18.1	4.0
158	429	−7.3	340	255	255	Calor	6.59	1.6	11.6	−1.9	5.8	−2.8	7.0
342	539	−1.3	222	169	174	Great Portland Estates	6.51	1.1	17.4	−0.3	3.5	54.9	16.6
434	168	−10.8	367	186	186	John Laing	6.45	1.6	11.9	−20.6	−14.3	−25.3	11.6
201	1,256	+1.0	248	173	179	Coats Viyella	6.42	1.7	11.3	−4.9	9.0	37.1	8.1
532	430	−3.8	299	245	279	Ocean Group	6.42	1.6	12.3	−4.8	30.6	16.8	8.9
675	914	+0.9	632	468	540	Southern Water	6.38	2.9	6.8	na	5.2	8.8	5.4
727	278	−6.2	267	188	188	Transport Development	6.37	1.6	11.9	−4.7	10.5	8.0	4.5
780	857	−0.0	336	263	277	Wessex Water	6.34	2.8	7.1	na	6.8	−4.4	6.1

first sieve therefore reduces our army of 350 to only twenty-six companies.

The sieving process for selecting a high-yielding portfolio is very different from the one you would use for growth shares. When focusing on growth, you try to select companies with strong balance sheets, a competitive advantage and an attractive price-earnings ratio in relation to their above-average growth rate. Any shares that do not measure up to these criteria, and the others that I have specified, are immediately eliminated with a view to leaving a select few which are 'officer' material.

With high-yielding shares, the risk factor is much greater. The companies in question are usually high-yielding for very good reasons, which include doubts about the future growth of what is probably a cyclical business, doubts about the dividend being maintained, doubts about the balance sheet (which perhaps has excessive gearing) and even doubts about the future survival of the company. You do not want to eliminate any companies simply because you have a *few* worries about them. If you did so, you would end up with hardly any shares in your high-yielding portfolio. Your main objective should be simply to remove the obviously hopeless cases and *spread* your money over the rest.

For security, you would normally need about ten shares in a high-yielding portfolio selected from the 350 Index.

Reverting to our list of twenty-six shares, it would be advisable to remove any with dividend cover of less than 1.5 times. (In the hardback edition of this book, I suggested cover of only 0.75, but in May 1993 there were fewer candidates and, on reflection, I chose too low a target figure.) This means that the residual list of companies will have the cost of their dividends covered at least 1.5 times by profits after tax. As you can see, the dividend cover is set out in the second column on the right hand side of the *REFS* table, so it is an easy exercise to reduce the list to the following seventeen companies:

Thames Water   Heywood Williams
BAT   T & N
General Accident   Powell Duffryn
North West Water   Anglian Water
Severn Trent   Lex Service
Man (ED & F) Group   Unigate
Hazlewood Foods   Tarmac
South West Water   Hepworth
Persimmon

HIGH GEARING

To reduce the risks still further, another important step is to eliminate any shares with excessive gearing. I normally suggest an upper limit of 50%, but to be on the safe side, we can reduce this to 40%. This will result in losing some promising companies, but it is a small price to pay to add to the safety level of your selections.

You can obtain details of the gearing of any company from its accounts, from brokers' circulars, from press comment such as the annual reviews in the *Investors Chronicle*, from the *Hambro Company Guide*, from *Company REFS*, or simply by asking your broker.

As you can see from the *Company REFS* table, the net borrowings criterion of not more than 40% would eliminate from our list Man Group with gearing of 241%, Hazlewood Foods with 90.4%, and South West Water with 74.4% and four other companies which were a little over the limit.

THE FINAL LIST

Here is the final list of ten residual companies from the leading 350 shares in March 1995:

Company	Price p	Yield %
General Accident	542	6.94
North West Water	507	6.78
Severn Trent	499	6.74
Persimmon	171	7.32
Heywood Williams	253	7.30
Powell Duffryn	454	7.21
Anglian Water	475	7.08
Lex Service	279	7.01
Tarmac	107	6.75
Hepworth	283	6.70
Average Yield		6.98

The next step is to ask your broker to make sure that none of the companies you have selected has issued a profit warning. If you subscribe to *Company REFS*, you can simply turn to the individual company entries in the Companies Volume to check that earnings per share forecasts are satisfactory and no profit warnings have been issued. You are not looking for massive growth in earnings – just reasonably stable levels.

An alternative is to make your selections more automatic. If you prefer this approach, you could devise another mild selection sieve such as 'forecast earnings per share not to be down more than 10% compared with the previous year' or 'forecast earnings per share to be at least the same as the previous year'.

We were originally searching for ten officers of high yield and we were lucky to find exactly that number. If we had only found nine, there would have been no harm in selecting the last company by relaxing one of the criteria. For example, Thames Water had net a gearing of 42.3% which was just over the 40% limit. However, there were already several water companies among the selections and as the regulator might turn nasty to investors (albeit nice to consumers), you might have decided instead to give the last place in your list to BAT.

As a result of all of your sieves, the companies you select will, according to the brokers' consensus forecasts, have prospective dividend yields of not less than 6.7% per annum, percentage gearing (net of cash) of under 40% and prospective dividend cover of not less than 1.5 times. For investors who needed a well above average yield of almost 7% in March 1995, the ten selected shares constituted a *relatively* safe portfolio with the hope of some capital growth and perhaps a re-rating.

I would like to emphasise that if you checked *Company REFS* today, or even the April issue instead of the March one, you would obtain a different selection of shares. For example, the highest yielder in the FT-SE 100 in March was Redland, which cut its dividend during the month. Share prices, prospective yields, forecasts and reported profits are constantly changing. The key point to grasp is the *approach* to analysis, so please bear in mind that the above list of shares is now very out-of-date and *is not in any sense a current recommendation.*

WEIGHTING THE PORTFOLIO

The basic principle of investing in high-yielding shares is a sound one. You must use a series of sieves to select the best shares and try to eliminate the obvious dangers. Whatever sieves you adopt, do not hesitate to adapt them from time to time for personal preferences, and on your broker's advice. The important caveat is to measure your results against the market and check regularly whether or not your sieves are working. If not, try to work out what went wrong with the failures and see if you can tighten your sieves to improve future results.

An alternative approach is to weight your investments towards those shares that satisfy a higher level of selective criteria. Instead of investing equally in each of the ten remaining shares, you can, for example, allocate one unit only for companies that fulfil all the basic criteria, 50% more for companies that have gearing of less than 25%, and perhaps another 50% if the dividend is more than twice covered or the company is forecast to increase earnings per share over the next two years.

INVESTORS CHRONICLE

You might be interested to know that, using rather different sieves, the *Investors Chronicle* selects a high-yield portfolio from time to time. Over the years it has been successful and, more often than not, outperforms the UK market as a whole.

In April 1995, the *Investors Chronicle* began another high-yield portfolio with the following *main* rules:

1. To buy the highest-yielding securities available in the London market (excluding 4:2 companies; financial, property and mining companies; and companies with one controlling shareholder).

2. To sell any stocks that pass their dividends and replace them with the same number of the next highest-yielding security available.

It also expanded its previous criteria to insist upon dividend cover of 1.5 times, consensus profit forecasts showing at least two years growth in both earnings and dividends, and above average cash flow.

The resultant portfolio was very different from the one obtained by using my sieves, mainly because the *Investors Chronicle* used a much wider universe than the 350 Index. Interestingly though, even amongst their leading company selections, there were no shares common to both portfolios. Another reason is that it had no sieve for levels of gearing, although some of its other criteria were much more stringent than mine. The one I found most interesting was the requirement of two years of forecast future growth in both earnings and dividends. My suggestion of not more than a 10% fall in future earnings was comparatively undemanding, but if I had applied this *Investors Chronicle* criterion to the ten shares that came through my sieves, only General Accident would have been a casualty. On reflection therefore, I believe that it makes sense to use this extra sieve in future. I have taken you through the evolution of my thinking on selecting high-yielding shares to show you how your own criteria can be developed and strengthened as you learn from both experience and example.

BEATING THE DOW

A very attractive alternative approach to high-yield investment is recommended by Michael O'Higgins, the American investor, who has written an interesting book, *Beating the Dow*. He argues that it is easy to beat the US market, if you use his system.

O'Higgins takes the ten highest yielding stocks from the Dow 30 Share Index and then selects the five with the lowest share prices. At the end of each year, he does the whole exercise again. His statistics show that if you had followed this system over a period of about eighteen years, you would have enjoyed an average annual gain of 19.43%, compared with only 10.43% for the Dow. The five-stock portfolio out-performed the Dow in fifteen years and lost money only in 1974 and 1990, when the Dow was also down. After adding dividends received, but with no charge for commissions, the cumulative gain before tax was more than 2,800% against only 560% for the Dow.

The underlying rationale of O'Higgins' simple approach is that the thirty companies in the Dow are all of a size and substance that should ensure their future survival, even in extreme circumstances. Union Carbide's Bhopal plant blowing up was, for example, only a very large setback for that company. For a smaller one, it could have been terminal.

The second argument is that stock markets over-react. On good news, greed propels shares to dizzy heights. On bad news, fear drives them downwards to bargain-basement levels. The highest yielders tend to be companies that are out of favour. They usually have good asset backing and, instead of froth in their share prices, there is often a discount for fear.

You might wonder why O'Higgins selects companies with the lowest share prices. He argues that they usually have smaller market capitalisations and therefore tend to register greater percentage gains than larger ones. This particular criterion seems a trifle primitive to me, but I share O'Higgins' enthusiasm for smaller companies. As I say in *The Zulu Principle*, 'Elephants don't gallop.'

I was so intrigued by O'Higgins' book that, with the help of Johnson Fry, I researched what would have happened if his system had been applied to the UK market. The results were all computed on a dividends-reinvested basis and were staggeringly good. Over the ten years ended 31 December 1993, the ten highest-yielders from the top thirty UK companies produced a 22.4% compound annual return against 18.8% for the UK market as a whole. The five lowest-priced shares selected from the ten highest-yielders produced a superb 26.1% compound annual return. Even after allowing for estimated costs of 4% per annum, the O'Higgins system substantially beat the market.

The main advantage of the O'Higgins approach is that it is an automatic way of applying contrary thinking. Without this kind of discipline, it is only too easy to become a member of the crowd and develop similar views on the market outlook and the investment appeal of individual companies. This may be the reason why the O'Higgins approach does not work so well if you tinker with it and try to apply value criteria or personal judgement. If you intend to use his system, you should stick to his rules to the letter.

I would like to make it clear that there is nothing magic about O'Higgins' approach – it is just another way of sieving and selecting top quality shares that are currently out-of-favour and are therefore high-yielding. All the companies in the Dow and almost certainly all of those in the top thirty in the UK share the distinction that they are likely to survive. As John Neff, the great American contrarian investor, puts it, the important point for investors is to 'get 'em while they're cold'.

My recent book, *PEP Up Your Wealth*, sets out the O'Higgins system in great detail and shows the research undertaken and the assumptions made by Johnson Fry. For anyone interested in high-yielding shares, the O'Higgins five lowest-priced from the ten highest-yielders selected from the top thirty shares takes a lot of beating. It also has the great virtue of being a very simple system to operate, requiring at the most only one hour of your time every year.

21

___

BULL AND BEAR MARKETS

Very few experts can forecast which way the stock market is heading, so concentrate upon selecting the right shares. Selection is far more important than timing.

As I have already explained, selection is far more important than timing. The good news is that selection is also much easier. To be a successful investor you have to remember three key points: selection, selection and selection.

You should not be unduly concerned about the level of the stock market as a whole. You should always keep about 50% of your patient money invested in well-chosen growth stocks. Otherwise, if you try to deal in and out, you risk making the wrong judgement about the trend. Remember that bull markets climb a wall of worry, whereas bear markets strike when the sky appears to be blue and everyone is confident about the future. Whatever your fears and hopes for the economy and the stock market, they are almost certainly in the price.

Even if it was possible to give you a few simple guidelines to help you to anticipate a bull or bear market, after a short while the formula would be of little use to you. As more and more investors became aware of the approach, the market would adjust to make it ineffective.

Crowd psychology moves markets far more than fundamental values. Greed takes prices up to dizzy heights. Fear does the opposite. Periodically, a kind of mania develops. At one time, conglomerates were the flavour of the month, then financials, then property and drug stocks and then the Japanese market. After a while, the mania peaks and fear begins to replace greed. As the downward movement gathers momentum, yesterday's favourites become the outcasts of the investment world. At one time, everyone wanted to have a foot on the property ladder, which appeared to lead only upwards. Now, to many people, property does not seem to be such an attractive investment.

How do normal, rational people get swept up in these manias? Charles Mackay, in his excellent book *Extraordinary Popular Delusions and the Madness of Crowds*, gives examples of the Mississippi Scheme, Tulipomania and the South Sea Bubble. Tulipomania has always been my favourite. In the early seventeenth century, many people in Holland were collecting tulips to such an extent that it was proof of bad taste for a man of fortune to be without a rare tulip bulb collection. The desire to possess tulip bulbs spread to the Dutch middle classes. By the year 1636, the demand for rare tulip bulbs increased so much that regular marts for their sale were established on the Stock Exchange in many of the principal cities. Prices continued to rise and many individuals who had speculated in tulips suddenly became very rich. People in all walks of life began to convert their hard-earned money into tulip bulbs. Tulipomania became rampant.

You may wonder how the Dutch people allowed themselves to be so carried away from reality. Your wonderment would have been shared by the unfortunate sailor who, having just returned from a long voyage, took a tulip bulb from a merchant's store, thinking that it was an onion, which, a few hours later, he ate with his herring breakfast. The tulip bulb in question was a *Semper Augustus,* then worth about 3,000 florins, which would have been sufficient to feed his entire ship's crew for over a year. The poor fellow had plenty of time to think about tulip bulbs during the months he spent in prison on the theft charge.

It is very important for you to realise that financial manias are not just an academic subject about events like Tulipomania that happened many years ago to other people who were silly. People are still silly today. In 1987, at the top of the utility boom, the Japanese Government floated NTT, the Japanese telephone monopoly. The price was Y1.6m per share on a multiple of 170 times earnings, with a dividend yield of 0.3%. At the peak price of Y3.18m the shares were quoted at about 340 times earnings, and the valuation of NTT was more than the entire German stock market.

Since then, the Japanese bubble has well and truly burst. NTT was a leading example of a mania in full cry. By mid-1995, the price had fallen to Y718,000 on a prospective multiple of 85 times earnings.

There are a number of ways of testing if a market is in a bullish or bearish phase. For example, when the bull is rampant, shares usually sell on historically high P/E ratios and at large premiums to book value. Furthermore, there is a high degree of speculation and a plethora of new issues of dubious value. But you have to understand that the bear is a wily animal, and each market cycle has subtle variations from previous ones. It would all be too simple if the bear was easy to recognise – he is out to trap you, so you can be sure that most people will not see him coming. Keep this warning firmly in mind, while I set out some of the more traditional signals that have heralded the top of *previous* bull markets and the bottom of *previous* bear markets. You will see that bull and bear market signals are like the reverse sides of the same coin.

SIGNS OF A BULL MARKET TOP

CASH IS TRASH

This expression was coined by American fund managers. The 'rubbishing' of cash and the consequent low institutional cash holdings are an obvious danger, signalling that most funds will be fully invested.

VALUE IS HARD TO FIND

The average P/E ratio of the market as a whole will be near to historically high levels. The average dividend yield will be low and shares will be standing at a high premium to book values. If you have been using my approach to investment, you will already have sold many of your shares and very few will measure up to your criteria.

INTEREST RATES

Interest rates are usually about to rise or have started to do so. In mid-1995, interest rates in both the USA and UK had been rising from historically low levels. Investors were wondering how much further they would rise before topping out.

MONEY SUPPLY

Broad money supply tends to be contracting at the turn of bull markets.

SIGNS OF A BEAR MARKET BOTTOM

CASH IS KING

At the bottom of a bear market, it is universally recognised that cash is the best possible asset to own. Institutional cash holdings are, therefore, usually at high levels and eventually that money has only one way to go – into the market.

VALUE IS EASY TO FIND

The average P/E ratio of the market as a whole will be near to historically low levels. The average dividend yield will be high and shares may be standing at a discount to book values.

In January 1975, at the bottom of the bear market, the FT Ordinary Share Index stood at 146, the lowest it had been since May 1954. The average P/E ratio was under 4 with a dividend yield of over 13%; ICI yielded 13.4%, Glynwed 24.0%, Tarmac 17.7% and Lex Service 43.6%.

INTEREST RATES

Interest rates are *usually* at a high level and are about to fall or have just begun to do so. At the bottom of the 1981/2 bear market, for example, long bonds in America were yielding a staggeringly high 15.23%. What a wonderful buy they would have been.

MONEY SUPPLY

Broad money supply tends to be increasing at the turn of bear markets.

INVESTMENT ADVISERS

The consensus view of investment advisers will be bullish.

REACTION TO NEWS

An early sign of a bull market topping out is the failure of shares to respond to good news. The directors of a company might report excellent results only to see the price of their shares fall. The market is becoming exhausted, good news is already discounted and there is very little buying power left.

NEW ISSUES

Offers for sale, rights issues and new issues are usually in abundance, with quality beginning to suffer and low-grade issues being chased to ridiculous levels. In early 1994, the new issues market in the UK reached a peak as companies rushed to take advantage of high share prices.

MEDIA COMMENT

The press and TV tend to give more prominence to the stock market and to be optimistic near the top. If prices appear high in relation to value, the argument is that 'it will be different this time.' The few bearish articles that warn of dangers to come are ignored by investors.

PARTY TALK

At the peak of a bull market, shares tend to be the main topic of conversation at cocktail and dinner parties.

INVESTMENT ADVISERS

The consensus view of investment advisers will be bearish.

REACTION TO NEWS

An early sign of a bear market bottoming is the failure of shares to fall on bad news. The weak holders will already be out of the shares, so there will be very little further selling to come.

NEW ISSUES

There will be hardly a new issue in sight. Entrepreneurs, who have built up private companies to a size sufficient to obtain a public quotation, wait for better markets to obtain higher prices for their businesses.

MEDIA COMMENT

Press and TV comment shrinks in response to lack of public interest. Most financial articles will be bearish and the odd bullish article will be ignored (probably on the grounds that the journalist who wrote it is demented).

PARTY TALK

The prevailing mood will be so dismal that most people will believe that there is no longer much point in owning shares. In a bear market no one wants to talk about the Stock Exchange.

CHANGES IN MARKET LEADERSHIP

A major change in leadership is often a prelude to a change in market direction. Near the top of a bull market, investors often move from safe growth stocks into cyclicals, which they buy heavily.

UNEMPLOYMENT

An interesting study by Matheson Securities of ten stock market turning points, demonstrates that eight times the stock market turned downwards an average of about ten months after the unemployment figures began to fall.

There are a few general points to be made about bull and bear markets:

a) You will be pleased to know that bull markets usually last longer than bear markets.

b) Bull markets take many years to build and then a long time to move from the massive over-valuations caused by greed to the substantial under-valuations that usually prevail in the fearsome conditions of a major bear market.

c) A great deal of money can be lost in a very short time in a vicious bear market. The average fall in the seven bear markets since 1964 was 34%, lasting an average of fifty-seven weeks, but in 1973–5 the fall was 73% for a very unhappy 136 weeks.

d) Bull markets frequently seem to last four to five years, which may have some connection with electoral cycles. There are many exceptions, however.

CHANGES IN MARKET LEADERSHIP

Sectors that have had many years of unpopularity often begin to show signs of life, which could indicate that they might be the leaders in the next bull market. For example, gold and other resource stocks have been out of fashion for many years now. In May 1993, *all the world's* quoted gold mines did not add up to the combined market capitalisation of British Telecom and Glaxo, so very little buying would have been needed to spark off a boom in gold shares again.

At the bottom of a bear market, growth stocks become ridiculously cheap as multiples crumble.

UNEMPLOYMENT

The converse of the Matheson Securities study is that rapidly rising unemployment can be a sign that a bear market is near to its end.

e) To my mind, there is no real difference between a major correction in a bull market and a mini-bear market. I suppose a technical purist would argue that because the market recovered from the 1987 crash and went above its previous high, the bull market was still intact, and the sharp fall in share prices was simply a major correction.

A major bear market is different – a prolonged period of at least nine months and sometimes as much as two to three years, during which bearish conditions prevail and you wish you were somewhere else.

f) In the 1980s, global markets seemed to move in step. During the days after the 1987 crash, one afternoon Wall Street might fall sharply, with a knock-on effect in Tokyo overnight – which in turn would weaken opening prices in London the next morning. But less than five years later, Japan had more than halved, while both Wall Street and London had reached all-time highs.

In the final analysis, no major country can succeed in isolation. If the world economy falls into a deep recession, there is no doubt that every major stock market will be affected. Nevertheless, there does seem to be more scope today for a number of individual stock markets to rise, even if some of the other major markets in the world are in a down-trend.

g) Both bull and bear markets have several different stages. In a bear market, for example, stage 1 is usually a sharp fall during which economic conditions remain positive. In stage 2, economic conditions deteriorate but the market becomes over-sold. There is then a sucker rally, powerful enough to persuade most investors into believing that the market has bottomed. During stage 3, the economic news becomes awful. Investors panic and sell at any price. The market declines very sharply as the downward spiral becomes self-feeding. Stage 3 is only over and ready as a springboard for the next bull market when investors abandon all hope for the future. The first positive sign will be that shares no longer fall on bad news.

All of this makes for gloomy reading, but it is important for you to realise that markets can come down as well as go up. Remember that bear markets carry almost everything down with them, irrespective of underlying value, so do not try to beat the trend. If you feel very bearish, you could prune your portfolio down to 50% of your *patient* money, but leave this invested in the best of your well-chosen growth stocks and wait for better times.

A SUMMARY OF MY ADVICE ON GENERAL MARKET STRATEGY:

1. By reading your daily and weekly newspapers, investment magazines and newsletters, you should be able to keep your finger on the pulse of the market.

2. You have seen the table of warning signals and must make up your own mind on the state of the general market. Try to avoid becoming a member of 'the crowd'.

3. If you feel bullish, invest 100% of your *patient* money. If bearish, 50%.

4. When pruning your portfolio down from 100% to 50%, keep

your more defensive stocks. This should happen naturally as you sell shares which fulfil your investment objectives. With a growth portfolio, keep the shares on the lower PEG factors. You do not mind the multiple remaining high, provided the growth is still there to support the price.

5. Unless you are an experienced investor, do not consider shorting stocks or buying *derivatives* (financial instruments such as options or futures which, because of their high gearing, magnify the fluctuations in the prices of shares, currencies and commodities).

6. Above all, do not allow a bear market to frighten you into taking your patient money out of your carefully selected super-growth shares that are continuing to perform well. Remember the Coca-Cola story – $40 to over $2m per share; $1,000 to $50m in an average man's lifetime. That is what investment is all about.

22

—

PORTFOLIO MANAGEMENT

Always measure your portfolio's performance against the market. Make a habit of running profits and cutting losses, and make sure you do not pay any unnecessary tax.

THE ADVANTAGES OF A SMALL PORTFOLIO

Private investors with small portfolios have a considerable advantage over institutions with massive funds to invest. The institutions have to spread their investments over hundreds of stocks. I recommend that, as a private investor, you should hold no more than ten to twelve shares at any time. Because of the disproportionately high commission charges on small bargains, it is unlikely to be economic to invest less than £1,000 in each share.

A portfolio of ten shares is far easier to manage. Your first choice is better than your tenth, which in turn is considerably better than your hundredth. Also, the fewer stocks in your portfolio, the easier it is to keep a really keen eye on them all.

SPREAD YOUR RISK

With a portfolio of ten shares, you should make it a policy to put no more than 10% of your money in any one. However attractive a particular investment may appear to be, you should always remember that investing in equities involves risk and that things can go wrong. You may suddenly find that your favourite company has infringed an important patent, the chief executive has decided to leave, or a major new product has encountered unexpected technical difficulties with consequently massive service charges and loss of reputation. If your portfolio is well spread, you will find unexpected setbacks of this nature much easier to handle both psychologically and financially.

GOLD

In 1993, there was a great deal of activity in gold and gold shares when George Soros, the investment guru of sterling devaluation fame, purchased a substantial shareholding in America's leading gold-producing company, Newmont Mining. The other major shareholder, Sir James Goldsmith, has been a gold enthusiast for a few years and is likely to remain so, but the world's gold markets became very excited in early 1993, when Soros (much more of a dealer and expert on timing) confirmed that he, too, believed that the time had come for gold to be re-rated. In fact, as the chart shows, the gold price has been broadly flat for two years now but some analysts were suggesting in mid-1995 that a new bull market was imminent.

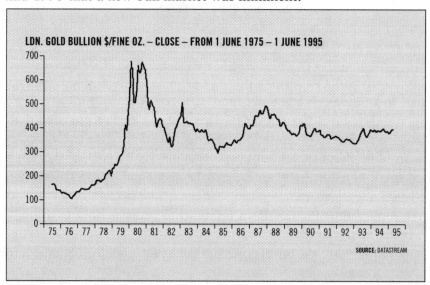

LDN. GOLD BULLION $/FINE OZ. – CLOSE – FROM 1 JUNE 1975 – 1 JUNE 1995

SOURCE: DATASTREAM

The attraction of gold is as a store of value, particularly in times of crisis. Gold bugs argue that world currency markets are in turmoil. Most countries have large deficits, so governments are tempted to print even more money. Inflation is rampant in many emerging economies, where people buy gold as a way of saving. Gold cannot be printed; it is universally accepted; it is likely to remain in relatively scarce supply; and it is no one else's liability.

Sceptics argue that gold is just another commodity and it is absurd to devote so much money and labour to extracting yellow metal out of the earth with a view to burying it again in the safes and vaults of world banks and under Indian and Chinese mattresses.

Central banks have been selling their stocks of gold and this has had a depressing effect on the price. Against this, the Chinese, with their double-digit inflation rates and substantial savings, are buying gold very strongly and are changing the balance of supply and demand from surplus to deficit. There are powerful arguments both ways.

The supply/demand position was summed up in a mid-1993 issue of the *Investors Chronicle* in the concluding paragraphs of an excellent article, the main arguments of which still hold true:

'The market's major preoccupation, however, is central bank selling and mining companies unwinding forward sales. A glance at the demand/supply situation (see table) reveals why. According to "Gold 1993", the definitive gold industry survey by Gold Fields Mineral Services, global gold demand would have exceeded supply in each of the last three years in the absence of central bank sales and hedging by miners. And the gap is increasing. From 187 tonnes in 1990, it had risen to 476 tonnes in 1991 and 725 tonnes last year.

GOLD SUPPLY AND DEMAND (tonnes)	1990	1991	1992
Supply			
Mine production	2129	2154	2217
Old scrap gold	508	419	453
	2637	2573	2670
Demand			
Fabrication (jewellery, electronics etc)	2616	2793	3107
Bar hoarding	208	256	288
	2824	3049	3395
Excess demands	187	476	725
Net official sales	184	131	568
Gold loans forward sales, option hedging	241	46	155
Investment	238	–	–
Disinvestment	–	299	2

Source: Gold Fields Mineral Services.

In 1992, net sales by central banks, totalling 568 tonnes, went a long way towards plugging the gulf between the demand and supply. The major sellers, the Dutch and the Belgians, argued that they wanted to reduce gold's share of total reserves to a level similar to that in neighbouring countries. Gold now accounts for 35 and 51 per cent of their reserves, respectively, more in line with the European average of around 40 per cent.

Further sales from the Netherlands and Belgium seem increasingly unlikely. Sentiment amongst European central bankers is becoming progressively pro-gold. The Italians were forced to abandon the idea of selling gold to fund the support of the lira. Meanwhile, Edouard Balladur, the new French Prime Minister, is a notorious gold bug. Helmut Schlesinger, President of the Bundesbank, recently argued that gold was a core holding for central banks and should not be sold. In the past week, the head of the Austrian central bank and Eddie George, Governor of the Bank of England, both went public in pledging not to sell their gold.

The attitude of the US Federal Reserve is harder to assess. Though it is the world's largest single owner of gold (8,144 tonnes, worth around $80bn), it has not been selling recently. However, during the 1970s gold bull run the Fed intervened in the market, selling gold in the hope of depressing the price and dampening inflationary expectations. Though the policy failed, the unflattering implications of further sharp rises in the gold price for President Clinton's control over inflation might prompt a repeat performance.

Sentiment amongst mining companies is also shifting. Throughout the 1980s the stars were those, like American Barrick, with successful hedging programmes (ie. using financial markets to lock in a selling price). Many would not have survived the decade without selling their production forward or using options to lock in favourable prices. Recently, however, the big movers have been unhedged mining companies, whose profits remain highly geared to a rising gold price.

Gold Fields Mineral Services estimates that gold mines have sold forward around 38m ounces of gold, or 1,200 tonnes. Some will be short below the current price. If they want to neutralise their positions, they will have to buy at above their selling prices. And as much as 300-400 tonnes may have been sold in the $380-400 range. Already, miners are feeling the pressure. Two weeks ago Lac Minerals covered 500,000 ounces, crystallising a $17m loss, though it is still short by around 2.4m ounces. Meanwhile, Dominion Mining covered a third of its forward sales, and was rewarded with a 16 per cent rise in its share price. Others will no doubt follow.'

As you can see, the gold price seems to hinge on the actions of the US Federal Reserve and other central banks and no one really knows what they will do, even if they know themselves. If they decide not to sell their gold, the price could easily go through the roof. Even if the Federal Reserve does sell, it can only do so once and it would be very weakening for the dollar to run its stocks too low. Therefore, it seems to me that the argument favours the bulls, who must find it comforting to be on the same side as Goldsmith.

Most major gold mines break even at prices ranging from $200 to $300 an ounce. In May 1995, the price of gold is just under $400, so if this level is maintained, the average mine can be expected to make a profit of $100–200 an ounce. A rise in the gold price to $500 would work wonders for them, lifting profits to $200–300 an ounce.

Gold shares are also in relatively short supply. They have been unpopular for many years, perhaps building a base for a major reappraisal before becoming a market leader in a few years' time. All the world's quoted gold mines added together do not equal the combined market capitalisations of British Telecom and Glaxo Wellcome, so a flicker of extra demand could trigger a massive upward status change.

The doomsters and gold bugs could be right and gold might fly again. Soros sold out in August 1993 (and was proved right), but there is still an argument for having 5–10% of your portfolio in gold shares as a kind of insurance policy. Any investment in gold shares would be a hedge, so you want to be absolutely sure that your investment would be safe and well spread. Investing in one or two mines could be a risky and unsuccessful policy; the best way, therefore, is through a well-established unit trust.

NEW ISSUES

A new issue of shares offered to the general public is usually priced at a level that will ensure the success of the issue. Unless the whole market tumbles, you can therefore normally expect a premium of at least 5–10% over the share price when trading commences. Sometimes, with a very popular issue, the premium can be very much more but, in that event, you will probably find it hard to get hold of a significant number of shares. In particular, an issue in a sizeable company or one with market leadership or a strong niche position is usually worth pursuing because of its likely appeal to institutional investors.

Until you have read *The Zulu Principle*, however, I would not advise you to subscribe for the general run of new issues. In bullish conditions, you will make money on most of them, but you will fare much better if first you learn how to value the shares of smaller companies.

The Government's privatisation offerings, like British Telecom and British Gas, are a different proposition altogether. The Government has not striven for maximum prices. General politics and wider share ownership have been the underlying motives and all concerned naturally want the issues to be successful. As a result, the investing public have been able to help themselves to substantial and safe premiums and sound investments at a discount to normal prices.

For the small investor, in particular, it makes good sense to apply for at least the minimum subscription of every Government offering in as many family names as possible. Usually, with Government issues, minimum subscriptions are favoured, so it is far better to apply for five lots of, say, 200 shares rather than one application for 1,000 shares. Multiple applications in one name are illegal, but there is nothing wrong with a man and his wife and each of their children applying in their own names. The dog, the cat and the budgerigar are not allowed to own shares.

An alternative approach is to apply for a larger number of shares in the hope that you will not be scaled down too much. This can work out well, but the loss of interest on your money can outweigh the gain on the extra shares you receive.

With issues like British Telecom and British Gas, the requirements of the institutions are not always fully satisfied by the offering. They, too, are scaled down, so they tend to top up their holdings later by buying in the market. Usually, after these kinds of issues, the stags quickly sell their shares at a small profit and the institutions and other long-term investors buy them quietly. The share price mills around for a few weeks and then the shares begin to move ahead as they find their proper place in the market. This may all sound too easy, but that is the way it has been with Government issues so far.

RECORD YOUR INVESTMENTS

I recommend that you purchase a small investment ledger from a stationer. As you make purchases and sales, record the details, which will be a great help to you when you come to complete your tax return. Also make a note of the level of the FT-SE Actuaries 350 Index on the days you make the transactions. This will give you a useful measure against which to gauge the performance of individual shares and your portfolio as a whole.

You should retain all contract notes as proof of transactions, in case there are any queries. Share certificates should be kept in your own safe or at your bank. Do not put them somewhere obscure that seems to be 'a safe place' at the time. It is so easy to forget the whereabouts of the safe place.

A WATCHING BRIEF

I always try to keep a watching brief on the stocks that constitute my portfolio. Needless to say, I read about all major developments and, through my broker, keep an eye on directors' share dealings. I also try to be aware of what is happening to the current trading of any company in which I am interested.

At one time I had some shares in Psion, the company that introduced the revolutionary palm-top computer. Whenever I was in a Dixons store, I would ask the assistant how sales were going, if they had any better alternatives to offer and whether or not they had many complaints about the product. There had been a few, but they turned out to be only teething troubles.

Even if you cannot check up personally on a specific point of worry, you will be surprised to learn that you almost certainly know someone who knows someone who knows the answer. I remember my Chairman at Leyland, Lord Black, saying that when he had his photograph taken for The National Photographic Gallery, he commented to the photographer that he was surprised to find that he knew personally all the famous people in the many photographs hanging on every wall of the studio. The photographer smiled and remarked, 'They all say that.' The world is a small place – with just one telephone call, most of those people would have been able to check up on a major new development in many different fields. If you really want to verify something about a company, you will soon find someone who knows someone who can answer your questions. You can also try telephoning the company secretary. Explain that you are a shareholder, and ask for clarification of any points that may be worrying you. Some secretaries are very helpful indeed, but they will naturally avoid giving you any 'inside information'.

If you can spare the time, there is another obvious way of acquiring information about a company in which you have invested – attend the Annual General Meeting. You will find this an interesting experience that will help you to get the feel of the company. Is the meeting well organised? Are the chairman and chief executive impressive and do they answer questions well? Is the mood of the meeting upbeat or downbeat? These are the kinds of general questions you should ask yourself. If you have any specific ones that remain unanswered, you can always stand up and put them to the chairman. An alternative is to wait until after the formal meeting is over and have a quiet word with him or another member of the board.

INSIDE INFORMATION

I mentioned earlier the dreaded words 'inside information' – a grey area that is constantly changing. From the investor's viewpoint, the main thing to avoid is using unpublished and price-sensitive information about a company's future results or a major development, such as an impending takeover. Acting upon certain knowledge of a coming unexpected rise or fall in a company's profits is illegal – tips based on this kind of information are therefore obviously best avoided. Takeover tips have an even more inside flavour as the parties involved are under an obligation to make an announcement as soon as they have agreed a deal subject to shareholders' approval (or the predator has unilaterally formed an intention to bid on specific terms). There is a profound difference between thinking that a company might not be doing so well, after studying the generally available brokers' consensus forecast or national retail sales, and *knowing* from a member of the board that profits are suffering. There is also an obvious difference between concluding that a company might be taken over one day because its assets are grossly under-valued and *knowing* that an acquisitive conglomerate is about to take it over. Acting upon unpublished, price-sensitive information is illegal. Acting upon your own judgement based upon generally available facts about a company is fair game and permissible.

CUT LOSSES AND RUN PROFITS

There is an old adage on the management of a portfolio: cut losses and run profits. Easy to say, but much harder to do. Warren Buffett, the legendary American investor, had a wonderful way of illustrating why you should follow this practice. He took the hypothetical case of being offered the future earnings for life of each and every member of his graduation class. Adapted for the UK, let us take a class of twenty and say that you could have bought all your classmates' life earnings for a fixed sum. Fifteen years elapse before you review the position. Two have died, two are drug addicts, one has AIDS, one is in prison and three are unemployed. Amongst the rest there is a priest, three accountants, two lawyers, a detective sergeant in the police and an actor. The remaining three are really in the money. Of the high flyers, one is already a captain of industry, another a leading financier and the last one is in line to be chief executive of a leading company. If you had to make a few sales at differing prices, would you keep the less fortunate ones, those who had performed reasonably well or the high flyers? I know your answer.

Let me show you a typical portfolio that illustrates how the discipline of running profits and cutting losses works in practice.

COMPANY	INITIAL INVESTMENT (£)	LOSS (%)	PROFIT (%)	FINAL VALUE (£)
A	1000	25	–	750
B	1000	–	160	2600
C	1000	–	60	1600
D	1000	25	–	750
E	1000	–	200	3000
F	1000	–	50	1500
G	1000	–	180	2800
H	1000	25	–	750
I	1000	–	90	1900
J	1000	–	35	1350
	£10,000			£17,000

I have assumed that £10,000 was invested in ten shares and, over a three-year period, three shares were outright winners, four were fair to medium performers and the other three were mistakes. By running profits and cutting the losses at the 25% level, the overall performance of the portfolio would still be a very satisfactory 70% increase. In addition, in practice, the proceeds of the sale of the three lossmakers would have been reinvested, lifting the overall gain to about 80%.

You can readily see that the alternative approach of running losses and snatching profits would, almost certainly, have been disastrous. Large profits would have been realised prematurely at the 25% level and losses might have grown substantially to eat up the much smaller profits.

THE STORY OF A STOCK

By 'the story' of a stock I do not mean an amusing tale. Whenever I buy a stock, I do so for very specific reasons and those reasons are 'the story'. If I learned that a major new competitor had entered the industry, or that growth had unexpectedly slowed down, or that a major overseas subsidiary had begun to falter, I would take my profit or cut my loss *without hesitation*. The story would have changed.

I also begin to worry if I see that any of the directors are selling a significant proportion of their shares, if the Chairman's Statement becomes more cautious, if a key executive suddenly leaves, or if the Balance Sheet shows an alarming increase in debt. Any of these factors might be sufficient to persuade me that the story has changed and that the reasons for my purchase no longer apply. As a result, the shares become an instant sell.

The essential point to grasp is that you do not simply select a share and go to sleep on it. You monitor your investments all the time, keeping an eye, in particular, on the ongoing validity of your reasons for buying the share in the first place. For example, you might have admired the chief executive, liked the company's freedom from debt and the absence of creative accounting. You have to make sure that these important factors remain in place.

So let us be completely clear on this vital point. If the story of a company you have invested in changes for the worse to a material extent, you should sell your shares *immediately*. Speed is of the essence – you do not want to be the last in the queue of disappointed enthusiasts. The share will probably have fallen and may be below your purchase price, but that is irrelevant. Cut your loss. You will enjoy a great sense of relief and your portfolio will make for much better viewing.

POOR RELATIVE STRENGTH OF YOUR SHARES

In the last chapter, we established that if you are bearish about the market as a whole, you should prune your portfolio so that only 50% of your patient money is invested. A far more difficult problem arises when, for no *apparent* reason, a particular share begins to perform badly. The market might be rising but the shares stand still or drop a little. If the market is falling, the shares might fall more quickly and show poor relative strength.

When this happens, and there is no identifiable reason, ask your broker to check with the market to see if he can find a satisfactory explanation. Your broker may not be able to find one, but you can *usually* be sure that something is afoot. The explanation often emerges a few weeks or even months later. The company might lose an important patent case, the chief executive might leave, or the interim results could be very disappointing. Before you heard the news, a number of other people knew about the problem and sold their shares.

There is no formula for dealing with apparently inexplicable losses. Whatever else you do, I strongly recommend that you do not average down and buy more shares. This practice is known as 'trying to catch a falling knife', a phrase which speaks for itself. Sell your shares maybe, sell half of them perhaps, but do not buy any more.

A possible solution is to decide in advance to sell your shares if they reach a predetermined trigger point – a kind of stop-loss. For example, 25% below your cost might be appropriate for a growth share, assuming that the market was reasonably stable. Another approach is to grit your teeth and hope that the company, and in due course the share price, will surmount the problem. In the end, I suppose it all comes down to judgement and feel which, in turn, comes from being in the closest possible touch with your investments.

TAKING PROFITS

I always find cutting losses easy and obvious in comparison with deciding whether or not to take a profit. You buy a share because it meets your criteria. As the price increases, the shares might no longer be a buy under your system, but they may not have matured sufficiently to become a sell. At that stage, they can best be classified as a hold.

Finding a really good growth share involves a great deal of trial and error. Once you have selected a share that has the capacity to churn out earnings growth of 20% per annum or more, you cannot let it go lightly. The compounding effect of rapidly increasing earnings will be so dramatic that you want to enjoy the ride to the full.

There are also other reasons for expanding the period during which you hold a share. The first is the expense of switching. Stamp duty, brokerage and the marketmaker's turn all take their toll and can add up to as much as 5% of the value of your investment.

The second factor is capital gains tax. When you take a large profit, the capital gains tax liability becomes payable on 1 December following the end of the tax year. While you run the profit, the Government is, in effect, making an interest-free loan to you of the tax you will eventually have to pay on the gain. You should savour this benefit, the extent of which does, of course, depend on your tax rate. The more you run your profit, the more the Government lends to you.

TAXATION AND PEPS

For the purpose of calculating the capital gains tax you owe, your gain is the difference between the selling price and the price you paid for your shares minus an element of relief to compensate for the impact of inflation. If the shares were bought before 31 March 1982, then their value on that date is assumed to be your purchase price.

The rate of tax you pay is the same as your top rate of income tax and each year you are permitted £6,000 of tax-exempt capital gains. Your spouse is, too, so do not forget to maximise your exemption by spreading gains between you.

Another way of reducing your potential capital gains tax liability is to sell some of your shares and immediately buy them back again. The disposal establishes either a gain to take you up to your tax-free limit or a loss to set off against other gains. The technique is called bed-and-breakfasting and can easily be arranged with your broker before the end of each tax year.

Small private investors should also take full advantage of personal equity plans (PEPs), which were introduced by the Government to encourage the public to invest in quoted companies. There are two advantages to PEPs: they allow tax to be reclaimed on dividends and capital gains on shares are tax free.

PEPs fall into two categories – general and single company. You can invest in each fiscal year up to £6,000 in a general PEP and £3,000 in a single company PEP. Therefore, for many small investors the tax advantages can apply to the whole of their portfolio. Again a man and his wife are both eligible for the full £9,000 allowance. Children cannot be included, unless over eighteen, and all participants must be resident in the UK for tax purposes. Full details of PEPs are given in Chapter 9.

Many investment management companies offer general PEPs through direct mail or advertisements in the national press. The success of these schemes does, of course, depend on the skill of the investment managers, as the investor has no say in the choice of stocks. However, most stockbrokers offer a service to enable investors to run their own schemes and choose their own quoted investments. PEPs are, therefore, an essential tool for anyone using my system of investment for growth shares. They are also attractive for investors requiring high income as specified corporate bonds and convertibles of UK non-financial companies and preference shares of non-financial companies incorporated in EC member states can now be held in a general PEP.

There are very few rules. Your broker will do everything for you – keep the records, look after the share certificates, collect the dividends, advise about rights issues and takeovers and provide you with regular statements. There is no limit to the length of time your PEPs need stay in existence. PEPs can be closed at will and all the funds withdrawn, without incurring any tax liability on profits and without the benefit of being able to set off any losses against taxable gains.

Of course, PEPs do not come free. Brokers charge for their services; typically, £30 for start up, usual dealing commissions, valuation fees of £3 per stock and cancellation fees if you close your account or transfer your PEPs anywhere. However, these charges would have to be very onerous indeed to exceed the tax benefits.

In the first edition of this book, I underestimated an important feature of PEPs – the compounding effect of reinvesting tax-free dividends. A statistical study by the stockbrokers, Hoare Govett, convinced me of the overwhelming advantage of doing so and persuaded me to devote my latest book, *PEP Up Your Wealth*, to this profitable subject.

Hoare Govett has an index covering the smallest quoted UK companies – the bottom 10% in terms of market capitalisation. It shows that, in 1955 £1,000 invested in the average small share in its index by the end of 1993 would have grown to £89,000 and, in addition, would have provided an increasing flow of dividend income. However, if that dividend income had been *reinvested gross* (free of any taxes as it would have been in a PEP), the £89,000 would have increased nine-fold to a staggering £800,000!

Another major factor that I underestimated previously was the size of the capital sum that can be built up from the combination of the seemingly modest annual PEP entitlement with tax-free capital growth and the reinvestment of gross dividends. The compounding effect, year after year, produces far better results than you might imagine.

I know many wealthy and sophisticated people who do not bother with PEPs because the annual allowances of £9,000 seem relatively trivial. Many other investors of more modest means are put off PEPs because they think their annual £6,000 capital gains tax exemption is sufficient to cover their likely capital gains. Neither group of investors has understood the *cumulative* effect of building PEPs.

At the present level of annual allowances, a married couple can invest a total of £180,000 over ten years. With capital growth and dividends reinvested (together with a bit of luck, especially in the single company PEPs) it is not difficult to see that £180,000 growing to a very substantial sum. I already know one investor whose wife has £300,000 in her PEP schemes and I have no doubt that in a few years' time there will be a growing number of PEP millionaires.

THE PEG FACTOR AGAIN

There is no doubt that, from time to time, the stock market becomes unduly excited about a particular company. The shares go higher and higher for no apparent reason and, at some future point, however good the company, the shares become over-priced. However, you should bear in mind that truly great growth companies can stand the strain of a high multiple. As they continue to churn out earnings increasing by 20–25% per annum, the fundamentals quickly catch up with the share price. Lesser companies might disappoint the market, perhaps only a little, to find that their share prices quickly tumble.

In *The Zulu Principle*, when describing how to sell a super-growth share, I hovered between suggesting that the right time was 'never' or 'on adulation'. We have already established that you should sell if the story changes materially for the worse. That is easy. The difficult decision arises if the story remains intact and the shares continue to rise. At what point should you take your profit, if at all?

If you are truly satisfied with your selection, there is an argument for holding on, whatever the temptation to snatch a quick profit. In the long run, this could be the best policy for less active investors to adopt. However, I believe that a constructive alternative is to use the PEG factor as a measure of adulation.

In *The Zulu Principle*, when buying shares in the SmallCap Index, I suggested selling on a PEG of 1.2. However, these companies were being bought on PEGs of under 0.66. We are buying 350 Index stocks only on PEGs of 1.0 or under – the prospective P/E ratios are not to be more than the estimated future growth rates. I therefore recommend upgrading the exit PEGs for 350 Index stocks to 1.5 – sell when the multiples are more than half as much again as the growth rates.

Let us analyse how this might work in practice. If you bought a growth share in the Mid 250 Index on a PEG of, say, 0.8, this could easily have been a company growing at 20% per annum on a P/E ratio of 16 (16 divided by 20 = 0.8). If the earnings were 10p, the price would have been 160p (16 times 10p = 160p).

Let us assume that, during the first year, earnings increased by 20% to 12p and the multiple rose to 1.5 times the growth rate, which is our exit point. For the PEG to be 1.5 with a growth rate of 20% per annum, the multiple would have risen to 30 (30 divided by 20 = 1.5). On a multiple of 30 with earnings of 12p, the shares would stand at 360p against our purchase price of 160p. You would have more than doubled your money while the company increased its earnings by only 20%. *The main reason, you would have made such a large gain was the rise in the multiple.* Unless there was a ready and obvious explanation, such as the hope of an acceleration in future earnings growth, this would be a case of adulation and, in my view, your money could be working better for you elsewhere. Time to move on, so bid the shares a reluctant *adieu*. Perhaps I should say *au revoir*, as you can always keep an affectionate eye on growth shares that have done well for you, while you wait for a better moment to repurchase them.

SUMMARY

1. Your portfolio should contain no more than ten to twelve shares.

2. Record your investments in a ledger and regularly measure the performance of your portfolio against the appropriate index (for beginners following my recommendations, the FT-SE Actuaries 350 Index). If, over a period of a few years, you find that you are

failing to match or beat the market, you should consider switching to a tracker fund or delegating the management of your equity investments to someone more expert than you.

3. Keep all your contract notes and share certificates in a very safe place.

4. Do not invest more than 10% of your total funds in any one share.

5. As a kind of insurance policy, there is a strong argument for investing 5–10% of your portfolio in a well-established unit trust concentrating on gold shares.

6. Take advantage of new issues by the Government by applying for at least the minimum subscription of new issues in your own name and for members of your family.

7. After purchasing a share, maintain a hands-on watching brief. People within your acquaintance know people who know people who can help answer your questions about your investments. You can also be very active yourself.

8. Run profits and cut losses.

9. Additional factors that make it desirable to run profits are the expenses of switching and the crystallisation of capital gains tax liability if you make a sale. The Government is, in effect, lending you the capital gains tax liability interest-free while you run the profit on your shares.

10. Profits on good growth shares should always be taken reluctantly. I recommend selling 350 Index stocks when the prospective PEG reaches 1.5. Keep an eye on the shares subsequently, as you wait for a better moment to repurchase.

11. Losses should be cut on all shares when the story changes for the worse to such an extent that you would no longer consider buying.

12. If the relative strength of a share is poor, with an apparently inexplicable fall in price, check the market position with your broker. If you cannot find the explanation, you have to use your judgement and feel to decide whether or not to cut the loss. If you are going to adopt a formula for automatically cutting losses, I recommend a 25% limit for growth shares.

13. To save capital gains tax and income tax on dividend income, take full advantage of self-managed PEPs, especially when investing in dynamic growth companies which you hope will become very long-term investments.

14. If you need high income, bear in mind that specified corporate bonds and convertibles of UK non-financial companies and the preference shares and convertible preference shares of non-financial companies incorporated in EC member states can now be held in a general PEP.

15. Remember to bed and breakfast sufficient profits each year to use up your annual allowance of free capital gains.

16. If you feel a bear market is imminent, increase the cash content of your portfolio up to 50%.

17. There is a safety factor in buying shares with relatively low PEGs of 1.0 or less, which should help your portfolio to out-perform a bull market and fare less badly in a bear market.

23

RECOMMENDED READING

Devote a few hours a week to reading about investment. Make a note of any particularly interesting points that might improve your investment technique.

THE BARE MINIMUM

If you invest directly in the stock market, your daily, weekly and monthly reading is an important aid to the effective management of your portfolio. There is a bare minimum that you should read: the *Financial Times* every day, another good daily, a leading Sunday paper and the *Investors Chronicle* every week.

The *Financial Times* is one of the finest newspapers in the world and an indispensable tool to the active investor. Even if you do not have time to read the FT thoroughly every day, be sure to read the weekend edition, which summarises the week's movements in major markets and contains excellent articles of a more reflective nature.

When you read the FT, you should pay particular attention to the reviews of both annual and interim results. Nowadays, you need to study the detailed comment on companies to make sure that earnings are all that they seem to be and that, from one year to the next, you are comparing like with like.

In addition, news of a more general nature might also concern you. On the front page of the section dealing with companies and markets, the FT has an index of all companies mentioned in the paper that day. You can, therefore, always quickly turn to the relevant page to see if there has been some significant news affecting one of your investments. The kind of event that should alarm you is the sudden departure of an excellent chief executive, a major patent expiring or a major new competitor entering the industry. Conversely, there might be the good news of a management change for the better, a major new product or a competitor failing and leaving the field wide open. It is important for you to get the feel of your investments, as you do not want to be the very last person to hear what has been happening to them.

In addition to the daily papers, you should not underestimate technical and trade magazines in the areas in which you specialise or have an interest. On occasions, you might notice a new brand or new invention that is doing particularly well. You might then be in a position to take advantage of the information well before the stock market becomes fully aware of the development.

The *Investors Chronicle* is the only weekly investment magazine and is an essential tool for the active private investor. The annual reviews of company results, with their five-year records, are of particular interest and now highlight changes in accounting to facilitate earnings comparisons.

ADDITIONAL READING

Now we come to additional reading, which is to some extent a matter of personal taste. To help you make up your mind, let me give you a brief outline of the main publications:

The Economist, which is published weekly, is an excellent magazine for keeping in touch with macro-economics and international financial developments. I particularly recommend to you the last couple of pages, which highlight economic and financial indicators, showing the performance of world stock markets, money supply statistics, world interest rates, trade balances, reserves, exchange rates, industrial production, GNP, GDP, retail sales, unemployment, consumer and wholesale price movements and wage increases on a week-by-week basis. In mid-1995 the annual subscription was £60.

Really Essential Financial Statistics (REFS) is available monthly or quarterly and provides private and institutional investors with the financial statistics and other corporate information that they really need to be aware of regularly. The Companies Volume covers *all* quoted UK companies excluding investment trusts and gives details of return on capital employed, profit margin, earnings per share growth over five years, cash flow, dividend yield, net asset value, percentage debt, sales to market capitalisation, research and development expenditure to market capitalisation, tax rate, consensus forecast and PEG. There is also a chart of the relative strength of the share price and its relationship to earnings per share, key dates, the place of each share in its index and whether or not it is a contender for demotion or promotion.

The Tables Volume covers the same companies and shows the best and worst shares in terms of dividend yields, asset values, percentage debt, return on capital employed, sales-to-market capitalisation, earnings per share growth and price-earnings ratios. There are also details of directors' dealings each month and vitally important sector statistics showing how each company compares with the averages and the other members of its peer group.

The Companies Volume of *Company REFS* is ideal for bottom-up investing. The key statistics in the individual company entries have calibrated sector and market moons beside them which indicate if a particular statistic appears to be good or bad from an investment point of view. If the moons are full and black, the statistics are attractive (eg. a high dividend yield, a low price-earnings ratio, a high ROCE, low gearing, etc). The statistics are also grouped to show those that are primarily of interest to growth investors and those that will appeal more to value investors.

Of course, nothing can replace judgement, but *Company REFS* does give investors all the facts they need to decide whether or not a company is worth investigating further. In that event, you should always make a point of then reading the last annual report of the company, getting a copy of any brokers' circulars and reading the *Investors Chronicle* or other investment reviews.

I could go on and on about *Company REFS*, but as I helped to devise the product I have to admit that I am very biased. In April 1995, the special introductory price for the monthly version was £475 per annum and £175 per annum for the quarterly one. If you want to obtain full details, telephone 0171 278 7769 or write to the publishers, Hemmington Scott Publishing Limited, City Innovation Centre, 26-31 Whiskin Street, London EC1R 0BP.

The Estimate Directory and the *Earnings Guide* are also available monthly or quarterly. Both give a consensus of brokers' estimates of future earnings and future dividends. They also indicate the individual brokers who are likely to have written circulars on the companies in question together with their detailed investment recommendations. The annual subscription to *The Estimate Directory* (Telephone: 0131 220 0468) on a monthly basis is £495 and, if you pay by direct debit, £130 for the quarterly version. The *Earnings Guide*, recently taken over by Hemmington Scott Publishing, is currently on special offer at only £210 for the monthly version and £75 for the quarterly. In April 1995, *The Estimate Directory* covered a few more companies than the *Earnings Guide*, but now that Hemmington Scott has taken it over, it will be increasing the number of brokers. In addition, the *Earnings Guide* will be much improved during the coming months.

The Hambro Company Guide is an invaluable quarterly publication that gives five-year profits and earnings per share figures for all UK quoted companies. There are also brief details of the balance sheets, gearing, return on capital employed, activities and key dates for announcements. Annual subscription £105. Telephone 0171-278 7769.

There are also a number of excellent newsletters and a monthly magazine, but they mainly cover companies in the SmallCap Index and below. They occasionally recommend leading stocks, but not often enough to justify a subscription if you intend to focus on the top 350 companies. I will mention the best of these publications now, so that you will be able to decide which of them to subscribe to when you progress to investing in smaller companies:

Analyst is an excellent monthly magazine, which has many interesting in-depth articles each month on investment systems and approaches as well as excellent company profiles and very detailed commentaries on small- to medium-sized growth companies. The annual subscription is £180, falling to £165 in the second year and £150 in the third. There are sometimes special offers. Telephone: 0171-247 4557.

Techinvest is a monthly investment newsletter which concentrates on high technology companies. The track record of its average recommendation is excellent and its model portfolios have performed extremely well. Most of its investment recommendations are for small- to medium-sized companies, but a few reach into the Mid 250 Index. The annual subscription is £129 and the publisher's address is Techinvest Ltd., Mill House, Millbrook, Naas, Co. Kildare, Ireland.

The Investors Stockmarket Letter is a very good fortnightly publication which has an above-average track record of investment recommendations. It tends to concentrate on smaller- to medium-sized companies. The annual subscription is £75 and in June 1995 there was also a special offer of a free copy of my new book, *PEP Up Your Wealth*. Telephone: 0171-247 4557.

Fleet Street Newsletter is published fortnightly and currently divides its recommendations into three sections. Only the first section concerns larger companies. The annual subscription is £45 for the first year and £96.50 per annum thereafter. Telephone: 0171-453 2211.

The Penny Share Guide is a fortnightly newsletter that concentrates entirely on penny stocks. This is a very specialised area in which it is positively dangerous to dabble, unless you understand investment principles and the risks involved. Penny shares can be very rewarding (as advertisements are prone to tell you), but operational risks are high and market liquidity of the shares is often very poor indeed. The annual subscription to *The Penny Share Guide* is £25 in the first year, rising to £59.50 in the next. (Telephone: 01932 354020.) I recommend leaving penny stocks alone until you have read *The Zulu Principle*.

The Wall Street Journal is a daily newspaper which is worth reading to obtain a global perspective. The European edition covers major UK companies, with articles on their results and the effects of recent or impending American legislation. For example, the extent to which the American subsidiaries of UK drug companies like Glaxo Wellcome are likely to suffer from price controls and special taxes.

The Bank Credit Analyst is an excellent monthly Canadian publication, which has been very successful at detecting major stock market and currency trends. The annual subscription is a hefty US$695 per annum. The Montreal telephone number is 001 514 398 0655.

I should stress that I have quoted for annual subscriptions at the prices available in mid-1995. They change quite frequently and are also often the subject of special offers. *Analyst*, for instance, has, on occasions, offered first-time subscribers a free copy of *The Zulu Principle*. If you are interested in any of the optional extra reading, I suggest that you keep your eyes open and watch for special offers by direct mail or through press advertisements. Remember, too, that as a member of ProShare you can obtain a discount on a number of the publications mentioned.

BOOKS

We now come to books on investment and the stock market. First, you must be *certain* that you understand the basics. If you are in any doubt at all, I suggest that you read *The Beginners' Guide to Investment* by Bernard Gray and/or *How to Read the Financial Pages* by Michael Brett. Both these books will give you a good grounding, which will, I hope, be rounded off by *Investment Made Easy*.

More advanced books on UK investment are difficult to find. It has always surprised me that there are so few British books on investment beyond the primer stage. In law, medicine, accountancy and banking there are hundreds of books covering every aspect of those subjects. In America, there are scores of excellent books on investment, outlining and analysing the approaches and methods of the most successful professionals. There is so much interest in them that many become best-sellers.

Both the *Financial Times* and the *Investors Chronicle* agree that my previous book, *The Zulu Principle*, 'fills a gap'. There are chapters on the common characteristics of growth shares and the criteria for selecting them; the price-earnings growth factor; cash flow; competitive advantage and relative strength. There are also chapters on the essential requirements for investing in shells, turnarounds, cyclicals and asset situations. If you are *seriously* interested in becoming a successful investor, I recommend *The Zulu Principle* to you.

My most recent book, *PEP Up Your Wealth*, gives all the details you need to know about PEPs and also explains the remarkable O'Higgins system of high-yield investment that has beaten the market substantially over the last twenty years in the USA and over the last ten years in the UK.

Another recent UK publication is Terry Smith's *Accounting for Growth*, which gives a comprehensive account of the various ways some companies boost their annual earnings. I recommend this book if you want to delve into the mysteries of company accounting. The other excellent book on this subject is *Interpreting Company Reports and Accounts* by Geoffrey Holmes and Alan Sugden, published by Woodhead-Faulkner. In both cases, you should double-check first with the retailer whether or not new editions are on the way, as accounting practice is a fast-changing scene.

All of the other books you might enjoy and find beneficial are American. I will list them in order of ease of reading:

1. *One Up on Wall Street* by Peter Lynch (Penguin). An excellent and very readable book by one of America's most successful mutual fund managers. His new hardback, *Beating the Street* (Simon and Schuster), is also full of practical advice and is a compelling read.

2. *The Midas Touch* by John Train (Harper & Row). A detailed exposition on the strategies that have made Warren Buffett America's pre-eminent investor. An easy and entertaining read.

3. *Beating the Dow* by Michael O'Higgins and John Downes (HarperCollins). A detailed exposition on Dow stocks and a method of buying those that are out of favour to produce returns that dwarf the market averages. The same technique can also be applied to leading UK stocks as explained in my book, *PEP Up Your Wealth*.

4. *Extraordinary Popular Delusions and the Madness of Crowds* by Charles Mackay (Farrar, Strauss & Giroux). First published in 1841 – a classic on crowd psychology. Fun to read and one of my favourites.

5. *The New Money Masters* by John Train (Harper & Row). A very readable account of the highly successful strategies of investment

giants like Soros, Lynch and Rogers. Train's previous book, *The Money Masters*, is also good value.

6. *The Craft of Investing* by John Train (HarperCollins). Explains in an easy-to-understand way growth investing, value investing, emerging markets, the psychology of the market, when to buy and sell and how to avoid losing strategies.

7. *The Buffett Way* by Robert Hagstrom Jr (John Wiley & Sons). An in-depth analysis of the innovative investment and business strategies behind the spectacular success of Warren Buffett.

8. *The New Market Wizards* by Jack Schwager (Simon & Schuster). Interviews with top traders in commodities and stock markets, concentrating upon their individual approaches and attitudes. *Market Wizards* is also on similar lines.

9. *Reminiscences of a Stock Market Operator* by Edwin Lefevre (Fraser Publishing Company). An amusing account of the early life of the famous speculator, Jessie Livermore, showing how important it is not to fight the market but to go with the force.

10. *The Intelligent Investor* by Benjamin Graham (Harper & Row). An investment classic which Warren Buffett believes is the 'best book on investment ever written'. The main subjects are the virtues of 'value investing' and a systematic approach. Not a quick and easy read, but full of revelations and intriguing ideas.

11. *Security Analysis* by Graham and Dodd (McGraw-Hill). The fifth edition brings this investment classic up to date. The book, which is very hard going, outlines in great detail the principles and techniques for measuring asset values, cash flow and earnings.

12. *Technical Analysis of Stock Trends* by Robert Edwards and John Magee (John Magee). An authoritative book on technical analysis, but a very hard read. Only for the dedicated.

The first seven books are a very easy read and entertaining as well as instructive. *The New Money Masters* and *The New Market Wizards* are also an easy read, but are more for international investors who are also interested in currencies and commodities. The last three are very hard going indeed, but well worth the effort.

Obtaining copies of some of these books can be difficult. I suggest that you begin by inquiring at a leading book store like W.H. Smith, Hatchards or Foyles, but, if unsuccessful, you should try a specialist in books on business and investment, such as Dillons City Business Store, 9 Moorfields, London EC2Y 9AE (Telephone: 0171-628 7479), or Books Etc., 30 Broadgate, London EC2 (Telephone: 0171-628 8944).

The important point to remember is that if you intend to become more knowledgeable about investment, you cannot escape from further homework. A few hours a week will suffice. I recommend that, as you progress, you make a written note of any particularly interesting and impressive points made by authors and financial journalists. In this way, you will be able to build your own handbook of maxims and guidelines to keep you on the straight and narrow path towards successful investment.

24

SHAREHOLDERS' PERKS

Perks are an attractive tax-free bonus. Find out what is on offer, but do not buy a share just for the perks.

Over 115 British companies offer perks to their shareholders. In some cases you need to own only one share; in others, many more, sometimes with a qualifying period, sometimes without.

The best-known example is the All-England Lawn Tennis and Croquet Club. Owners of its debenture stock are entitled to centre court seats at the Wimbledon Tennis Championships. No other company offers such an attractive perk, but there are many others that are well worth having.

You might already own shares in a company that offers perks to shareholders, or you might be considering making an investment in such a company. Whatever your views about perks, it must pay you to know and understand the full range of privileges you can obtain simply by becoming a shareholder.

BOOKLET OF CONCESSIONARY DISCOUNTS

Henry Cooke, Lumsden, (HCL) the stockbroker, publishes annually an excellent booklet that sets out all the details of shareholder perks on offer. Here is a typical extract from its 1995/96 edition:

Allied Domecq – 6
A range of offers with the Reports & Accounts including vouchers towards meals in selected Company pubs and restaurants and vouchers offering discounts on various wine, spirit and beer purchases through Victoria Wine and Haddows off-licences.
Samples of the company's products are available for consumption by shareholders attending the AGM.
AGM.
Discount is available to Nominee Shareholders provided the nominee manager advises the Company of the number of beneficial holders they require vouchers for.
Div: Feb. Aug.
No minimum shareholding required: all shareholders
Share price at 1.5.95, 550p

Ann Street Brewery (Rule 4.2 (a)) – 7
25% discount on bed and breakfast for two persons, even if the booking is on half or full board basis, at St. Pierre Park Hotel, the Greenacres Hotel and La Trelade Hotel, all in Guernsey C.I. (Company shareholders must designate beneficiary's name).
Concessions are available to Nominee Shareholders provided that when the booking is made the registered holder confirms in writing that the person making the booking is the beneficial holder of not less than 100 Ordinary shares.
Minimum shareholding required: 100 £1 Ord.
Share price at 1.5.95, 345p

Argos – 8
A discount voucher has historically been sent out to all registered shareholders in August, with the Company's interim report. This has entitled shareholders to a once-off discount depending on the amount of the sale transaction (i.e. £2 on a purchase of £20-£40, £4 on a purchase of £40.01-£60, £6 on a purchase of £60.01-£100, £10 on a purchase of £100.01-£150, £15 on a purchase of over £150.01).
Vouchers have a limited life. In 1993 they were valid until 27 November and 1994 until 26 November and they can only be used for purchases of merchandise (not gift vouchers or postal purchases).
The decision on whether or not to offer a voucher, and the levels of discount, is taken every year. Whilst the Company has provided a voucher every year since flotation, it does not guarantee such in future years. Voucher sent to registered shareholders only.
Voucher not eligible to Nominee Shareholders.
Div: May. Nov.
Minimum shareholding required: all shareholders.
Share price at 1.5.95, 413p

As you can see, the HCL booklet shows the minimum shareholding required, the details of each perk, and the qualifying period (if any). In many cases, the offer applies to *all* shareholders – even one share would be enough.

This excellent publication costs £5 and if you want a copy you should write to Henry Cooke, Lumsden PLC, Piercy House, 7-9 Copthall Avenue, London EC2R 7EH. HCL also offers a comprehensive range of other services to private clients.

Hargreaves Lansdown Asset Management Limited, Embassy House, Clifton, Bristol BS8 1SB produces a less comprehensive booklet, which usually sells for £3, but is sometimes offered free.

RANGE OF PERKS

The shareholder perks on offer include discounts on carpets, clothing, clocks and watches, DIY goods, dry cleaning, furniture, groceries, holidays, home furnishing, hotel bills, jewellery, cars and spares, shoes, silverware, sporting goods, wines and spirits, and travel. They range from a free lunch or small hamper of company products at the AGM to P & O's 50% discount off the fare for a trip for four with a car on the cross-channel ferry.

Among the more useful and significant benefits, you will find Airtours and other travel companies offer 10% off holidays, Asprey's allows a 15% discount, Austin Reed 15%, Burton 12.5% (including sale goods), Forte, Ladbroke and Vaux Group offer 10% off hotel accommodation and restaurant bills, Johnson Group Cleaners and Sketchley 25% off dry cleaning. Lonrho offers 30% off Metropole hotel bills and a wide range of other benefits, Meyer International 10% off building supplies and Moss Bros 10% off formal wear hire charges. Next has a one occasion discount of 25%, P & O remarkable discounts of up to 50% on the cross-channel ferries and major discounts on other ferry crossings, Park Foods 20% off Christmas hampers, Signet 10% for jewellery and Trafalgar House a 10-15% discount for selected Concorde flights and QE2 cruises together with certain other discounts. Even fish and chips are catered for, with Harry Ramsden's 20% off restaurant meals on Mondays to Thursdays.

HOUSEBUILDERS AND CAR DEALERS

You will notice that I have not included the discounts offered to shareholders by housebuilders like Barratt and Bellway. Nor have I mentioned discounts on new cars offered by a number of companies. Everyone knows that it is only too easy to negotiate a discount with most car dealers and housebuilders. Most of them would be surprised if you did not try. If you find it difficult to ask, begin to edge away and you will find that they will do all the talking.

I noticed among the car dealers, for example, that Alexanders Holdings, a main Ford dealer in Glasgow, offers a 2% cash discount on motor vehicles which they say could increase to 14% dependent on availability. I would be prepared to wager that the discount offered would vary far more with the determination of the buyer and the skill of the salesman.

Barratt Developments offers a £500 discount on every £25,000 (or part thereof) on the purchase of a new or part-exchanged Barratt house. In uncertain times for housebuilders, I believe that a reasonably determined buyer would have a very good chance of improving on this.

NEGOTIATING DISCOUNTS

I may have been unfair to car dealers and housebuilders, as in the list of perks I have included car hire, furniture, hotel rooms, air tickets and clothes. During the recession it has become commonplace to request and to obtain discounts for all of these goods and services. Discounts on hotel rooms, for example, are easy to negotiate, but discounts on restaurant meals could be potentially embarrassing and therefore difficult. It is very convenient, though perhaps a soft option, to receive an automatic discount, but you must always evaluate its worth against the discount you could obtain by growling a little.

Dry cleaning is an interesting one. Sketchley's and Johnson's 25% seems attractive, especially if applied to the whole family. However, I have no idea what kind of discount you could obtain by simply suggesting that if the price was right, you might be prepared to give them all of your family's business. I imagine that it could be quite substantial.

Another pertinent point is the pricing policy of the company offering the discount. In some cases, their prices will be sufficient to enable them to offer very generous discounts. However, you are only interested in the net price you have to pay, in comparison with the cost of the same or very similar goods from other sources.

In today's tough commercial world, you do not have to be a shareholder in a company to buy houses, cars, furniture and clothes on attractive terms. The same applies to hiring cars and booking hotel rooms. Steel yourself to be tough and be prepared to shop around. When you have negotiated the best *net* prices you can obtain, that is the base against which to measure the apparent perk being offered preferentially to company shareholders.

FINANCIAL OUTLAY REQUIRED

A further factor in measuring the benefit of a shareholder's perk is the financial outlay required to enjoy it. How many shares do you have to buy to qualify for the perk; how much will they cost, and are the shares likely to prove to be a worthwhile investment?

A minor perk in exchange for a weighty investment is a poor proposition. The example of ADT illustrates this well. An investment in 750 shares in September 1989 at £20.90 per share would have cost £15,675 and given the owner the right to enter a ballot for one of 250 places reserved for ADT shareholders in the London Marathon. By June 1995, the shares were worth just 720p, having been as low as 295p in 1991, so anyone influenced by the chance of a place in the race would have been better advised to run 26.2 miles in the opposite direction.

BUYING ONLY ONE SHARE

Signets' 10% off all purchases from any branch of H. Samuel, Leslie Davis and Ernest Jones would, at one time, have seemed to be a most attractive proposition as the perk applies to all shareholders. During the last two years, the shares have fallen from 143p to 15.5p, but you needed to buy only one share to qualify for the discount.

In mid-1995, the price of Signets' shares was only 15.5p but the company's outlook is very uncertain. In addition, you have to factor into the cost the small bargain charge of £25 for buying only one share. You would have to buy over £250 worth of their jewellery to make it worthwhile. Also, you have to consider that you might have been able to negotiate a discount anyway or bought similar goods elsewhere at an equally attractive net price.

TAX ADVANTAGE

A key factor in evaluating the worth of any benefit to you is the tax-free nature of shareholder perks. For example, in mid-1995 P & O's Dover-Calais ferry crossing for five people with a car at near-peak times costs £308 return. A 50% discount would therefore save £154. Normally, for a family trip, that money would have had to be taken out of taxed income. At the higher rate of 40%, the benefit in terms of taxable income is over £250 and over £200 at 25%. Any dividend paid to you would be subject to taxation, so, in comparison, a substantial perk is of more value than might appear at first sight.

While on the subject of tax, you should bear in mind that for administrative reasons, shareholder perks are not usually available to investors purchasing their shares through a PEP scheme.

ONE-OFF AND RECURRING PERKS

There is obviously a tremendous difference between a few vouchers for a total benefit of £16 offered by a company like Iceland Frozen Foods and a recurring discount of 12.5% offered by a company like Burton on all purchases (excluding food, drink, tobacco and certain services) made in branches of Burton, Top Man, Top Shop, Evans, Dorothy Perkins, Principles, Debenhams and Principles for Men. Most importantly, Burton extends its 12.5% to sales goods whereas most other clothing companies exclude them. Maximum purchases are £5,000 per annum per shareholder and, to qualify for Burton's discount, you would need to own 1,000 ordinary shares which, in mid-1993, would have cost 74.5p each for a total outlay of £745 plus brokerage.

You can see from the example of Burton that fine detail is important. The HCL booklet is most informative in this respect. However, I have given the list of names in Appendix 3 of all companies that offer shareholder perks in 1995. You should use this as a checklist to see if any of your investments are offering perks. You can then check the fine detail by contacting the company or obtaining a booklet.

UTILITIES

You will see on the list a few utilities, as well as Eurotunnel. These companies offered perks to *original* subscribers when the companies were made public. The benefits are not transferable to new shareholders.

SUMMARY

1. If you want comprehensive details of all UK companies offering shareholder perks, apply to Henry Cooke, Lumsden for its comprehensive £5 booklet or write to Hargreaves Lansdown for its free booklet.

2. Otherwise check the list in Appendix III. If you have an investment in one of these companies, you can ascertain details of the perks directly from the company secretary.

3. In evaluating the perks, first negotiate the best *net* terms you can achieve in the normal course of business. This is the base against which to measure the value of any perks. Nowadays it is possible to negotiate discounts on most purchases of goods and services, so in many cases the perks have very little, if any, real value.

4. Bear in mind that perks are tax free, which, according to your tax rate, increases their value in your hands. Also remember that shareholder perks are not usually available to investors purchasing their shares through a PEP scheme.

5. Although some perks are offered to all shareholders, the cost of buying one share will be substantially increased by the bargain charge, which is usually about £25 per transaction.

6. Distinguish between one-off discounts and recurring across-the-board discounts. The former have very limited appeal, but the latter can be valuable.

7. The perks offered by the utilities companies and Eurotunnel were only available to *original* subscribers when the companies became public and the benefits are not transferable.

8. It is very rarely worth buying shares in any company *just for the perks*. The exception is when your way of life results in an above-average use of the goods or services, which are subject to substantial shareholder perks. For instance, if you and your family are likely to use the cross-channel ferry frequently, you should consider an investment in P & O preference shares.

9. More often than not, perks should be looked upon as an attractive tax-free bonus. It is important to know what is on offer and to take full advantage of any perks after first establishing that they are real rather than illusory.

25

—

SUMMARY

Remember the words of Elmer Letterman: 'Luck is what happens when preparation meets opportunity.'

I hope you will not feel that the title of this book, *Investment Made Easy*, has misled you in any way. Perhaps I should have called it, *Investment Made as Easy as Possible*, but that might have been too much of a mouthful for the booksellers.

Learning the language of finance and learning to read accounts is simple enough. It is also easy to see that to be a successful investor, you need a discipline, a method that you can temper and refine and make your own.

As I write in early 1995, we have not had a vicious bear market since 1987. However, American studies show that, for their market at least, bear markets come on average every 5.3 years. Another one might be due soon, but even with this risk in mind I hope that I have made it clear to you that the stock market has been an excellent long-term investment and is likely to remain so in the future. I have also tried to demonstrate that companies with a competitive advantage, a proven growth record, an optimistic outlook and a strong balance sheet are likely to be far better investments than those with no special advantage, a choppy record, an uncertain future and too much debt.

The aim is to buy a share that fulfils your criteria, especially one having an attractive P/E ratio in relation to its growth rate. Unless you have overlooked something important, a share like this should be *relatively* cheap. You hope that, as growth continues at an above-average rate, the market will begin to appreciate the merits of the company. The shares will then command a higher rating and the price will go up.

All this is straightforward and easy to understand. The difficulties arise with creative accounting and the fact that you cannot rely upon a company's reported earnings as a base upon which to make your calculations when deciding whether or not a company's shares are good value.

I had to take you through Chapter 17, on price-earnings ratios, growth rates and price-earnings growth factors, without telling you that reported earnings are often unreliable. If I had warned you beforehand that earnings are not all that they appear to be, you might have wondered why you should bother to read a chapter about calculations based on figures that can sometimes be so misleading as to be meaningless.

I make no apology, though – as a result of your reading the chapter on price-earnings growth factors, you now understand how to measure the growth rate of a share and determine whether or not it is fully reflected in the P/E ratio and the share price. You know that, in early 1995, the average growth share in the FT-SE 350 Actuaries Index was on a prospective P/E ratio of nearly 13 with a future growth rate of about 12.5% and a consequent PEG factor of 1.0. You know that if a company is only growing at 10% per annum, it should not command an above average P/E ratio of 20; you know that a company growing at more than 20% per annum is worth a well above average P/E ratio. You also understand that you cannot completely rely upon reported earnings per share and that, in particular, FRS3 brackets extraordinary and exceptional items together. Both are now deducted from profits when reporting earnings per share, which need interpreting carefully by reading the detailed accounts (there will be fuller explanations than there used to be) and studying press and, when available, broker comment.

The vital point to grasp is that FRS3 is a step forward. Excellent companies that made no use of creative accounting will continue to make no use of it. The kind of companies that use creative accounting extensively have always been suspect. Now, at least, most investors know that the value of a company cannot be judged from one suspect figure of earnings per share compared with another equally suspect figure the following year. The profits and earnings each year need adjusting in line with the IIMR recommendations before they can be used as a basis of comparison.

Now that the press and brokers have become more used to FRS3, reporting and analysis have adapted to the new accounting regulations and the investor's task is much easier as a result.

It is important to take note of Sir David Tweedie's advice not to judge a company just by its earnings per share. The strength of the balance sheet and the reconciliation of operating cash flow with operating profits should also be taken into account and become a routine check.

I hope that the chapters on share selection and high yielders will have shown you how to use a series of sieves to reduce a large number of shares to a select, much smaller number. It is this approach that is all important, as the sieving process is the essence of effective investment analysis.

A hundred or more points have been made in Chapters 12–24 dealing with direct share investment. Any summary must inevitably leave out the majority of them. At the risk of oversimplification, I will end on the note of suggesting a few very basic, broad guidelines:

1. If you decide to invest in growth shares, stick to the leading 350 companies, until you become more expert. There is more safety in the size and stature of the leading companies, so you are less likely to invest in a complete failure.

2. Set aside a few hours a week to read the financial press, the detailed accounts and any brokers' circulars you receive on the growth shares in which you are interested. Refine and improve your approach to investment, as you learn from both your successes and your mistakes. It may help you to keep a notebook to write down key points.

3. Allocate from your available resources a sum to invest – patient money that you can spare and afford. Your aim is to avoid being pressurised into having to make a premature sale.

    Invest between 50% and 100% of your patient money at all times. When you believe the outlook to be exceptionally bearish, you can reduce your investments to 50% of your portfolio, if it makes you feel more comfortable.

4. Choose a broker who understands your objectives. You may decide upon execution-only, but a more traditional broker can be an invaluable ally. The choice depends upon how much help you feel that you need.

5. Invest in a maximum of twelve shares which meet your criteria. Ten is the recommended minimum, with a maximum investment of 10% in any one share. There is also a strong argument for investing 5–10% of your portfolio in a well-established unit trust concentrating on gold shares.

6. If you want to handle your own investments, but spend a minimum amount of time on them, the O'Higgins system of high-yield investment is designed especially for you. It beats the market more often than not and takes only an hour a year to select the five shares for your annual portfolio. If this approach appeals to you, I recommend my latest book, *PEP Up Your Wealth*.

7. Use your annual PEP allowances to the maximum possible extent and, if you can afford to do so, be sure to reinvest the dividends.

8. If you need a high income, bear in mind that specified corporate bonds and convertibles of UK non-financial companies and preference shares and convertible preference shares in non-financial companies incorporated in EC member states can now be held in a PEP.

9. Take advantage of new issues by the Government by applying for at least the minimum subscriptions of new issues in your own name and for members of your family.

10. With any system based on small- to medium-sized growth stocks, you are seeking to identify a few super-growth shares and hold on to them through thick and thin. Selection is far more important than timing.

You are searching for companies with strong business franchises that enjoy an excellent return on capital employed and generate plenty of cash. In addition, you must ensure that the other criteria set out in detail in Chapter 16 are satisfied to a sufficient extent to provide you with an adequate safety net.

11. Your final check on any share is to make sure that you can buy at the right price. You are seeking shares which have attractive P/E ratios in relation to their growth rates – shares in the leading 350 with PEGs of not more than 1.0. You do not want to buy when the prospective P/E ratio is higher than the future growth rate.

12. FRS3 appears to have complicated the issue. You now know for certain that you cannot rely upon reported EPS. Reading the accounts amplified by press and broker comment should give you a far better picture of real growth rates and current P/E ratios.

13. You should also heed Sir David Tweedie's advice and take a broader view of a company. In particular, note the strength of the balance sheet and reconcile the selected company's trading profits with its net operating cash flow. Remember that cash is the only indisputable asset and that when making an investment you should consider the downside first.

14. After you have purchased a share, maintain as much of a hands-on approach as you can manage. You should be able to find someone who knows someone who can answer your questions about most companies. Be active in monitoring your portfolio.

15. Growth shares should be held for the long term unless the market goes mad and awards your chosen company a PEG of over 1.5. Sell if the prospective P/E ratio rises to 50% more than the growth rate or if the story changes very much for the worse. In general, it pays to run profits and cut losses.

In the foregoing chapters, you have been given a backcloth of investment know-how on important aspects of share investment such as competitive advantage, balance sheet strength, cash flow, growth rates, PEGs, creative accounting and relative strength. The better you understand the essentials of investment, the better your judgement is likely to be and the more likely you will be to develop a feel for the market and an instinct for financial preservation.

As you progress, you may decide that you would like to explore the world of cyclicals, turnarounds and smaller companies. In that event, I recommend you to read *The Zulu Principle*, followed by some of the American investment books I have described. You should also consider subscribing to *Company REFS*, at least on a quarterly basis. This will give you all the facts and figures you need to select shares for further investigation and to monitor your portfolio regularly.

The more you read about investment, think about it and talk about it, the more likely you are to succeed in beating the market. As Gary Player says, 'The more I practise, the luckier I get.'

APPENDIX I

THE CONSTITUENTS OF THE FT-SE 100 INDEX IN MID-1995

3i Group
Abbey National
Allied Domecq
Argyll Group
Arjo Wiggins Appleton
Asda Group
Associated British Foods
BAA
Bank of Scotland
Barclays
Bass
B.A.T. Industries
Blue Circle Industries
BOC Group
Boots
British Aerospace
British Airways
British Gas
British Petroleum Co
British Steel
British Telecommunications
BTR
Burmah Castrol
Cable & Wireless
Cadbury Schweppes
Caradon
Carlton Communications
Commercial Union
Courtaulds
De La Rue
Eastern Group
Enterprise Oil
Forte
G K N
General Accident
General Electric
Glaxo Wellcome
Granada Group
Grand Metropolitan

Great Universal Stores
Guardian Royal Exchange
Guinness
Hanson
HSBC Holdings
Imperial Chemical Industries
Inchcape
Kingfisher
Ladbroke Group
Land Securities
Legal & General Group
Lloyds Bank
Marks and Spencer
MEPC
National Power
National Westminster Bank
North West Water Group
Pearson
Peninsular & Oriental Steam
   Navigation
PowerGen
Prudential Corporation
Rank Organisation
Reckitt & Colman
Redland
Reed International
Rentokil Group
Reuters Holdings
Rexam
RMC Group
Rolls-Royce
Royal Bank of Scotland Group
Royal Insurance
RTZ Corporation
Sainsbury (J.)
Schroders
Scottish & Newcastle
Scottish Power
Sears

Severn Trent
Shell Transport & Trading
Siebe
Smith & Nephew
Smithkline Beecham
Southern Electric
Standard Chartered
Sun Alliance Group
Tate & Lyle
Tesco
Thames Water
THORN EMI
TI Group
Tomkins
TSB Group
Unilever
United Biscuits
Vodafone Group
Warburg (SG) Group
Whitbread
Williams Holdings
Wolseley
Zeneca Group

APPENDIX II

Airtours
Albert Fisher Group
Alliance Trust
Allied Colloids Group
Amersham International
Anglian Water
Anglo & Overseas Trust
Argos
Associated British Ports Holdings
Babcock International Group
Baird (Williams)
Bankers Investment Trust
Barratt Developments
BBA Group
Beazer Homes
Berisford
Berkeley Group
BET
BICC
Boddington Group
Body Shop International
Booker
Bowthorpe
BPB Industries
Bradford Property Trust
Brake Bros
Britannic Assurance
British Assets Trust
British Biotech
British Land Co
British Vita
Brixton Estate
Brown (N) Group
Bryant Group
BTP
Bunzl
Burford Holdings
Burton Group

Caledonia Investments
Calor Group
Camas
Capital Radio
Capital Shopping Centres
Charter
Chelsfield
Christies International
Chubb Security
Coats Viyella
Cobham
Compass Group
Cookson Group
Courtaulds Textiles
Cowie Group
Cray Electronics Holdings
Croda International
Daily Mail & General Trust
Dalgety
Danka Business Systems
Delta
Devro International
DFS Furniture Company
Diploma
Dixons Group
Dunedin Worldwide Investment Trust
East Midlands Electricity
Edinburgh Dragon Trust
Edinburgh Investment Trust
Electra Investment Trust
Electrocomponents
EMAP
English China Clays
Eurotherm
Eurotunnel
Fairey Group
Farnell Electronics
Fine Art Developments

First Leisure Corporation
Fisons
FKI
Fleming Far Eastern Inv. Trust
Fleming Japanese Inv. Trust
Fleming Mercantile Inv. Trust
Fleming Overseas Inv. Trust
Flextech
Foreign & Colonial Investment Trust
Foreign & Colonial Pacific Inv. Trust
Gartmore
Gestetner Holdings
Glynwed International
Govett Oriental Investment Trust
Govett Strategic Investment Trust
Great Portland Estates
Greenalls Group
Halma
Hambros
Hammerson
Harrisons & Crosfield
Hays
Hazelwood Foods
Hepworth
Hewden-Stuart
Heywood Williams Group
Hickson International
Highland Distilleries Co
Hillsdown Holdings
House of Fraser
Howden Group
Iceland Group
IMI
INVESCO
Johnson Matthey

Kleinwort Benson Group
Kleinwort European
   Privatisation Inv. Trust
Kwik Save Group
Kwik-Fit Holdings
Laird Group
Laporte
LASMO
Lex Service
Lloyds Chemists
London & Manchester Group
London Electricity
London Insurance Market Inv.
   Trust
London International Group
London Merchant Securities
Lonrho
Low & Bonar
Lucas Industries
M & G Group
Macallan-Glenlivet
MAI
Man (E D & F) Group
Manweb
Marley
Marston, Thompson &
   Evershed
Matthew Clark
McKechnie
Medeva
Menzies (John)
Merchants Trust
Mercury European
   Privatisation Trust
Mercury World Mining Trust
Mersey Docks and Harbour
   Company
Meyer International
MFI Furniture Group

Midlands Electricity
Mirror Group
Monks Investment Trust
Monument Oil & Gas
Morgan Crucible Co
Morrison (Wm) Supermarkets
Murray Income Trust
Murray International Trust
Murray Smaller Markets Trust
Next
NFC
Northern Electric
Northern Foods
Northern Ireland Electricity
Northumbrian Water Group
NORWEB
Nurdin & Peacock
Ocean Group
Pentland Group
Perpetual
Pilkington
Powell Duffryn
Powerscreen International
Premier Oil
Provident Financial
Racal Electronics
Redrow Group
Refuge Group
RIT Capital Partners
RJB Mining
Rothmans International
Rugby Group
Salvesen (Christian)
Savoy Hotel
Scapa Group
Scotia Holdings
Scottish American Investment
Scottish Eastern Investment
   Trust

Scottish Hydro-Electric
Scottish Investment Trust
Scottish Mortgage & Trust
Second Alliance Trust
Securicor Group
Securities Trust of Scotland
Sedgwick Group
SEEBOARD
Sema Group
Senior Engineering Group
Slough Estates
Smith (David S.) (Holdings)
Smith New Court
Smith (W.H.) Group
Smiths Industries
South Wales Electricity
South West Water
South Western Electricity
Southern Water
Spirax–Sarco Engineering
St Ives
St James's Place Capital
Stagecoach Holdings
Stakis
Storehouse
T & N
Takare
Tarmac
Taylor Woodrow
Telegraph
TeleWest Communications
Templeton Emerging Markets
   Investment Trust
Tibbett & Britten Group
TLG
TR City of London Trust
TR Smaller Companies
   Investment Trust
Trafalgar House

Transport Development Group
Travis Perkins
Trinity International Holdings
TT Group
Unichem
Unigate
Unitech
United Friendly Group
United News & Media
Vaux Group
Vendome Luxury Group
Vickers
Vosper Thornycroft Holdings
VSEL
Wassall
Watmoughs (Holdings)
Weir Group
Welsh Water
Wessex Water
Wickes
Willis Corroon Group
Wilson Bowden
Wilson (Connolly) Holdings
Wimpey (George)
Witan Investment Co
Wolverhampton & Dudley
    Breweries
WPP Group
Yorkshire Electricity Group
Yorkshire Water
Yule Catto & Co

APPENDIX III

LIST OF COMPANIES OFFERING SHAREHOLDERS PERKS IN 1995/96

Abercorn Place School (unquoted)
Aberdeen Trust
Airtours
Alexanders Holdings
All England Lawn Tennis Ground (Rule 4.2(a))
Allied Domecq
Ann Street Brewery (Rule 4.2(a))
Argos
Laura Ashley
Armour Trust
Asprey
Associated British Foods
Austin Reed
Bank of Scotland
Barr & Wallace Arnold Trust
Barratt Developments
Bellway
Bensons Crisps
Bentalls
Berisford
Berry Birch & Noble (USM)
Bluebell Railway (unquoted)
Boots
British Airways
British Telecommunications
Brooks Service Group
N Brown Group
H P Bulmer Holdings
Burton Group
Burtonwood Brewery
Coats Viyella
Community Hospitals Group
Country Gardens (Rule 4.2(a))
Courts
Eldridge, Pope & Co. (USM)
EMAP
Emess
Eurotunnel
Fired Earth
Forte

Friendly Hotels
Fuller Smith & Turner (USM)
General Accident
Stanley Gibbons Holdings (Rule 4.2(a))
Gieves Group
Goldsmiths Group
Green Catalogue Corporation (unquoted)
Greenalls Group
Greene King
Greenstar Hotels (Rule 4.2(a))
Groupe Chez Gerrard
Hartstone Group
Hawtin
Hi-Tec Sports
Hodgson Martin
Hollas Group
Iceland Group
Invesco
Isle of Man Steam Packet Co.
Johnson Group Cleaners
Thomas Jourdan
Jurys Hotel Group
Kwik-Fit Holdings
Ladbroke Group
Lex Service
Lloyds Chemists
Lonrho
Lookers Group
S. Lyles
Mallet
Manchester and London Investment Trust
Merrydown
Meyer International
Moss Bros Group
Mount Charlotte Investments
Next
Norcros
North Norfolk Railway (unquoted)

P & O
Park Food Group
Park Lane Hotel
Perry Group
Persimmon
Psion
Queens Moat Houses
Quicks Group
Harry Ramsden's
Rank Organisation
Reed International
Regina (USM)
Romney Hythe & Dimchurch Railway (unquoted)
Royal Bank of Scotland Group
Ryan Hotels
Savoy Hotel
Scandinavian Seaways
Scottish & Newcastle
Sears
Securicor Group
Sefton Hotel (Rule 4.2(a))
Severn Valley Railway Holdings (Rule 4.2(a))
Sharpe & Fisher
Signet Group
Sketchley
Specialeyes
Stakis
Storehouse
Stylo
Sunleigh
Thorntons
Tottenham Hotspur
Toye & Co.
Trafalgar House
Upton & Southern Holdings
Vaux Group
Whitbread
World of Leather

APPENDIX IV

RETAIL PRICE INDEX FIGURES FOR CAPITAL GAINS TAX CALCULATIONS

RPI (Jan. 1987=100)	1982	1983	1984	1985	1986	1987	1988
Jan.		82.61	86.84	91.20	96.25	100.0	103.3
Feb.		82.97	87.20	91.94	96.60	100.4	103.7
Mar.	79.44	83.12	87.48	92.80	96.73	100.6	104.1
Apr.	81.04	84.28	88.64	94.78	97.67	101.8	105.8
May	81.62	84.64	88.97	95.21	97.85	101.9	106.2
Jun.	81.85	84.84	89.20	95.41	97.79	101.9	106.6
Jul.	81.88	85.30	89.10	95.23	97.52	101.8	106.7
Aug.	81.90	85.68	89.94	95.49	97.82	102.1	107.9
Sept.	81.85	86.06	90.11	95.44	98.30	102.4	108.4
Oct.	82.26	86.36	90.67	95.59	98.45	102.9	109.5
Nov.	82.66	86.67	90.95	95.92	99.29	103.4	110.0
Dec.	82.51	86.89	90.87	96.05	99.62	103.3	110.3

	1989	1990	1991	1992	1993	1994	1995
Jan.	111.0	119.5	130.2	135.6	137.9	141.3	146.0
Feb.	111.8	120.2	130.9	136.3	138.8	142.1	146.9
Mar.	112.3	121.4	131.4	136.7	139.3	142.5	147.5
Apr.	114.3	125.1	133.1	138.8	140.6	144.2	149.0
May	115.0	126.2	133.5	139.3	141.1	144.7	149.6
Jun.	115.4	126.7	134.1	139.3	141.0	144.7	
Jul.	115.5	126.8	133.8	138.8	140.7	144.0	
Aug.	115.8	128.1	134.1	138.9	141.3	144.7	
Sept.	116.6	129.3	134.6	139.4	141.9	145.0	
Oct.	117.5	130.3	135.1	139.9	141.8	145.2	
Nov.	118.5	130.1	135.6	139.7	141.6	145.3	
Dec.	118.8	129.9	135.7	139.2	141.9	146.0	

Figures prior to 1987 are rebased on January 1987=100 and are given to two places of decimals for greater accuracy.

The RPI figures can be used to calculate the indexation 'uplift' (i.e. how much you can add to your original purchase price to allow for the change in retail prices since purchase.) The formula is:

$$\text{Indexation factor} = \frac{\text{RPI in month of disposal} - \text{RPI in month of acquisition}}{\text{RPI in month of acquisition}}$$

For further details, see "Portfolio Management System".

The above details are supplied by ProShare to its members for use with its portfolio management system.

INDEX

CREDITS

The author and publisher would like to thank the following for permission to reproduce figures, tables, graphs and articles: Company REFs, Datastream, *Financial Times*, Henry Cooke, Lumsden, *Investors Chronicle*, Geoffrey Holmes and Alan Sugden *Interpreting Company Reports and Accounts* (Woodhead-Faulkner), *Housing Finance*, the London Stock Exchange, ProShare.